A Kinder and Gentler Tyranny

A Kinder and Gentler Tyranny

Illusions of a New World Order

D. Michael Rivage-Seul
and Marguerite K. Rivage-Seul

Foreword by Franz Hinkelammert

Westport, Connecticut
London

Library of Congress Cataloging-in-Publication Data

Rivage-Seul, D. Michael.
    A kinder and gentler tyranny : illusions of a new world order / D.
Michael Rivage-Seul and Marguerite K. Rivage-Seul; foreword by Franz Hinkelammert.
        p.   cm.
    Includes bibliographical references and index.
    ISBN 0–275–95201–0 (alk. paper)
    1. Sustainable development—Developing countries.   2. Developing
countries—Economic conditions.   3. Economic history—1990–
I. Rivage-Seul, Marguerite K.   II. Title.
HC59.72.E5R58   1995
330.9172′4—dc20   95–3341

British Library Cataloguing in Publication Data is available.

Library of Congress Catalog Card Number: 95–3341
ISBN: 0–275–95201–0

First published in 1995

Praeger Publishers, 88 Post Road West, Westport, CT 06881
An imprint of Greenwood Publishing Group, Inc.

Printed in the United States of America

Copyright Acknowledgments

The authors and publisher are grateful for permission to reprint excerpts from the following copy-
righted materials:

Jeremy Brecher and Tim Costello. "People's Transnational Coalition." *Third World War*. Hong Kong:
Christian Conference of Asia—International Affairs (1991): 73–78.

Franz J. Hinkelammert. *Crítica a la razón utopica*. San José, Costa Rica: Editorial DEI, 1984.

Franz J. Hinkelammert. *Democracia y totalitarismo*. San José, Costa Rica: Editorial DEI, 1987.

Franz J. Hinkelammert. *La fe de Abraham y el Edipo occidental*. San José, Costa Rica: Editorial DEI,
1991.

Contents

Foreword

I am pleased to introduce *A Kinder and Gentler Tyranny* by Mike and Peggy Rivage-Seul. It intends to develop for English-speaking audiences the latest work of the Departamento Ecuménico de Investigaciones (DEI) of San José, Costa Rica. In 1992, the Rivage-Seuls worked with us for a semester at the DEI. They were the first North Americans to participate in our annual workshop for invited researchers. In the fall of 1994, they returned to us for further research. In our work together, their manuscript attracted my attention as creatively interpreting for North American audiences DEI themes surrounding the free market fetishism which marks the so-called New World Order (NWO).

Since 1977 the DEI has been tracing international capitalism's drive to self-destruction inherent in its treatment of products as persons and consumers as things. All during the 1970s and 1980s, the system's necrophilia necessitated unprecedented human sacrifice at the hands of the National Security States which functioned to make conditions safe for capitalism throughout the Third World. The efforts of the then-reigning military dictatorships were papered over with a "veil of appearances." The disguise enabled the cult of death to be portrayed as a celebration of life. The veil theologically misrepresented the biblical God as requiring blood libations on behalf of the worldwide system of private property.

Obviously, the world has changed drastically since the DEI's foundation. To most, capitalism now appears stronger than ever. Its alternative has apparently disappeared with the simultaneous demise of the Soviet Union and the discrediting of historic socialism. "Democracy" has reportedly displaced both National Security States and communist dictatorships. In the words of Francis Fukuyama, we have finally reached "the end of history." Utopias are dead. Capitalism has no alternatives. It stands triumphant for all to see.

These are the NWO illusions which *A Kinder and Gentler Tyranny* tries to dispel. Here the Rivage-Seuls offer nothing less than a trenchant critique of Western culture and its underlying spirituality. The book relentlessly focuses on DEI themes of the "impossibility" of the capitalist system, and of the "human sacrifice" the free market requires for its maintenance. Additionally, this book centralizes the destructive nature of "market totalitarianism" and its inevitable tendency to "marginalize" environmental concerns. It shows how the New World Order creates a global underclass of "debt slaves" "excluded" from a "utopian" universalization of the American Way of Life. Yet the system persists, legitimated by a bastardized Christianity which exacts payment rather than forgiveness of debts.

Emphasizing historical perspective, the argument here is that the New World Order is not that new. Of course, there is the new technology -- information superhighways and the accompanying publicity. There is also the intensified internationalization of markets. Such developments are novel to some extent. But the theory and practice which accompanies them are dreadfully familiar. Theoretically, Adam Smith's "invisible hand" makes a reprise as President Reagan's "magic of the market place." "Trickle down" theory is repackaged as "supply side economics." International "Free Trade" refers to a highly regulated system of neo-mercantilism and colonialism-revisited which in the context of the North American Free Trade Agreement takes hundreds of pages of turgid prose to delineate.

In practice, the changes of the nineties attempt to reinstitute a modernized version of the world order which preceded capitalism's own *perestroika* which beginning in the 1930s incorporated elements of socialism to insure capitalism's very survival. That older order was Darwinian -- governed by the "law of the strongest," by survival of the fittest. It was a world without legal labor unions, prohibition of child labor, provisions for minimum wage, social security, workplace compensation, public education, health care, housing subsidies, unemployment insurance, paid vacations, 40 hour workweeks, environmental protection, etc. The rich lived in opulence excluding and blaming the poor for their inability to compete. On the analysis of the Rivage-Seuls, these same conditions represent the utopian vision celebrated by today's powerful advocates of the New World Order.

So in recapturing the 1890s, "Coketowns" reappear as *maquiladora* communities featuring cardboard shacks and inhumane living conditions, all justified in terms of the "social costs" and "structural adjustments" necessary to "integrate" the Third World into a system of which it has been an essential part for 500 years. The resultant "sacrifice" of the world's most vulnerable is defended in terms of not caving in to "special interests." Allegedly these include labor union members, women, students, the homeless, sick, impoverished, racial minorities, the indigenous, the unemployed, etc. Meanwhile, the "general interest" is unquestioningly understood as represented by rich investors and entrepreneurs.

In all of this, the overriding fiction maintains that "Growth" is the answer to worldwide poverty. Uncontested New World Order math implies that the Third World can achieve the level of consumption self-righteously flaunted by the U.S. where 40% of the earth's product is already devoured ravenously. The earth itself is assumed capable of absorbing the garbage produced by the universalization of consumption levels achieved in America's shining "city on a hill."

More particularly, NWO calculations overlook the "champagne glass" distribution of world resources reflected in the U.N. Human Development Report of 1992. It pointed out that 20 percent of the world's population controls nearly 83 percent of the world's income. Only 6 percent is left for the bottom 60 percent. Moreover, the gap is widening rather than narrowing, as NWO rhetoric might lead us to believe. This is shown in the following Figure:

"The Champagne Glass"

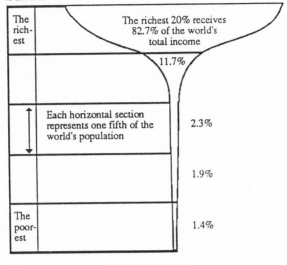

World population according to income

The rich-est	The richest 20% receives 82.7% of the world's total income
	11.7%
Each horizontal section represents one fifth of the world's population	2.3%
	1.9%
The poor-est	1.4%

The poorest 20% receives 1.4% of the world's total income

Commenting this reality, DEI scholar, Xabier Garostiaga observes[1]:

> It is impossible to "universalize" the world under these circumstances, to "globalize." If the poorest 80 percent of humanity were to adopt the patterns of consumption presently enjoyed by the richest 20 percent, we would face an ecological social and political disaster. Even so, the sole intent of the World Bank, the International Monetary Fund, the North American Free Trade Agreement and the General Agreement on Tariffs and Trade is to create a so-called homogeneous, global world. Such a feat is structurally and politically impossible under the present scheme. You cannot liberalize markets and create a level playing field for trade when an elite 20 percent of the world controls the bulk of the wealth, the technology, the military and political power available to humanity. Globalization in this context is like placing a shark and a sardine on the same fish scale: the sardine is being devoured. (12)

The Rivage-Seuls' *Kinder and Gentler Tyranny* elaborates these points in the clearest possible way. The authors present analysis of market triumphalism sadly lacking in the dominant culture's mainstream sources. In easy to understand language, they show how the market's logic (its "invisible hand") indeed supplies rich rewards for the few. However, it does so (inevitably) at the expense of the world's impoverished majority. At book's end, the Rivage-Seuls suggest bold new directions for correcting the market's automatic tendencies. The key, they hold, is found in rescuing the Judeo-Christian tradition from its perversions which since Augustine and Anselm have increasingly legitimated human sacrifice, the payment of crushing debt and the devastation of the natural environment.

Mike and Peggy are educators and peace activists of the kind we attempt to nourish at the DEI. Their familiarity with Third World thinkers makes them excellent conduits for the ideas and visions of those they present as living outside the West's "cultural cave." Having listened carefully to "outsiders" not sharing their own culture's allegience to shadow and illusion, they challenge North Americans to re-envision their world and its reigning spirituality.

Franz Hinkelammert
San José, Costa Rica
May, 1995

NOTE

1. See Xabier Garostiaga. "World Has Become a 'Champagne Glass' " *The National Catholic Reporter* (27 Jan. 1995): 3. See also Heinz Dietrich Steffan, "América Latina entre el capitalismo utópico y la democracia mundial." *Pasos* 51, (Jan./Feb. 1994): 9-13.

Preface

This book arises from an identity crisis experienced in our local peacemaking community in Berea, Kentucky. We call ourselves "The Berea Interfaith Taskforce for Peace." Like similar groups throughout the country, we started up in the early 1980s in response to the Reagan administration's arms buildup and its counterinsurgency and proinsurgency wars in El Salvador and Nicaragua respectively.

However, after 1989 we lost direction. Our sense of "task" vanished with the breakup of the Soviet Union. Gone was the urgency of the nuclear FREEZE "house parties" we sponsored to mobilize opposition to the bankrupting military policy of the 1980s. Neither were the regular demonstrations at our congressman's office in Lexington, Kentucky necessary to protest U.S. policy in Central America. Our issues had disappeared. Unwittingly, our "peace group" became a kind of innocuous discussion club. This month our post-potluck speaker might address Somalia; next month, Bosnia; the following month who knows?

To some extent, we felt good about this turn of events. It showed we had done our job well over a decade and more. After all, the Cold War had ended. So had the nuclear arms race as we knew it. The Soviets were no longer our enemies. Formal democracy was spreading throughout Central America. South Africa had ended apartheid. Even the Israelis and Palestinians had shaken hands in the White House Rose Garden. It was a new world. Presidents Bush and Clinton told us so.

And since peacemakers throughout the country had a hand in that, perhaps, some thought, we should declare victory, throw a party, and disband to enjoy the "normalcy" of the "New World Order" that our presidents proclaimed. As one of our Taskforce members put it, "The enemy is no longer 'out there,' a government doing things we can't agree with. The problem of peacemaking has moved from the realm of politics to the interior life, to dealing with sources of hatred and violence within each of us. In a sense, we've got to tend our own gardens."

That observation and the vision behind it was not unique to our local group. It remains widespread throughout the peace community. But however common and understandable it might be, it strikes us as almost uniquely "First World" -- able to originate only from those who still think everyone will benefit from the emerging international arrangement of economics and politics. However, the complacency of "tending our own gardens" becomes ludicrous when the world is revisioned from a Third World standpoint.[1]

Third World peace activists do not wonder "What's to resist now that the Cold War has ended?" For them, the dawning of the "New World Order" is fearful. In many ways it is less hopeful than the old world order. Its "free trade" cornerstones like the North American Free Trade Agreement must be resisted at every turn. As rebels in Chiapas, Mexico put it, the new trade pacts amount to "World War III" against the planet's poor. Its advocacy of unrestrained, untargeted "growth" wreaks the equivalent of nuclear devastation on the natural environment. Stated more historically, the new order is like the return of a much older, Dickensian economic arrangement that preceded the Cold War.

Members of our peace group have had trouble accepting these views. Consequently, we have been immobilized. We lack a consistent stand on issues of justice, peace, and war, be it a shooting war, or the New World Order economic arrangements Susan George terms "financial low intensity conflict." We have had trouble deciding, because unlike our Third World counterparts, we lack a coherent vision of the world and how it works. Or rather, our vision tends to be pragmatic. Its ideology tells us to decide issues on a case-by-case basis. So each time a crisis arises, we must decide again which side we are on. In Somalia we might stand with our president. In Iraq, we perhaps should oppose him. Regarding the New World Order in general, we just do not know. In all cases, it takes us a long time to decide.

First World complacency about the New World Order juxtaposed with Third World alarm reminds us of Plato's "Allegory of the Cave." As we will see in Chapter 1, that image is central to our argument that peacemakers need acquaintance with Third World political theory. Plato described the human condition in terms of prisoners in a cave mistaking the shadows projected by their keepers for reality. First World shadows tell us the unfolding New World Order is beneficial. Unlimited economic growth can lead to U.S.-style prosperity for everyone. Millions of deaths each year, as a result of lost jobs and the consequent hunger from poverty are the price we (the poor among us) must pay to arrive at the projected utopia. Meanwhile, fears about impending environmental disaster reflect the timid concerns of paranoid extremists. A little voluntary tinkering here and there is all that is required to "save the planet."

The vision is quite different once we step "outside the cave" and into the Third World. There peace activists have a coherent understanding that enables them to see the impossibility of the New World Order and its reliance on "market" as the solution to virtually every human problem. Our thesis is that effective peace activism in the First World is intimately connected with that Third World vision. We have to exercise "moral imagination" by changing our viewpoint (Chapter 1); we must sharpen our understanding of how the international market works and why it necessarily excludes the least well-off (Chapter 2); this demands developing historical perspective revealing that the "triumphant" system of international capitalism is a colossal failure (Chapter 3), that its basic ideology is genocidal and destructive of the natural environment (Chapter 4), and that it relies on a religious understanding that turns the West's most basic religious heritage on its head (Chapter 5). Finally, Chapter 6 will synthesize the critical vision we think peace activists must develop in the face of the New World Order. It will present the direction toward replacing that New World Order with what we call a New Earth Order based on human welfare and environmental sustainability.

Our goal, then, is "political education." Third World intellectuals, activists, teachers and students see such education as foundational to any effective work for peace and justice. Our point is to share the political education we have received from such people. A glance at the works cited in this book makes it clear to whom we listened. We draw heavily upon publications by Costa Rica's *Departamento Ecuménico de Investigaciones* (DEI), a research institute founded in 1977 by Chile's Hugo Assman. We have been reading DEI books and journals for years, and in 1992 we had the privilege of studying with DEI scholars at their center in San José, Costa Rica. We did so in the company of a dozen other invited researchers from various Latin American and European countries. Ongoing conversation with them sharpened our own thinking and some late drafts of our book.

Even more, our thought was given edge by the DEI's permanent scholars. The analysis of Pablo Richard, Elsa Tamez, Carmelo Alvarez, Raquel Rodriguez, Arnoldo Mora, Julio de Santa Ana, Enrique Dussell, Fernando Mires, Raúl Vidales, Ingemar Hedström, Richard Shaull, Janet and Roy May and others from the DEI play central roles in the reflections presented here. Above all, what follows shares the insights of Franz Hinkelammert, the heart and soul of the DEI. Along with many throughout Latin America, we regard him as one of the great thinkers of the contemporary West. The final stages of our work benefitted immensely from the guidance of Helio Gallardo, an incomparable social analyst, who patiently read, critiqued, and generally inspired our work during our time in Costa Rica. Needless to say, responsibility for what is said here belongs entirely to us.

NOTE

1. In most of our study, we will refer to these countries as the "Third World." We do this fully aware that with the virtual disappearance of the "Second World" as the antagonist of "the West" in a bipolar configuration of dominant powers, the phrase "Third World" has lost much of its meaning. We retain the designation, however, because the sources we cite characteristically use the phrase. Toward the end of our book, having presented reasons for doing so, we change our terminology to "Two-thirds World," reminding us of the widespread nature of world poverty and hunger and that the "development" experienced in the United States and Western Europe is a decidedly minority phenomenon.

1

Illusion: Everyone Is Better Off without the Soviets

The sudden and profound changes that have shaken the world over the last few years are unfortunately ambivalent. On the one hand, these largely unforeseen events are cause for great rejoicing. They indeed signal the dawning of a New World Order with enormous potential for the achievement of lasting peace. On the other hand, though, our era's seismic shifts provoke seriously concerned second thought. This becomes apparent when the brave new world of the 1990s is examined with what this study calls "moral imagination," the ability to "revision" the world through the eyes of its victims, especially those inhabiting the so-called Third World.

The exercise of imagination in this sense reveals that work for peace and justice is now more urgent than ever. The employment of moral imagination uncovers the fact that the dawning New World Order mortally threatens the world's poor and the very biosphere all of us inhabit. The institution of that order amounts to the prosecution of "World War III" against the poor. It is a conflict waged by the developed countries of the West and their allies in the South. The insight provided by the exercise of moral imagination suggests that a *change in worldview* is in order for peacemakers. The comprehensive nature of the paradigm shift must be commensurate with the widely hailed new international relationships.

FOUR KEY DEVELOPMENTS: TWO VIEWS

The urgency of peace and justice work remains hidden for most U.S. citizens. It is especially shrouded by four recent developments which have engendered the following complacent convictions now nearly universally held throughout the West:

1. *The end of the Cold War has removed the greatest single obstacle to peace.* Following the failure of "historic socialism," nearly fifty long years of Cold War have finally drawn to a close. The Berlin Wall has been torn down. Troop reductions have long since become the order of the day. A new spirit of cooperation between the United States and Russia has taken hold. The United

States is now even extending "foreign aid" to the former USSR. The world is no longer living "under the gun." All of us can breathe more easily.

2. *The newly triumphant capitalist system remains the only realistic possibility for achieving world prosperity.* In the aftermath of communist failure, the Western system of free enterprise and democracy has emerged triumphant from its death struggle with communism. Whole peoples enslaved in Eastern Europe have been liberated from totalitarian systems that have kept them in chains since World War II. At the very least, this signifies that Soviet communism and the Stalinist interpretation of Marxism have unequivocally collapsed. Less cautiously put, it seems that Marxism and socialism are themselves dead. Meanwhile, a neoliberal economics of growth is achieving nearly unquestioned dominance throughout the world. Free market capitalism, in other words, has no viable alternative. Even with all its faults, it remains the best of all possible systems. Hence, the principal barrier to eventual world prosperity is continued government interference with the "magic of the market."

3. *The threat of planetary holocaust has become remote.* The end of the Cold War has largely stopped the threat of worldwide destruction. Whole classes of weapons that a few short years ago profoundly threatened Europeans both East and West, as well as North Americans and the environment itself, have been eliminated. Even before the official Soviet demise, the United States and USSR appeared to be engaged in a kind of reverse arms race, striving for leadership in arms reduction rather than in arms production and deployment. As a result of this, the day seems fast approaching when humankind need no longer fear total destruction of our planet's environment.

4. *The function of war and the military is now truly one of peacekeeping.* In the kinder and gentler setting following the end of the Cold War, it remains now for the United States to employ its military might to foster a "New World Order." With preoccupation directed away from The Russians, the military can now turn its attention to other areas of more immediate concern. This happened, for instance, in the 1991 Gulf War as well as in Libya and Panama. Each "action" involved bringing to heel a recalcitrant and nearly diabolical international terrorist -- Saddam Hussein, Mu'ammar Gadhafi and Manuel Noriega. Additionally, military resources can now be redeployed to such socially beneficial missions as controlling and eventually eliminating the international drug traffic, which so disastrously undermines the foundations of our culture. Thus the interests of our government, of the military, and the peace activists seem to be converging at last. This promises a new era of cooperation between ordinary citizens on the one hand, and national leaders on the other. Happily, the need for the past's unremitting opposition to government policy seems less imperative.

As noted in our introduction, such developments have led some to draw the conclusion that like the U.S. system itself, peace activism has apparently triumphed. The meetings, civil disobediences, the letter writing and phone calling, the demonstrations and teach-ins have all borne fruit. The peace community can evidently rest on its laurels to some extent, while continuing to exert pressure to keep our politicians' feet to the fire of continued negotiations aimed at making our planet safe from the threat of destruction by war. In other words, the work of peacemakers has come to a rather successful end--or at least to a resting place.

Another Vision

And yet, there are disturbing signs that such conclusions may be unwarranted and even dangerous. Coming principally from the Third World, the indicators in question are the very signs interpreted so positively in settings like our own - the end of the Cold War, the triumph of capitalism, the reversal of the nuclear arms race, and the shift of enemies from "the Russians" to "Rogue State" madmen. It is not that recent developments are not welcomed as hopeful. Instead, each has a dark underside that adversely impacts the poor of the Third World. Once again, consideration of these shaded sides suggests that work for peace and justice is far from over, but may simply be entering a new phase. Consider the following points of reasoning.

1. *The end of the Cold War is ambivalent for the Third World.* While the conclusion of the Cold War signals a reduction in East-West tensions, it does not hold the same promise for North-South conflicts. In fact, the achievement of peace in many areas of the Third World now seems more remote than ever. One component of the Cold War's end is termination of commitment on the part of former socialist countries to liberation struggles in the less developed world. This removes an important counterbalance to the designs of the United States, the poor nations' historically inveterate foe. Absent the threat of Soviet reprisal, the United States can focus its attention more intently on its perceived enemies to the South. It can even more freely intervene in that sphere to protect the system that treats so many harshly. Intervention often entails expanding the gunboat diplomacy, which, as we will see, has been the hallmark of its twentieth-century relationships with less developed nations. The poor of the Third World, in other words, cannot emphatically breathe more easily because the Cold War has ended. They have lost their staunchest ally. This is nowhere more clearly illustrated than in Nicaragua and Cuba (Girardi 1989, 23).

2. *Capitalism is a failed and impossible system.* From the viewpoint of Third World peace activists, free market capitalism has failed miserably. Moreover, as a system it is entirely incapable of achieving success. Its apparent triumph is the very root of what is wrong with the Third World. Capitalism's so-called victory merely masks the destruction historically wreaked by the cult of free markets among the planet's majority. In fact, the very reason for widespread Marxist-inspired resistance has been and continues to be capitalism's 500-year demonstration of its inability to meet the needs of working people. Put otherwise, if Eastern Europe's economic disaster after three-quarters of a century is taken as proof of communism's failure, what are we to think of capitalism's 500-year probation in the Third World? After all that time, the gap between the local rich and the poor, and between poor nations and developed ones is growing daily. From the perspective of the Third World, then, the so-called "victory of capitalism" is totally illusory. Girardi has made this observation in the form of a question:

Is it that the reasons which over the last two centuries have given rise to the communist, socialist and Marxist search for a global alternative have somehow lost their validity? Has the oppressive, marginating, and alienating character of capitalism which made finding an alternative so urgent, ceased to be true? If one responds as inevitably one must from the Third World perspective, that those characteristics, those contradictions, those problems are today more acute than ever, then one can only reject with indignation the thesis of those who consider the search concluded and problem merely historical. (37)

Of course this viewpoint runs entirely counter to the spirit of the times as experienced in the United States. This is no accident, for the reality is purposely hidden from those of us living in developed countries. As Girardi says, "(I)t is not for nothing that the multinational information sources are an essential part of the capitalist system" (37).

Neither is it an accident of history that free market capitalism has failed. As Costa Rica's Franz Hinkelammert has pointed out, the system simply *cannot* succeed. It is impossible. This is because only feasible economic systems *can* persist. They are feasible only if they can maintain and renew the means by which they exist over the long haul. These means include meeting the subsistence needs of workers and the protection of the natural environment. However, without the control that is antithetical to the notion of "free enterprise," the market system consumes precisely those elements. It first of all fails to provide employment for available workers. Thus in many Third World neoliberal regimes, unemployment commonly reaches fifty percent or more of the workforce. Such statistics are directly related to massive deaths within the working class, especially of children. Moreover, even those holding jobs do not escape system-related death because capitalist wages are routinely inadequate to support workers' families. In addition, capitalism everywhere consumes the natural resources by which and from which its products are made. On the first point, Hinkelammert writes:

> The current world economic crisis demonstrates the incapacity of the capitalist system to secure full employment and adequate levels of income distribution. The capitalist system cannot achieve such ends as full employment or income distribution which permits satisfaction of basic necessities. The system finds its flexibility unilaterally in its capacity to produce this or that product and to apply this or that technology. However as far as employment and income distribution are concerned, it is the least flexible system which has ever existed. (*Democrácia* 50)

For this reason, Third World critical theorists presently admit that there can be no viable alternative to socialism. Helio Gallardo defines socialism's meaning in this context: Socialism, he says:

> is not a discourse nor an ideology nor a science. It is rather a practice of *liberation* whose agents are the exploited, the rejected, the segregated, the oppressed by the systems, institutions and actors of the actual organization of the world, be they economic, social, political or ideological. Socialism is the name which is given to Agrarian Reform or the New International

Economic Order, or the liquidation of patriarchal domination when such revolutionary practices block and interrupt the logic of capitalist accumulation, the logic of profit and of sacrifice directed against the human being. We ought to term *socialism* and *socialist* the practices and movements by which people resist, combat and politically invalidate the institutions and the actors which demand the victims necessary to bring about, for example, development, to form the State, to achieve peace or to ensure the "magic of the market." (*Crisis* 17)

This, however, does not mean that capitalism's panacea of "total market" must be replaced by "total planning." That remedy has already been tried with disastrous consequences in the countries identified as "historically socialist." Hinkelammert writes:

The market as such cannot be replaced by anything else. At the same time, if we ask for alternatives to the planned economies of the countries of historic socialism, we must not succumb to the temptation to abolish economic planning as such. Attempts at total solutions by the abolition of the problem itself, only reproduce the crisis whose solution is sought. (*"Capitalismo sin alternativas?"* 11)

In other words, Hinkelammert recognizes the problems of both historic capitalism and historic socialism. Total abolition of either system, he says, is no solution. Some combination of both systems is required. But in view of the problems of an unregulated market, planning must regulate market. The socialist goals of full employment and environmental protection, that is, must be given priority.

On behalf of the natural environment, U.S. geologian Thomas Berry, echoes Hinkelammert's call for a socialism that departs from the distortions and limits of its East bloc embodiments. However, in Berry's opinion, the socialism in question must extend further still.

[A]n awareness should exist that the present system is too devastating to the natural fruitfulness of the earth to long supply human needs. Alternative programs are being elaborated and becoming functional. If the moral norm of economics is what is happening to the millions of persons in need, then these more-functional economic developments are required not only by those excluded from the present system, but also by the entire nation community, by the entire human community, and by the entire earth community. This is not a socialism on the national scale, nor is it an international socialism, it is *planetary socialism*. (79 emphasis added)

3. *Capitalism's economics of growth threaten planetary holocaust.* This third point is connected with elements extremely important to reorienting the vision of peace activists--with the continued menace of nuclear weapons, and with capitalism's devastating environmental impact. First, nuclear arms constitute a powerful image revealing capitalism's unfeasible nature. Again it is Hinkelammert who points out that a system whose defense depends on nuclear weapons cannot really endure (*Demócracia* 19). This is because the weapons' efficacy hinges on their controllers' freedom from human error and weakness

(including insanity, nervous breakdowns, drug addiction, and alcohol abuse). Moreover, the effectiveness of nuclear weapons depends on elimination of technical malfunction. In human systems, all of these elements are clearly impossible. To deny this represents the worst kind of naive utopianism.

Nevertheless, the utopianism persists. Despite recent developments, the United States as well as countries such as Israel and Brazil, continue to develop and deploy nuclear weapons. They persist in husbanding arsenals still capable of destroying our planet many times over. And why? None of the usual "rational" responses ring true any more, if ever they did. Previously, the "free world" had claimed that the earth's destruction was worth risking in order to save humanity from the fate of losing its freedom to the absolutely evil and immutable system of international communism. It was the "better dead than Red" philosophy writ large. But now that communism has demonstrated its extreme changeability and possibly even its mortality, such claims should be impotent. In fact, one would think that communism's demonstrated mutability might lead opinion makers to reflect sagely on what a colossal error waging nuclear war might have been on the many occasions it was contemplated. In the light of subsequent history, was the Korean War worth nuclear holocaust? the Cuban missile crisis? Vietnam?

Such reflections, however, are entirely absent in the mainstream. For some reason, the presence of nuclear weapons continues to be accepted as "realistic," even though the rationale for their use has virtually disappeared. In the absence of those reasons, one can only conclude that the remaining purpose of nuclear weapons is to protect the present world order whose maintenance has been elevated to the status of an absolute value. In theological terms, that status quo has been divinized. That is, in order to protect what is apparently perceived as the absolute good of the present world order, that order's "leaders" are still willing to risk the absolute evil of the world's total destruction.

The second element important to reorienting the vision of peace activists is capitalism's "nuclear" impact on the environment. The apparent madness of divinizing the current world order is only unmistakably *imaged* by nuclear weapons. The psychosis , however, finds much deeper roots. It is located at the very heart of the West's industrial system, of which nuclear weapons are merely a sign. More particularly, reigning policies reflecting the West's commitment to "progress" daily cause extinctions and other environmental tragedies that amount to "nuclear" devastation carried out in slow motion. Thus Fernando Mires explains that by the turn of the century processes related to modern industry will eliminate between 500,000 and one million presently living species (*El discurso* 138). Every minute fifty acres of tropical rain forest, the habitat of fully half the earth's living species, are irrevocably destroyed (131). This constitutes total war against entire segments of creation. Thomas Berry has perceived this as well.

> For humans to assume rights to occupy land by excluding other lifeforms from their needed habitat is to offend the community in its deepest structure. Further, it is even to declare a state of warfare, which humans cannot win since they themselves are ultimately dependent on those very lifeforms that they are destroying. (166)

In other words, the outworking of the newly triumphant economic system is simply total warfare by other means. It represents holocaust that human beings wage against their environment and ultimately, of course, against themselves.

4. *The function of war and the military is to enforce capitalism's discipline as its leaders prosecute World War III against the poor.* The outworking of the capitalist system also involves more immediate attacks on the human species. This returns us to the fourth development so optimistically assessed in the developed world, but perceived in a less sanguine fashion in underdeveloped countries. Here the reference is to the nature of war and to the "peacekeeping" role of the military in the New World Order. From the Third World standpoint, fulfillment of this assignment dictates that wars against the species' majority continue unabated. In this connection, the view from the developed world sees only the minor "brushfire" engagements earlier mentioned. Often these latter are referred to as "low-intensity conflicts." However, in the less developed world where the wars commonly take place, they are experienced as major conflicts of extreme high intensity. Nicaragua's Contra War provides an example.[1]

But why are such "actions" carried out? Usually we are told their purpose is to defend traditional American values of freedom, justice, democracy, or for more concrete ends such as making our cities drug free. However, on other occasions, what Third World analysts see as the more believable cause of all such wars stands unveiled for all to see. The Gulf War is a case in point. There pretexts about liberty and justice could not withstand even the slightest scrutiny. In Kuwait and Saudi Arabia, it was a question of defending feudal dictatorships of the worst kind. So U.S. officials had to admit: "Its about oil." Third World scholars would say, the Gulf War was like most of the other wars fought by the West. Its purpose was to preserve a way of life largely dependent on universally disproportionate consumption patterns. Chile's Fernando Mires has energetically indicated the dimensions of the consumption in question:

> One United States citizen consumes twice the energy as a German; six times more than a Hindu; 160 times more than a Tanzanian; and 1,100 times more than a Rwandan. In the face of such unequal consumption of energy, there remain only two alternatives: the first is the one proposed by the "theoreticians of growth:" that all countries of the earth achieve the level and style of life enjoyed by U.S. citizens. But is anyone so dense as to think that this planet will not resist energy loss on such a scale? The other alternative would be working on behalf of politics aimed at reducing energy wastes, above all in the more industrial countries, and at the use of renewable energy resources on a massive scale. The only problem is that this [second] alternative requires extraordinarily radical changes in economics, politics and culture. (*El discurso* 29-30)

To prevent such radical changes, the United States prosecutes its wars against the poor who are understandably desirous of increasing their share of consumption in order to transcend their abysmal poverty. More than forty years ago, George Kennan, then head of the State Department's Policy Planning Staff, implied the "necessity" of such "lifestyle wars" when he wrote:

We have about 50 percent of the world's wealth, but only 6.3 percent of its population. In this situation, we cannot fail to be the object of envy and resentment. Our real task in the coming period is to devise a pattern of relationships which will permit us to maintain this position of disparity without positive detriment to our national security. To do so we will have to dispense with all sentimentality and day-dreaming and our attention will have to be concentrated everywhere on our immediate national objectives. We need not deceive ourselves that we can afford today the luxury of altruism and world benefaction. We should cease to talk about vague and unreal objectives such as human rights, the raising of living standards and democratization. The day is not far off when we are going to have to deal in straight power concepts. The less we are then hampered by idealistic slogans the better. (Chomsky *Turning the Tide* 48)

But the West's way of waging war on the Third World has lately become more subtle and covert than Kennan might have imagined. For its leaders have discovered a mechanism for gaining control of Third World resources, without firing a single shot in conflicts of either high or low intensity. Instead, all that is required is to allow capitalism's automatic processes to unfold. Those processes alone end up placing Third World peoples in the traditional position of nations who have lost on international battlefields. The key "mechanism" here is the Third World's external debt. As Fidel Castro announced in 1985, that obligation is totally unpayable. But the banking industry's continued insistence that the obligation be met has placed Third World peoples in a kind of debt servitude where, like the losers of wars, their national policy may be dictated by the victors without consulting the will of those the policy directly impacts. Hinkelammert describes it this way:

[T]he one who falls into an unpayable debt loses his or her liberty. There remains not a single moment of life which he or she is able to self-determine. The creditor holds everything in his hands. The debtor falls into slavery and, historically speaking, unpayable debts have always been one of the main reasons for slavery. The unpayable debt has transformed Latin America into a Sysiphus who can never arrive at his destination, but who at the same time can never relax. Therefore Castro's announcement of the debt's unpayability was for the international banking system and for the countries of the center an announcement of its definitive victory. Meanwhile for Latin America, it was the announcement of its defeat in the long run. For the region, the payment of the debt is a war lost before it has begun. (*La deuda* 59)

As we shall see, the debt crisis and its consequences are so severe that it has driven Hinkelammert and others to use it as an entry point to reinterpret the entire history of Western civilization. The reinterpretation makes it clear that far from being the apex of "the ascent of man," the Western tradition represents the ideological superstructure of the most devastating political economy that has ever existed.[2]

MORAL IMAGINATION AND THIS STUDY

Once again, it is our position that the developed world must listen closely
to the understandings of its Third World counterpart, contradicting on virtually
every point received wisdom about the nature of the brave new world we have
just entered. Doing so is an exercise of moral imagination.

The exercise of this faculty entails breaking away from the developed world's
exclusive view of recent world-shaking events. That view might be characterized
as taking place "from the veranda." There, well-to- do white males (joined by a
few friendly women and people of color) spend their "happy hours" overlooking
the city or estate discussing how what they see works. They speak of their
investments and of the centrality of such speculations to general world
prosperity. Comfortably stirring their drinks, they discuss how the events
unfolding below might be directed to serve more smoothly their own interests.
Those interests, of course, are invariably identified with the common good.

Meanwhile, things look different from the street or the field. Problems are
different. A central worry is not a return on an investment, but rather the
sacrifices necessary to pay a suffocating debt incurred by others. Western history
is different. It is not an account of capitalism's triumph, but of 500 years of
misery induced by that allegedly victorious system. The earth itself is often
different -- especially for tribal peoples who are marginalized in every westernized
culture. For traditional peoples, rather than an inert mass open to exploitation
in the name of progress, the earth is a living being endowed with dreams that can
be shared, and with discourse that should be heard and respected. Enemies and
allies are different. The United States often ends up wearing the black hat; our
designated foes, the white one. In broader terms, solidarity with slum dwellers in
São Paulo, with their counterparts in Johannesburg, with Palestinians in the
Mideast, or with the earth itself as a living organism, uncovers interpretations of
the world that set on their heads analysis issuing from "above."

However, the contention here goes further still. It asserts that attempting to
view the world from the street or from the field does not merely yield difference;
it gives more accuracy as well. Fernando Mires makes this point. Speaking of
Western modernity, he observes that those who analyze and laud it are generally
modernity's beneficiaries. These analysts concentrate on the advantages
industrialism and high technology have brought Western society. Their
concentration generally excludes the voices of the majority whose experience as
victims has been radically other. It is this excluded majority, Mires argues,
whose voices communicate essential truths otherwise ignored (*El discurso.* 12,
72, 142). It is easier for a system's victims to detect what is wrong with the
offending structure and to determine what must be done to remedy the harms
inflicted. At the very least, those voices express more truth because they
complete the conventional picture.

Plato's Allegory of the Cave

This idea that those living on the periphery of political-economic activity
provide *entre* to levels of truth not accessible to those "at the center" was long

ago suggested by Plato, the father of Western intellectual history. In fact, Plato provides us with a remarkable, if somewhat neglected, image for understanding this privileged knowledge of society's outsiders.

In *The Republic's* "Parable of the Cave," Plato describes what he takes to be the human condition. He asks his readers to imagine a group of people dwelling in a cave since birth, completely unaware of the light of day. There they are shackled alongside each other so that they sit in a row facing the back wall of the cave, unable to see their companions or to view their own bodies. On the wall the prisoners are forced to face, shadows move constantly, produced by a fire that burns behind their backs. The only images the prisoners have of themselves are their shadows cast on the wall from the light of the fire. But other shadows appear as well. Unseen by the prisoners, people pass on a bridge in front of the fire carrying statues of wood and stone. The prisoners' own shadows, those of these statues and their bearers are all the captives know of reality.

But then one of the prisoners is released from bondage, forced to stand up and face the blinding fire for the first time. The released one discerns the people on the bridge with their statues and recognizes the situation of the other cave dwellers. Dragged forcibly out of the cave, the escapee resists, tripping and falling all the way. Once outside the cave, however, the released captive is nearly blinded by the sunlight. But with eyes finally adjusted, the escapee is introduced to an entirely new world. With a new understanding of reality, the prisoner is moved to free the others still shackled inside the cave. The escapee returns to share the news of the world outside. But instead of welcoming the report, the prisoners in the cavern are angered by this would-be liberator who disturbs their peace. They swear to resist violently anyone who attempts to convince them to leave their safe haven.

The Vision of the Outsider

Plato's parable leaves us with a multitude of images for making sense of what we are describing here as a disastrous "New World Order." Most significant is the vision of the outsider -- the one who escaped from the cave. The escapee points out that there exists a reality that calls into question the cave's shadows. Without contacting that reality, moral vision is impossible. For Plato, attaining this critical standpoint meant accessing a world of unchanging ideas that exists apart from the sensory world of day-to-day experience. He wrote: "the prison-house is the world of sight, the light of the fire is the sun, and you will not misapprehend me if you interpret the journey upwards to be the ascent of the soul into the intellectual world" (307).

Plato, then, thought the world of experience was fundamentally misleading in the search for truth and morality. Justice was found only by escaping the material world and achieving contact with the world of pure ideas. On this point, we think Plato was exactly wrong. Justice is not found in some abstract world of ideas but by redirecting attention to the historical, material world. This is particularly true in the highly ideologized situation of a World Order dominated by abstract television images and government "perception management," where the real movement of imagination becomes escape from the world of ideas to confronting the "real world" of flesh and blood. This was illustrated in the 1991 Gulf War. There, the abstract world of ideas and images became the major obstacle to the experience of real life -- to hearing the screams of dying children, to seeing the blood and smelling the burning flesh of the incinerated thousands. The real world, in other words, remained invisible despite inundation with abstractions and images reminiscent of Plato's cave. Truth-seekers had to "imagine the real" in order to begin apprehending it at all.[3] Hinkelammert writes, "Whereas reality is an approximation of the idea in the cave myth, the idea is an approximation of the reality of real life" (*Ideological* 60). The point of moral imagination's exercise is perceiving life as it is experienced daily by others that our culture renders abstract.

In another context, Plato himself suggested that the ideal outsider to help begin the process of critical thought is the foreigner -- someone from outside Athens. For like the parable's central figure, people from countries not our own usually do not benefit from the particular lies we are brought up on; they have nothing to lose by calling them into question. Their observations help us see our own reality with new eyes -- with those of a foreigner. That, in fact, is the way Plato defined educated persons -- those who have the ability to see their own cultures as a foreigner would. The outsiders facilitate the exercise of moral imagination.

CONCLUSION

What follows attempts to expose the vision of the outsider, of the excluded, of the marginated, of the victim -- of those negatively affected by the New World Order. The point is to stimulate new thought and a sense of urgency empowering peace activists, educators, and students to seize initiative in the face of a totalitarian global system working against the interests of our planet's majority and of the planet itself. The moment must be grasped before it is too late.

NOTES

1. In relation to Nicaragua's population, the percentage of persons maimed and killed actually surpassed the percentage of those similarly affected in the United States during World War II.

2. All of this means that it is no exaggeration to say that the policies of free market capitalism amount to an actual world war against the world's poor. Leaders in both the developed and underdeveloped worlds have employed that image themselves. In 1979, for instance, the Committee of Santa Fe advising the incoming Reagan administration wrote:

World War III is almost over. The Soviet Union, operating under the cover of increasing nuclear superiority, is strangling the Western industrialized nations by interdicting their oil and ore supplies and is encircling the People's Republic of China. Latin America and Southern Asia are the scenes of strife of the third phase of World War III. The first two phases --

containment and détente -- have been succeeded by the Soviet strategy of double envelopment -- interdiction of the West's oil and ore and the geographical encirclement of the PRC. America's basic freedoms and economic self interest require that the United States be and act as a first rate power. (Committee 1)

On the same topic, but from the Third World side, Brazilian labor leader, Luis Ignacio Silva has connected World War III more directly with the underdeveloped world's external debt and with nuclear devastation.

The Third World War has already started -- a silent war, not for that reason any the less sinister. The war is tearing down Brazil, Latin America and practically all the Third World. Instead of soldiers dying there are children; instead of millions of wounded there are millions of unemployed; instead of destruction of bridges there is the tearing down of factories, schools, hospitals, and entire economies. It is a war by the United States against the Latin American continent and the Third World. It is a war over the foreign debt, one which has as its main weapon interest, a weapon more deadly than the atom bomb, more shattering than a laser beam. (Buchanan 93)

3. In the previous decade of peace education the need to "imagine the real" was the focus of psychiatrist Robert J. Lifton's campaign to awaken the U.S. public to the dangers of the nuclear arms race. (17) Lifton diagnosed the North American public as suffering from "psychic numbing" -- a learned disability preventing us from understanding nuclear reality. These, of course, are simply other terms for describing life in the cave. Our suggestion here is that "imagining the real" in the decade of the nineties may involve refocusing our imaginations in the direction of the outsider.

WORKS CITED

Berry, Thomas. *The Dream of the Earth*. San Francisco: Sierra Club Books, 1988.
Buchanan, Keith and Anne. "Global Class War: A Review Article on *A Fate Worse than Debt*." *Race and Class* 30, no. 3, (Jan.-Mar. 1989): 91-97.
Chomsky, Noam. *Turning the Tide*. Boston: South End Press, 1985.
Committee of Santa Fe. *A New Inter-American Policy for the Eighties*. Washington, D.C.: Council for Inter-American Security, 1980.
Gallardo, Helio. *Crisis del socialismo historico: ideologías y desafíos*. San José, Costa Rica: Editorial DEI, 1991.
Girardi, Giulio. *La conquista de América: con qué derecho?* San José, Costa Rica: Editorial DEI, 1989.
Hinkelammert, Franz J. "Capitalismo sin alternativas?" *Pasos* 37, (Sept./Oct. 1991): 11-23.
_____. *Democracia y totalitarismo*. San José, Costa Rica: Editorial D.E.I., 1987.
_____. *The Ideological Weapons of Death*. New York: Orbis Books, 1986.
_____. *La deuda externa de América Latina: el automatismo de la deuda*. San José, Costa Rica: Editorial DEI, 1988.
Lifton, Robert. "Beyond Nuclear Numbing." *Teachers College Record*, 84 (1982), 15-29.
Mires, Fernando. *El discurso de la naturaleza: ecologia y política en América Latina*. San José, Costa Rica: Editorial DEI, 1988.
Plato. *Dialogues of Plato*. Translated by B. Jowett. 2nd ed. Vol 3: *Republic*. Oxford: Clarendon Press, 1875.

2

Illusion: The Poor Are To Blame

Most of us have trouble grasping the structures of the New World Order (NWO), of understanding how it works. Many Third World activists, on the other hand, do not share our difficulty. Instead, they explain the world system in clear terms of a Third World War against the poor. Though invisible to us, this conflict permeates all aspects of life in economically underdeveloped countries (UDCs). As Brazil's Ignacio Luis Silva has indicated, World War III's most devastating battles involve no shooting at all. Its weapons are more often computers than AK47s. Its generals and even the foot soldiers in most cases, wear pin-striped suits; they seldom leave the insulation of their plush offices; they never get their hands dirty. Even when guns are fired and bombs dropped, the crucial acts are typically performed by surrogate armies of UDC locals and developed world mercenaries for whom no government accepts responsibility. In all cases, operations are covered by the rhetoric of New World Order, peace, cooperation, and harmony. It is Plato's Cave all over again.[1]

When the devastations of World War III are recognized, the shadows in our cave present familiar "stories" explaining away any responsibility for their existence. We are led to believe that overpopulation, laziness, and backward religious beliefs are to blame. None of us, experts say, has any real control over those elements as they impinge on the world's poor. We can only suggest solutions of education, birth control, and enlightenment. At the same time, we are led to understand miseries associated with high unemployment as the natural, essentially short-term outworkings of the Free Market. No one really bears responsibility for what the market decrees. Eventually, we are told, the market is capable of answering needs and discouraging unacceptable behavior. Unlike "moral solutions," allowing the market, rather than human decision, to take care of "development" problems is uncoercive. Though its short-term effects may be regrettable, humanly speaking, they respect the individual freedom that Westerners prize so highly. U.S. Assistant Secretary of State for Inter-American Affairs, Alexander F. Watson, indicated this in a 1994 address before the Institute of the Americas:

> Market-based economic reform is a major part of the recipe for improving

governance and controlling corruption. With privatization of state enterprises and the elimination or liberalization of controls on prices, foreign exchange and trade, economic decisions are shaped by impersonal market forces rather than bureaucracies which can become subject to improper influence. (157)

There are, then, two principal dimensions to the "shadow accounts" that prevent even peace activists from critically examining the New World Order. The first explains why there is poverty in the world. The second tells how the market solves problems naturally. Each is contradicted by Third World analysts.

With this in mind, the chapter that follows offers studies in contrast. The first part directly juxtaposes First and Third World accounts of why poverty exists. The second part of the chapter then presents analysis eliciting judgment that the story originating from the Third World is closer to the truth. Finally, part three of this chapter will summarize the worldwide structures of the international free market that lie at the heart of the New World Order. We will show why these institutions necessarily neglect the requirements of the most needy and perpetuate their misery. Grasping these points must be a major focus for peace and justice activists.

THE TWO STORIES BEHIND THIRD WORLD POVERTY

The Explanation of Third World Poverty Originating in the Developed World

1. Good and ill fortune (or God's blessing or its absence) divide rich nations from the poor.

2. Poor nations are "unfortunate" in that their land and/or weather are not generally suited to production of food or of wealth in general.

3. For some reason, Third World citizens irrationally insist on having large families which they are unable to afford.

The Explanation of Third World Poverty Originating in the Underdeveloped World

1. A long history of exploitation of the poor by the rich divides rich nations from the poor nations.

2. Virtually every country has land capable of providing food and subsistence for its own population.

3. Large families are often welcome in the Third World since they (a) provide assistance in making a day-to-day living, (b) compensate for high rates of infant mortality, (c) supply disability and old age insurance.

4. In their dependence, the poor look to rich nations for help.

4. Third World peoples look to the rich nations for justice--for reparations for past exploitation (e.g., colonialism) and for the cessation of present aggression.

5. The leaders of rich countries want to eliminate poverty and hunger in poor nations, so that the poor might eventually become self-sufficient.

5. In fact, rich nations, especially the U.S., have little practical interest in eliminating hunger from the poor countries, or in helping them to become self-sufficient. Such possibilities would deprive multinational companies of valuable markets.

6. To this end, the rich countries supply massive amounts of humanitarian foreign aid, especially in the form of trade and loans.

6. World trade and debt payment transfer more food and money from the Third World to the developed world than poor countries receive in foreign aid.

7. Efforts at direct food aid are frustrated because corrupt and unenlightened local governments typically fail to distribute the food, so that it ends up on local black markets instead of in hungry people's stomachs.

7. Corrupt and unenlightened local governments are regularly placed and maintained in power by developed countries against the wishes of the majority of local people.

8. In addition, poor countries are politically unstable and under constant threat of being taken advantage of by foreign powers which seek to draw them into their orbits.

8. The political instability of poor countries is created by local situations of extreme maldistribution of wealth and by unjust practices on the parts of local governments and of wealthy elites working in collusion with developed world governments.

9. For this reason, rich countries find themselves obliged to maintain military presence in underdeveloped countries--to prevent their takeover by hostile foreigners.

9. Most often rich countries arm Third World countries and maintain military presence in them to prevent uprisings of the nations' own people against unpopular and oppressive local governments which create good business climates for corporations based in developed countries.

| 10. First World people simply do not know what to do to help their less fortunate neighbors. | 10. Inhabitants of the developed countries are kept from knowing what to do about Third World poverty through official promulgation of the (shadow) story on the left-hand side of these pages. Media, schools and churches assist the promulgation. |

THE INVISIBLE STRUCTURES OF THE NEW WORLD ORDER

To achieve a more detailed understanding of the structures of World War III as seen from the field and street, we recommend Frances Moore-Lappé's and Joseph Collins' books, *Food First* and *World Hunger: Twelve Myths*. In addition, we have found Jack Nelson-Pallmeyer's *Hunger for Justice*, *War against the Poor*, and *Brave New World Order* wonderfully conducive and pertinent to the exercise of moral imagination in the way we are recommending here. Though all but the last mentioned of these books predate the emergence of the "New World Order," they provide rich images of the institutional factors behind World War III as they are experienced in UDCs. Those structures, though vastly oversimplified, are reflected in Figure 1, where dots represent population concentrations.

FIGURE 1
THIRD WORLD ECONOMIC ORGANIZATION

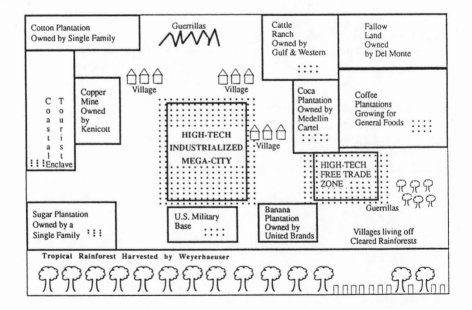

Figure 1 represents a typical country victimized by World War III. The diagram indicates the key elements responsible for the country's situation of destitution that are so closely connected to campaigns of counterinsurgency, pro-insurgency, and of low-intensity conflict both military and financial. The model shows that the hostile conditions in question include most prominently the elements of food, external debt, foreign investment, population, organized guerrilla resistance, and the counterguerrilla strategy used to combat it.

Food

Figure 1 makes it obvious that this representative UDC has a predominantly export economy. Its bananas, beef, sugar, coffee, cotton, and coca are not for local consumption, but for buyers in countries such as the United States and Western Europe. The copper from the model's mines and the goods from its high technology factories will be exported to the same destinations.

All of this is in accordance with the classic economic principle of comparative advantage whose logic is so emphasized in the NWO. This theory of comparative advantage has each country concentrating economic activity on producing what its geographical location, climate, and workforce character suggest as most efficient. Tropical countries with their longer growing seasons will thus produce fruits, vegetables, and luxury crops like coffee and sugar -- mostly for export. With foreign exchange gained from such sales, the exporting countries can then purchase wheat and corn along with other products and services which are most efficiently produced in nontropical locations. Thus the realities of comparative advantage ensure the prosperity of all concerned.

That is the theory. Its outworking, however, has traditionally spelled disaster for Third World majorities. For the dynamics of private ownership have ensured that money exchanged in the "free trade" just described will not benefit those most in need. To begin with, earnings from the sales of luxury crops are not usually invested in local economies in ways that favorably impact the majority. Much less are profits expended on food for local needs as the theory of comparative advantage suggests. Instead, following good capitalist strategy, entrepreneurs reinvest their money where it is promised the best return. Locally, this often means carving out tourist enclaves with luxury hotels catering to foreign visitors who remain well insulated from surrounding endemic poverty (see "west coast" of our model). Though installations of this type provide some jobs for locals, they do so on a very limited scale. Moreover, the logic of private ownership dictates that the earned foreign exchange (i.e., dollars) be more frequently invested abroad instead of locally, because it is in the developed economies that investments are likely to earn far higher returns. The upshot of all this is a net outflow of capital from most UDCs. As we shall see, that outflow is aggravated by the dynamics of massive external debts.

The situation just indicated is well illustrated in the case of El Salvador depicted in figure 2:

FIGURE 2
LAND USE IN EL SALVADOR

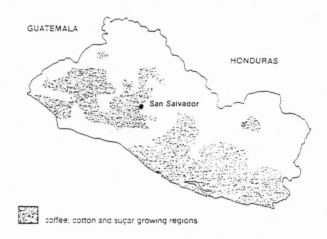

coffee, cotton and sugar growing regions

Here El Salvador's best land is taken up by export production of coffee, sugar, and cotton. The land has been traditionally owned by the country's famous "Fourteen Families," the Creole descendants of El Salvador's original Spanish settlers, who sell their products mainly to multinational corporations. The remaining (predominantly marginal) land is left for the country's rural peasants who for that reason, have constituted the hungriest population in Central America according to Bread for the World (Vanderslice 1981, 1) . Demands for land reform in El Salvador have consistently been met with cosmetic reforms or harsh reprisals from the U.S.-backed Salvadoran government. The reprisals have mostly taken the form of death squads and military action against the opposition indiscriminately dubbed "communist" both by the local oligarchy and by U.S. officials, despite the fact that many so designated are not communist but are the individuals and groups already mentioned who bore the brunt of U.S. counterinsurgency strategy during the 1980s (church workers, priests, human rights advocates, mothers of disappeared Salvadorans, union organizers, and the like).

Nevertheless, the harsh anti-communist stance of the Salvadoran government made it a favored recipient of U.S. foreign aid in the form of grants and loans, for both military and economic purposes. In fact, during the 1980s, El Salvador received more such U.S. assistance per capita than any other country in the world, with the exception of Israel. El Salvador got a million and a half dollars per day from the United States. But despite such volume, the country remained on the brink of economic ruin and ever deeper debt.

External Debt

Because of its centrality to World War III against the poor, we will give this topic special attention in the chapter that follows. Here suffice it to note that the debt is largely fictitious and unpayable. Currently, it is the central tool of control employed by the developed world over its underdeveloped counterpart, both economically and politically. The debt represents an automatic mechanism for transferring capital from the Third World to the First World at a rate that far exceeds U.S. aid to Europe during the heyday of the Marshall Plan. Once again, as the words of Luis Ignacio Silva noted earlier, the debt system is more devastating to the Third World and easily claims more lives there than did World War II in all its battles combined.

Foreign Investment

The Free Market aspects of the system at hand involve foreign investment by multinational corporations (MNCs). As the diagram suggests, such investment entails the location of agribusiness operations in the UDCs. In the past, this has meant outright ownership of hundreds of thousands to millions of acres by foreign companies for their export crops. More recently, however, land has been leased, typically from the local oligarchy or from the government; and crops have been grown for the MNCs on a contract basis (Moore-Lappé and Collins, *Food First* 299-300). In this way, modern capitalism more firmly entrenches the type of feudal arrangement just described.

Since the early 1960s and increasingly under NWO free trade agreements, multinational presence involves relocation of high technology installations, such as electronics, textiles, and auto factories to the Third World. The standard defense of this practice is that it brings the benefits of modernization and increased employment to the countries involved. But such rosy apologetics paper over not only the loss of jobs in the home countries of the MNCs but also the horrific consequences of such investment practice on the lives of Third World inhabitants. More importantly, they obfuscate the driving reasons for transnational flight to the underdeveloped world.

Relative to employment, capital investment by MNCs can easily be seen as negatively impacting the Third World and as replicating the horrors of the Industrial Revolution there. Along with multinational presence comes the same enclosures of land that characterized nineteenth-century Europe (indicated in Figure 1 by the Gulf and Western, United Brands, and Del Monte holdings) and the consequent loss of employment by the millions of peasants who formerly worked the land (Rothstein 59). Circumstances of this type end up herding the displaced families to the burgeoning megacities that increasingly characterize the Third World. In fact, the modern movement of millions from the rural countrysides to huge urban centers all over the world, represents the largest mass migration in the history of the world.

Once in these megacities, former peasants become a surplus workforce of unemployed and underemployed. Their sheer numbers exercise massive downward pressure on the wages paid in the increasingly high tech-factories. Consequently, workers end up living in cardboard hovels and in the most unhygienic of circumstances. Crime, prostitution, and child labor run rampant. Moreover, lack of government-imposed safety regulations lead to widespread maiming of workers (Lernoux 250), and the absence of environmental protection causes the extreme fouling of the atmosphere. Thus, the scenes confronting visitors to São Paulo or Mexico City are absolutely Dickensian, reminiscent of the worst conditions described in *Hard Times* .

Of course, these circumstances are not unforeseen externalities uncontrollable by the MNCs in question. Rather, they are the predictable outcomes of free trade logic. Low Third World wages are the biggest attraction to MNC investment. For instance, according to Witness for Peace, the Ford Motor Company of Mexico pays its workers $1.03 per hour instead of the $16.50 per hour demanded according to union contract in Detroit (1). Arrangements like that amount to a kind of slavery for Mexican workers. If one assumes that the Detroit pay scale roughly represents the value of work performed in the manufacture of Ford automobiles, then workers in Mexico earn their weekly wage of approximately $40.00 in the first two and a half hours of work each Monday morning. For the rest of the week they are effectively paid nothing at all.

Other factors also draw transnational investment to UDCs. They include tax breaks given MNCs by local governments in the host countries. As representatives of the elite who profit from multinational presence, Third World governments often declare tax holidays of twenty years or more in order to attract the transnationals. Additionally, antiunion and antistrike legislation in the host countries make them attractive shelters from the profit-reducing wage, benefit, and safety demands imposed where labor possesses more power. Unrestricted "pollution rights" in the UDCs also cut costs and increase profits tremendously. All of this has been illustrated in the North American Free Trade Agreement (NAFTA) and in the most recent discussions surrounding the General Agreement on Tariffs and Trade (GATT).

Once inside Third World settings, transnationals turn out to be uncontrolled in other ways as well. Frequently the individual entities represent more financial resources than possessed by the host country itself. And with such economic power at their disposal, the MNCs can exercise a crucial political influence for maintaining "stability" in circumstances of poverty and hunger that cry out for drastic social change. By force of gifts, bribes, threats, and friends in high places, companies such as United Brands in Guatemala and ITT in Chile can virtually run their host countries. They routinely establish and overthrow governments. For instance, in 1954, United Brands with the help of the CIA and the marines, brought down the Guatemalan government of Jacobo Arbenz when he introduced mild social reforms of the type taken for granted by workers in the United States. Something similar happened with Juan Bosch in the Dominican Republic just prior to 1965. And in Chile ten years later, ITT conspired to weaken and eventually overthrow the democratically elected government of Salvador Allende because of social changes geared to benefit the workers there.

Population

Land usage, the export demands of MNCs and transnational industrial investment are all intimately linked with population pressures -- the factor (indicated by the dots in Figure 1) most often interpreted as the principal cause of world hunger and poverty. Here the common perception is that countries like the one depicted in Figure 1 are overpopulated, and that lack of common sense, moral conscience, self-control, and economic responsibility prompts Third World people to beget children they cannot afford to feed. But this superficial analysis proves false on several counts.

To begin with, the country represented by the model is not characterized by overpopulation. There are not too many people for the land available for habitation or cultivation. Look at that fallow land owned by Del Monte. Look at the acreage controlled by Gulf and Western. For that matter, notice the space taken up by the U.S. military base. Rather, Figure 1 depicts a country victimized by surplus population, or more people than the economic organization can support. There would be plenty of land to meet local needs with a surplus for export, if the population were somehow redistributed, and if fallow and inefficiently used fields were employed to meet those requirements. Instead, land use patterns in the diagram have deprived the country of the food necessary to feed its own people. Land usage has caused population concentrations where sufficient jobs cannot possibly be generated by the formal economy. The result is hunger and desperation for the country's majority.

The consequence is also the creation of *economic incentive* for poor families to have more children. This gives rise to rapid population growth, which has the census figures of the South growing at roughly twice the rate of their northern counterparts. In a situation with little prospect of work in the formal sector, even small children can increase family income by performing odd jobs and by begging. Moreover, where on-the-job accidents are frequent, and where there is no unemployment insurance or disability compensation, more children represent replacements for a family's main breadwinners should they become incapacitated while at work or elsewhere. Finally, without systemic provision of retirement pay, parents must take steps to provide for their own futures; children are the best social security policies available to them. In other words, it is not economic or moral irresponsibility that drives Third World parents to have so many children. It is just the opposite -- prudence and provision for the future. At times the calculus represented can be quite exact. In India, for example, to be 95 percent sure that parents will have a son survive to care for them in their declining years, it is necessary for families to average 6.3 children. In fact, the average family in India has 6.5 offspring (Nelson 125).

The War Against the Poor

All of the factors indicated so far -- land use, food shortages, concentration of wealth, multinational investment, high-density urban populations, poor housing, low wages, virtually nonexistent employment benefits, and widespread joblessness -- combine with other factors like low literacy rates, poor health care, and grossly inadequate social services to produce powder kegs of social unrest throughout the Third World. These in turn give rise to citizens' movements for change stimulated by church workers, teachers, union organizers, human rights groups, and by peasant, feminist, and student associations. Contrary to uninformed perception, Third World peoples are not inactive or passive (Moore-Lappé and Collins, *12 Myths* 94-101). They frequently organize massively, often putting their lives on the line in the process (see, e.g., *I Rigoberta Menchú*). The Nicaraguan revolution of 1979 is a case in point. Though typically peaceful in origin, such movements and activists are not viewed kindly either by the landowning oligarchy or by the multinationals who lease estates from the elite or who buy their crops. Neither is the desire for reform welcomed by the U.S. government, pledged as it is to protecting the property and profits of its own business communities.

Government by Force of Arms

All of this has led our country to support unpopular regimes throughout the Third World and to keep them in place by bribery and force of arms. The tenure of these governments depends to a great extent on providing stable investment climates for the MNCs. As a result, governments propped up by the United States normally pay more attention to the latter's needs than to those of the host country's own people. Government officials are handsomely paid for the service. By the same token the United States typically opposes local movements of protest and for social change on behalf of the poor and hungry wherever they are. Usually such mobilizations of the poor demand higher wages, better housing, health, education, welfare, and retirement provisions. And since these provisions invariably cut into the profit margins that constitute the very reason MNCs locate in less developed regions in the first place, the provisions are regarded as threatening to U.S. "national interests."

Finally, the local army, which throughout the Third World tends to be independent of the government but aligned with the oligarchy, stands ready to employ force to bring change to a screeching halt. Often it does this through death squads and by the systematic "disappearances" of social activists. The idea is to terrorize the local population into quiet submission. In all of this, the local militaries find support from their counterpart in the United States, which provides training in police and counterinsurgency tactics, and which furnishes weapons and other equipment to be used against socially troublesome elements. This leads to the adoption of a military strategy that ends up oppressing the majority in the country represented in Figure 1.

This military strategy has produced "Low-Intensity Conflicts" throughout the Third World. As described by Jack Nelson-Pallmeyer:

> Low-intensity conflict integrates economic, psychological, diplomatic and military aspects of warfare into a comprehensive strategy to protect "U.S. valuables" against the needs and demands of the poor. It is a totalitarian-like system designed to control the hearts and minds, the economic life, and the political destiny of people. It uses terror and repression to intimidate or punish, cosmetic reforms to pacify or disguise real intent, and

disinformation to cover its bloody tracks. It defines the poor as enemy, consciously employs other peoples to die while defending "U.S. interests," and makes use of flexible military tactics. (*War against* 42)

Since the end of World War II, this element of the configuration has depended for its effectiveness on an ideology of anti-communism. This ideology became widespread not only in the United States but throughout the underdeveloped world controlled by regimes aligned with the United States. According to Robert White, former U.S. ambassador to El Salvador, the activation of this ideology has rendered the word "communist" meaningless, at least throughout Latin America. There, White says, virtually all opponents of the status quo, whether clergy, teachers, union organizers, human rights advocates, members of women's organizations, students, or peasants have been labeled "communists" regardless of their motivation or their familiarity or lack of acquaintance with the theories of Marx and Engels. Taking up the same theme, Noam Chomsky observes that the term "communist" came to be

a broad-ranging concept that has little relation to social, political or economic doctrines but a great deal to do with a proper understanding of one's duties and function in the global system. In brief, the "Communists" are those who attempt to use their resources for their own purposes, thus interfering with the right to rob and to exploit, the central doctrine of foreign policy. (*Ideology* 10)

The Drug War

Recent developments in the Soviet Union and Eastern Bloc countries have undercut the power of communist-related epithets to mobilize developed world populations against the planet's poor. Absent the threat of "Russian" expansionism, the question of how to convince the public that movements for social change in the Third World represented real threats to U.S. security was left problematic.

A way out of this conundrum was discovered with the declaration of the "war on drugs" during the 1980s and 1990s. Establishment leaders moved to replace the Soviets with the drug lords as the focus of evil. Moreover, this change in strategy showed promise of at long last overcoming the hamstringing of interventionist policy associated with the "Vietnam syndrome," which made U.S. citizens reluctant to support the commitment of their sons and daughters to combat in Third World situations. The drug problem entered U.S. family life with an immediacy absent from all other pretexts including the perennial threat of communism. Because of this immediacy, the declaration of the drug war had U. S. citizens themselves calling for military intervention in Latin America, and according to newspaper surveys, it made them willing to give up some civil liberties at home in order to curb the scourge of drugs.

But it was particularly when combined with the communist evergreen that the drug war theme evinced its unique power. This energy was unleashed when Third World guerrilla movements were charged with linkage to drug dealers in places like Colombia, Peru, and Bolivia. The linkage provided pretext for military intervention in Latin America and elsewhere. Thus in 1987, Colonel John D. Waghelstein intoned a telling anthem when he charged that "There is an alliance between some drug traffickers and some insurgents," and "dollars accrued to the drug dealers find their way into some guerrilla coffers" (Klare and Kornbluh 73). By reason of this double-barrelled theme, the incipient antidrug crusade promised to co-opt or at least to further marginalize opposition to Third World intervention originating from groups perhaps most threatening to transnational business interests, namely, the churches and academics. According to Klare and Kornbluh:

> By emphasizing this connection in official statements [Waghelstein] suggested the Pentagon would obtain "the necessary support to counter the guerrilla/narcotics terrorism in this hemisphere." This approach, moreover, would provide the Pentagon with an "unassailable moral position" from which to oppose those "church and academic groups" that have resisted U.S. intervention in Central America . (73)

Drugs and Land Use

None of this recognizes that the production of drugs in the Third World is but another facet of land usage problems there caused by MNCs. The issue pits impoverished peasants on the one hand striving to meet their families' subsistence needs against a wealthy oligarchy on the other, whose members prefer to use their estates for export cropping. Here coca represents one more (albeit especially lucrative) export crop, along with others such as sugar, coffee, cotton, and bananas. Similarly, entities such as the infamous Medellin Cartel represent but another multinational corporation controlling huge tracts of land required by peasants, once again merely to survive. Cocaine producers in Colombia, for example, have appropriated more than two and a half million acres of the country's fertile Magdelena Medio to nurture their harvest. This, of course, is so much land taken out of production to meet local needs.

In other words, the drug war element of World War III is one more piece in the land, food, and poverty puzzle depicted in Figure 1. It is soluble only by radical agrarian and other social reforms within both drug producing and drug consuming cultures. The other puzzle parts are familiar: starving peasants working at exploitation wages for wealthy landowners; multinational corporations (e.g., the Medellin Cartel) buying from the landlords; obscene profits for both wholesalers and retailers; Marxist insurgents siding with small-time growers in their quest for just prices and a better life; a counterinsurgency backlash by the right wing supported by the local military and its death squads; U.S. aid programs to landed classes in the form of weapons, communication equipment, advisers; and "information management," which identifies the drug producers with communists rather than with free marketeers.

In all of this, landlords, the drug lords, and the U.S. overlords are more natural allies than drug producers and guerrillas. What unites the various "lords" is a shared allegiance to capitalism in its most primitive form. The narcotics trade represents monopoly capitalism at its rawest: commerce is completely laissez-faire; the law of the jungle prevails; immense personal fortunes are accumulated; social conscience is largely absent; all taxes are avoided; the sweatshop fields force peasants to labor for slave wages; enemies of the system are vilified as "communists," and the government police and judiciary are bought or intimidated into cooperation. In fact, what escapes most in these days of triumphantly celebrating capitalism while heralding the failures and *fin de socialisme,* is the fact that the narcotics trade along with the unpayable Third World debt unmask the oppressive face of neoliberal capitalism on the international scale.

In summary, then, the drug war theme has conferred on those with war-making authority yet another powerful tool in the conflict we have been calling "World War III." The tool is employed to convince the public of the need for continued military spending, for extended aid to authoritarian and reactionary regimes, and for the eventual direct involvement of U.S. troops in a highly moral crusade against an all-too-evident evil often directly experienced in their neighborhoods and families. Thus, the drug war has filled the ideological vacancy created by the demise of the Soviet Union. A new pretext has enabled the United States and its allies to justify continuing World War III, even in the absence of Soviet threat.

WORLD WAR III: GETTING THE BIG PICTURE

The elements described in Figure 1 suggest a worldwide economic structure that must be understood in order to grasp the nature of the NWO and of World War III. The conflict's battlefronts are often neighborhood stores and supermarkets. A homey example taken from simpler times might get us started.

Think of the neighborhood store some of us knew growing up. But change its venue to a Third World urban setting. In simpler times, customers enter the store looking for whatever they need. If they ask for beans, rice, flour, milk, and vegetables, the storekeeper makes sure to stock such items, going to local farmers and purchasing the goods. In this way, the farmers get a "demand" message from consumers filtered through the storekeeper. Accordingly, farmers continue to produce the items asked for: beans, rice, flour, milk, and vegetables. Necessary goods like salt, sugar, and oil normally have to be purchased from farther away -- perhaps from another country. But they are bought and consumed in such relatively small quantities that they are nearly considered luxuries. The storekeeper, however, does not stock real luxury items such as sugared ready-to-eat cereals or canned foods. These are unavailable because customers do not know about them; in any case, such products are priced beyond the patrons' budgets.

Compare this reality with the modern supermarkets that can be found in any large Third World city. The stores are stocked with twenty varieties of sugared cereals from Corn Pops to Count Chocula; the aisles are lined with canned, boxed, frozen, and otherwise highly processed foods and other items like paper products and cleaning agents. Customers know about these products because of television, radio, and newspaper advertising. These items, however, are not purchased from local producers but from other countries. Most prominently, they are imported from the United States. Meanwhile, stock so central to the neighborhood store -- unprocessed vegetables, rice, corn, and beans -- occupy only very small sections of the supermarket. Sometimes they are found on only a portion of a single shelf.

The clientele of the store have changed too. They are well dressed, in a way that indicates they belong to the middle or upper classes. Very often they have a "gringo" look about them. This too accounts for the stocking of the supermarket. In reality, the inventory is responding to the "demand" of developed world people. In the process, local poor people have been driven out of the store; their faces, when seen at all, appear mostly at the entrances and exits, with their hands out, begging for spare change. Most often, they beg not because they are lazy or lack self-esteem but because they have no jobs. As already indicated, unemployment in cities we are describing runs between 25 percent and 60 percent.

The "spare change" money given beggars and the relatively low salaries of the employed are spent not at the *Supermercado,* but at the farmers' market. There, especially on weekends, poor people continue to buy the unpackaged food they need: beans and rice, flour, corn, vegetables, and fruit. But even shoppers at the farmers' market discover that prices have gone out of sight. Locals must often "do without" because the price of a kilo of rice has risen a few centavos. Rumors have it that the country is now importing rice as well as beans. Everyone wonders why the motherland is no longer producing its own staples. Figure 1 suggests the answer.

The Internationalized Free Market

Things have changed from the days of the simple neighborhood store because under the New World Order, the Third World market has been more closely than ever integrated into the international Free Market. That happened because beginning around 1980, UDCs typically fell into huge debt with the international banking community. (We will see why in Chapter 3.) And the terms of loan repayment set by the International Monetary Fund (IMF) stipulate that the debtor country must open its market to foreign competition. Moreover, public spending in the form of food subsidies that make rice and beans, bread and milk accessible to the poor must be curtailed. This frees up government funds to repay the country's loans.

Opening the market to foreign competition means that international purchasers can, for example, buy and rent land more freely and make more autonomous decisions about what to produce. They can produce the crops that bring them the highest return, without consulting local needs. So if carnations are in demand in the United States, carnations will be grown in Colombia, even if on land formerly used to grow corn, and even if that means that corn must now be imported from the United States at much higher cost to the ordinary consumer. Susan George comments:

In Colombia, a hectare devoted to the raising of carnations brings a million pesos a year, while wheat or corn brings only 12,500 pesos. As a result, Colombia, like most other poor countries in Latin America, must use scarce foreign exchange to import basic foodstuffs. Rich sources of protein like fishmeal, which could perfectly well be used for human food, are processed and exported by agribusinesses like General Foods, Ralston Purina, Quaker Oats, or Swift & Armour to feed America's 35 million dogs and its 30 million cats. The Pet Food Institute, the trade association of dog-and-cat-food manufacturers, estimated the 1974 U.S. grocery bill for pet food at $2.1 billion. Any rich mongrel or pampered puss is a better customer for agribusiness than a poor human being. Little has changed since William Hazlitt, replying to Parson Malthus in 1807, stated that the dogs and horses of the rich "eat up the food of the children of the poor." (*How the Other* 46)

The reference to the "purchasing power" of dogs and cats is important. It illustrates what is basically wrong with the internationalized Free Market -- why it does not work. That fundamental malady is illustrated in Figure 3:

FIGURE 3
FREE MARKET RESPONSES

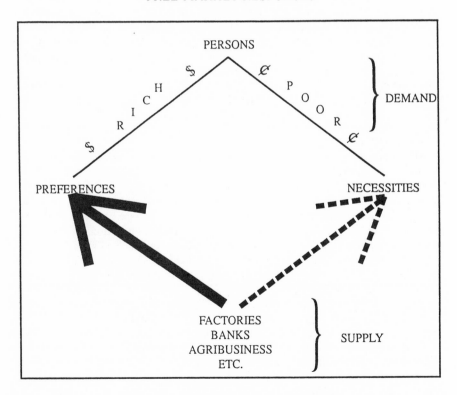

The market (international or not) starts out with human beings (along with dogs and cats) and their needs. We might think of it as a huge supermarket. Women and men enter its doors and declare their demands. In effect, they "vote with their dollars" for the products they want and the market responds with great efficiency. "Will it be New Coke or Old, sir?" More realistically, though, the question is, "Will it be an Apple Computer, or beans and rice?" Millions ask for Apple Computers (or highly processed foods), billions request beans and rice. So beans and rice is what the market produces, right? After all, it is a question of "supply and demand" here, isn't it? Wrong! The market supplies more computers and expensive highly processed foods.

This is because the market is, in effect, blind. It cannot distinguish between preferences and necessities. It cannot tell the difference between individual products at all. It reduces everything to abstractions -- to numbers and company names on the "Big Board." Computers and pork bellies, beans and Corn Pops, artificial fertilizers and cow manure, computer chips and potato chips could just as well be widgets. The market treats them all the same.

Though the market is blind, it is not deaf, however. It has acute hearing and can detect the most minute differences in the clang and rustle of money. If more money lands on the preference side of demand, then Rolls Royces, refrigerators, Coke and Pepsi, roses and cocaine are what the market produces. In the process, it becomes less responsive to necessities, even when that means products responding to fundamental human needs will become scarce and that their prices will go through the ceiling as a result -- even though it means the death of millions. In all of this, the crucial factor is not the number of *people* who request certain products in the market, but the number of dollars people (including pet owners) can spend. This does not deny that people do indeed "vote with their dollars." But this is an election where some are empowered to "vote early and often" while others cannot even get to the polling place, or if they get there, find that their single vote is rendered insignificant compared with the multiple votes of others.

In other words, the single international market has a strong side (indicated by the heavy framing of Figure 3) and a weak side (indicated by the dotted-line framing). International investment overwhelmingly puts its money on the strong side. In the process, it unwittingly condemns to hunger, sickness, and early death those whose needs cannot be met because these needy lack money. Moreover, transnational business constructs a "New International Order" that increasingly solidifies the dynamic in question. This is indicated in Figure 4.

The first thing to note about Figure 4 is that it is controlled not by elected governments but by international private enterprise. It operates in both the over-developed and underdeveloped worlds. In the overdeveloped countries (ODCs), for instance, it builds factories, buys and rents land, and invests in the stock market. It also makes public investment. Entrepreneurial campaign contributions, for example, make sure that government officials friendly to free enterprise projects are elected. Some would say this is the way international business purchases governments and the apparatus governments control. Thus, as employees of the business community, a President Reagan, Bush or Clinton, a General Schwarzkopf, or a Justice O'Connor will make the country and the world safe for the free market.

FIGURE 4
THE INTERNATIONAL MARKET SYSTEM

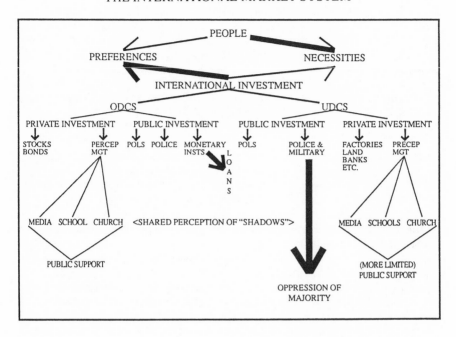

For historical reasons, which will become clearer in Chapter 3, safety is bought at the price of keeping the overdeveloped world's large middle class and labor force content. So despite resistance on the parts of the business community and the officials they employ, workers in the United States and Europe cut into free enterprise profits by way, for instance, of minimum wage laws. Retirement benefits, social security, health care, and education services also do their part to secure the majority's endorsement of the reigning system. Cooperation of the working class is reinforced by sophisticated "perception management" by which multinationally owned media provide assurances that the system "works." Almost by definition, they reiterate that the in-place system is better than alternatives invariably found to be "utopian" and "unworkable.

Meanwhile, something similar happens in the underdeveloped world where there is corresponding public and private investment. In fact, the structures and personnel of the ODC are replicated fairly exactly. Officials are created and purchased. They are sold to the public via transnationally owned media. President Bush or President Clinton has his counterpart; so does General Schwarzkopf and Sandra Day O'Connor. The difference is, however, that the middle class in the UDCs is almost invariably miniscule (and shrinking in size). This means that the perceived "winners" in the system are few, especially since the "benefits" received by Third World workers are nothing like those enjoyed by European and U.S. workers. So more and more people feel themselves excluded. True, the media, mainstream churches, and schools do their part to reverse such sentiment. Nevertheless, many remain unconvinced.

Often the unconvinced organize, demonstrate, and exercise the right of petition (where it exists). But they are typically identified as "communists" and made the objects of repression by their U.S.-backed governments. Some of the marginated literally "take to the hills" to constitute guerrilla bands. This justifies increased military aid from the United States to the inadequate and repressive governments. But the victims of such increased armed force are usually private citizens who simply want to work and earn a wage capable of supporting their families. Such are the structures of World War III.

CONCLUSION

The world described in the foregoing pages corresponds very little to the "normal" one we are used to imagining. Our "normal," in other words, is completely reminiscent of Plato's cave. As suggested earlier, in order to escape its bonds, we need moral imagination transcending the categorical limits our culture imposes. Imagination in this sense reveals not only a strange new world far from home but an equally foreign reality closer by. The "story" we are used to telling ourselves about the causes of Third World devastation is thus put into perspective. We are made to see the connections between that devastation and our own apparent prosperity. The chapter that follows will show that such connections are by no means new.

NOTE

1. Using Franz Hinkelammert's reinterpretation of Plato's parable can help us realize that common First World analyses of Third World problems not only run the risk of superficiality and naivety; they have alternatives. From "verandas" in Berea, (Ky.), Chicago, Ontario, Sidney, London, Berlin, or Tokyo, we typically diagnose World War III devastation as caused by simple food shortages, by natural disasters, by overpopulation, by the external aggression of our "enemies," or by the apathy and laziness of the impoverished themselves (Moore Lappé and Collins, *World Hunger* passim). Accordingly, we sagely advise birth control. We advocate induction of peasants into the wonders of modern technology -- into high-tech agricultural practices. We suggest employment of miracle seeds, extended use of irrigation, and heavy application of pesticides and fertilizers. We prescribe consolidation of farmland so that economies of scale might work their magic. We counsel extension of free market mechanisms, increased exports by Third World producers, and more "foreign aid" from the developed countries. We would steer the hungry away from "ideologies" that link underdevelopment to free market capitalism and that find poverty's cure in market controls.

Such "common sense" diagnosis and treatment contrasts sharply with the view "from the fields" of Nicaragua, Chad, Laos, Iraq, and "from the streets" of São Paulo, Bogotá, Johannesburg, and Manila. There our advice seems off the mark, irrelevant, and even obscene. Often it mistakes the disease for the cure, and in some cases, the cure for the disease. Characteristically, it prescribes individualized, psychologized responses to problems that are structural at base, making them well beyond the control of isolated individuals. By contrast, UDC analysts connected with grassroots movements typically find the principal causes of Third World problems at the level of economic and political structures deeply implicating countries like the United States, and lifestyles like our own. That puts our government and ourselves squarely on the front line of World War III, launching assaults on the war's victims.

WORKS CITED

Chomsky, Noam. *Ideology and Power: The Managua Lectures.* Boston: South End Press, 1987.

Freire, Paulo. *The Pedagogy of the Oppressed.* London: Sheed and Ward, 1972.

George, Susan. *How the Other Half Dies.* New Jersey: Rowman and Allanheld, 1977.

Klare, Michael T., and Peter Kornbluh, eds. *Low Intensity Warfare.* New York: Pantheon Books, 1987.

Lernoux, Penny. *Cry of the People.* Middlesex, England: Penguin Books Ltd., 1982.

Menchú, Rigoberta. *I, Rigoberta Menchú: An Indian Woman in Guatemala* . Edited and introduced by Elisabeth Burgos-Debray, translated by Ann Wright. New York: Verso, 1984.

Moore-Lappé, Frances, and Joseph Collins. *Food First.* New York: Ballantine Books, 1977.

_____. *World Hunger: Twelve Myths.* New York: Grove Press, 1986.

Nelson, Jack. *Hunger for Justice.* New York: Orbis Books, 1980.

Nelson-Pallmeyer, Jack. *Brave New World Order.* New York: Orbis Books, 1993.

_____. *War against the Poor: Low-Intensity Conflict and Christian Faith.* New York: Orbis Books, 1989.

Rothstein, Richard. "Free Trade Scam." *Trading Freedom: How Free Trade Affects Our Lives, Work and Environment.* John Cavanaugh, John Gershman, Karen Baker and Gretchen Helmke, editors. San Francisco: the Institute for Food and Development Policy (1992): 58-61.

Vanderslice, Lane. "Land and Hunger: El Salvador." New York: Bread for the World, Background Paper #54 (June 1981).

Watson, Alexander F. "U.S.-Latin America Relations in the 1990s: Toward a Mature Partnership." Address before the Institute of the Americas, La Jolla, California, March 2, 1994. U.S. Department of State Dispatch, Vol. 5 #11 (March 14, 1994): 153-157.

Witness for Peace. "Free Trade Agreements." Washington: Witness for Peace, 1993.

3

Illusion: Market Is the Solution Not the Problem

The New World Order (NWO) has a familiar story to justify its drive to incorporate the entire world into free trade relationships. The story holds that Third World nations need economic integration into the developed world if those poorer countries hope to share in the prosperity the market economy has so successfully brought to the developed world. According to this account, less developed countries are poor because they are like counterparts in Western Europe before the advent of capitalism. They remain precapitalist due to enduring feudal or semifeudal social arrangements stubbornly defended by backward oligarchs. Meanwhile, only the modern industrialized countries of Western Europe, the United States, Canada, Australia, and Japan are acknowledged as truly "free market."

Not all accept this easy assessment. Voices from outside the cave, like Franz Hinkelammert's, challenge it on three counts. Historically, they argue that the Third World has been a functioning part of international capitalism from the beginning -- for 500 years! Socially, they point out that "backward" dominant classes have often been kept in power by international business concerns, despite the contrary wills of LDC populations most of whom would long since have drastically modified or replaced the market dynamics to which they have been subjected for half a millennium. Logically, Third World analysts characterize thinking behind the received story as patently circular. For example, Hinkelammert observes:

> If a country is not industrialized and dynamic, capitalist ideology defines it as not capitalist; instead it is a question of precapitalist countries,whose stagnation is explained in terms of the simple inertia of its traditional structures. It would never occur (to capitalist theorists) that this Third World is a product and an integral part of the world capitalist system, and that (the underdeveloped world) is making desperate efforts to escape the strangulation inflicted by the centers of the capitalist world. (*Dialectica* 154-55)

As we will see below, Hinkelammert and others go on to appeal to the historical record to support their contentions. That record shows that something like the New World Order has been in place for centuries. Gallardo also explains why it is so important for NWO apologists to ignore that fact. Its acknowledgement would uncover the fundamental sickness of the overall system:

> [W]hen anyone wishes to determine one's fundamental state of health, he or she usually goes to a physician. The doctor however doesn't focus on what can be the patient's splendid appearance. Instead the physician orders examinations of the patient's urine and feces. Such tests say more about one's basic health than do examinations of outer appearance. This is an image of what follows if one submits the triumph of capitalism to fecal examination. In the real world these feces, this excrement is called the Third World. (*Crisis* 52)

With such critique in mind, the chapter at hand represents "fecal" examination. It will illustrate the Third World's essential character as part and parcel of the capitalist system for the last 500 years. History will show that. So will examination of Third World indebtedness and the impact of free market practices on Third World environments. The thesis here is that the New World Order is not really new. It is merely an intensification of a 500-year-old system. If half a millennium of integration into the free market has led to underdevelopment, more intense incorporation during the twenty-first century will lead to more intense underdevelopment.

HISTORIC LINKS BETWEEN CAPITALISM AND THE THIRD WORLD

Historically speaking, the prerequisite of the West's industrial system-- capital accumulation--has always depended on the enslavement and exploitation of "inferior" peoples. Predominantly, these have been located in the West's former colonies. In fact these possessions comprise the very Third World we so often speak of. Most of us do not make that connection. But the fact is that less developed countries are those of Latin America, the Caribbean, Africa, South Asia, and the Pacific -- the very ones that during the last 500 years have served as privileged fields of capital accumulation on the parts of the industrial giants principally located in Europe and the United States. Consider the stages of capitalist development:

The Pre-Industrial Stage

Capitalism's earliest relationship with what came to be considered the Third World began with the crusades. Those military expeditions opened up trade routes between the West and the East. The riches that merchants and craftsmen subsequently gained from traffic with the Mideast, India and China made possible early capital collection that distinguished merchants, craftsmen, and bankers as a specific middle class separate from the royalty and peasantry. However, by the middle of the fifteenth century, the Turk's Ottoman Empire closed eastern overland trade routes to Europeans (Mora 12). This made it imperative for Europe's nouveau riche and the royalty using middle class services, to find other routes to India. Isabel and Ferdinand of Spain, for instance, responded by commissioning Christopher Columbus to reach the East by sailing West. However, most of the sixteenth century "voyages of discovery" were financed by the decidedly nonroyal explorers themselves or by middle-class merchants and bankers in Germany, Genoa, Flanders, and Spain (Galeano, *Las Venas* 20, 34). Even the Spanish crown used bourgeois money to pay for its famous adventures. Here banking establishments like the powerful Fugger House typified the growing power of the business classes, who were gradually becoming the sovereigns of Europe.[1]

When Columbus "discovered" the New World instead of India's back door, he and the conquistadors and settlers who followed immediately set about despoiling the newly discovered peoples of their personage (through slavery), of their land, and of their gold and other precious possessions for purposes of enriching Europeans. This original accumulation was based on the destruction of whole populations, namely, the first nations of the Americas. The "Indians" supplied free labor (in mines and fields) leading to capital accumulation in the banks of the Medicis and Fuggers. As a result 90 percent of the New World's first peoples were annihilated (Girardi 31). The sacrifice of their lives, however, built up the precapitalist fortunes of Europe.

To make up for the free labor lost in the genocide of the original peoples in the "frontier," slaves imported from Africa enabled plantation owners in the U.S. South and elsewhere to develop the textile industries of Great Britain and the United States. In 1776, 20 percent of the entire U.S. population were slaves. Two-thirds of the 20 million slaves brought from Africa perished before even reaching their final destinations (Hinkelammert, *Sacrificios* 46-47). On average they survived seven years "on the job." Once again, such unpaid slave labor and human sacrifice translated into fortunes that remain to this day.

> The most formidable motor of European mercantile capital accumulation was American slavery. For its part, this capital became "the fundamental rock on which the gigantic industrial capital of contemporary times was founded" (Quote from Bagú). From the Potomac to the Rio de la Plata, the slaves built their masters' houses, cleared forests, cut and processed sugarcane, planted cotton, cultivated cocoa, harvested coffee and tobacco and panned the river beds in search of gold. (Galeano, *Las Venas* 125)

In summary, the settling and development of the New World provided a mighty stimulus to the further development of Europe's entrepreneurial classes. Gold and silver stolen from sacred temples or extracted from mines at the cost of untold human sacrifice poured into bank accounts across the continent. Old World craftsmen made ships, tools, weapons, and other instruments for New World settlers. Merchants sold them fabric, wines, and European finished products to help the settlers feel at home even there in the far off Wild West. Shipping companies and slave merchants joined forces to traffic in a lucrative market for human beings. The nascent banking industry especially benefited. The colonies were part of the capitalist system from the beginning. Although they "would show some formal features of feudalism, they functioned at the service of emergent capitalism in other districts. From start to finish, not even in our own times can the wealthy centers of capitalism explain themselves without the existence of the impoverished and subjected peripheries: both are integrated in the same system" (45).

The Stage of Colonial Accumulation

With the spread and expansion of industrialism, the capitalist system increasingly required an abundance of cheap raw materials and unpaid and underpaid labor. This requirement spurred further intervention outside of Europe in the form of nineteenth-century colonialism. This highly organized system of plunder largely financed the next stage of Western industrial development. The Third World countryside was as much a part of the system as were the great industrial centers of Great Britain or the United States.

Colonial exploitation under the British flag occurred principally in India, Africa, China, the West Indies, and the Caribbean. The French also colonized Africa, Southeast Asia, and the Carribbean. Meanwhile, the United States was expansionistic from the outset, particularly intent on incorporating Latin American countries into the U.S. system of political economy. Alexander Hamilton, for instance, envisioned an American Empire uniting his country with South and Central America. U.S. imperial influence would connect the Old and New Worlds, he thought, and by means of its superior power shape relationships between Europe and the transoceanic frontier (Gallardo, *Elementos* 171).

Toward realizing Hamilton's ambitions, President James Monroe (1817-25) formulated his famous Monroe Doctrine in 1823. Unilaterally, without consent of the other sovereign states making up the Western Hemisphere, the Monroe Doctrine claimed for the United States exclusive right to control economic and political affairs in that half of the globe. Of course, the original enemy here was not international communism, but European colonial rivals of the United States. Accordingly, the doctrine signaled U.S. opposition to European intervention in the affairs of Western Hemisphere governments. In practice, as we shall see, the Monroe Doctrine was the means by which the government of the United States claimed political guardianship of the Western Hemisphere. In the process, the doctrine frustrated attempts by Latin Americans to use their resources for their own benefit (165).

Banana companies like United Fruit were the first beneficiaries of Monroe Doctrine application. But other commercial, naval, railroad, and banking interests got their turn as well. In this way, the United States became industrialized and its expansion westward continued with the acquisitions of Alaska and Midway in 1865, of the Philippines and Hawaii in 1898, and of Guam in 1899. The purpose of these later additions was to facilitate commercially inspired military interventions along the coast of Asia, as for instance, happened in Japan in 1854 and in China in 1900 (170).

Under President Theodore Roosevelt (1901-09), the Monroe Doctrine received some of its most vigorous applications. Roosevelt understood his country's role in terms of hemispheric, and even global policeman intervening, he said, wherever necessary to bring civilization, democracy, and order to nations less able to govern themselves. He based his understanding on the concept of "Manifest Destiny" that had been central to the consciousness of Alexander Hamilton. The idea had been that God himself has designated the United States as the civilizing influence in the Western Hemisphere. Thus divine power was joined to that of the U.S. Navy and Marine Corps to make the earlier-mentioned interventions possible (171). Roosevelt added a corollary to the Monroe Doctrine in 1904. It claimed for the United States the right to intervene in the internal affairs of other countries should the latter prove chronically incapable of governing themselves (170). Under this corollary, Roosevelt instituted his "Big Stick Policy."

Chief among the interventions under the "Big Stick" was the 1903 fomenting of a revolution in Colombia and the subsequent use of this trouble to judge the Colombian government incapable of maintaining order in the western part of the country, which extended into the Central American isthmus. In order to protect the commerce and traffic of "civilized nations" in that area, the United States recognized the independence of western Colombia, and in the process effectively created the country of Panama. The United States controlled this new country through the agency of "Panamanian" officials installed and maintained in power by threat of U.S. intervention. Of course, doing so gave the United States control of the hemisphere's most important shipping lane (170).

Further incorporation of Latin America into the U.S. system of capitalism occurred under Roosevelt's successors, William Howard Taft (1909-13) and Woodrow Wilson (1913-21). Under these presidents continuation of the Big Stick Policy became known as "Open Door Policy" and "Gunboat Diplomacy." Both were characterized by the historic U.S. tendency to identify its own interests with those of private enterprise. Taft, for instance, was particularly protective of banking interests south of the border. Recognizing the great natural resources of Latin America, Taft justified intervention in terms of laying a sound financial base so that the objects of intervention might realize the potential of their countries and prosper accordingly (172). Such realization and prosperity, of course, never occurred. Nevertheless, while claiming concern for the benefit of the countries involved, the United States invaded Nicaragua, Equador, and Cuba, as Taft also admitted, to secure profit from commercial and private enterprise opportunities there (172).

For his part, Woodrow Wilson advocated worldwide free trade under the rubric of an Open Door Policy. In doing so, he emphasized the civilizing mission of the United States. That mission, however, was invariably connected with U.S. armed interventions, occurring where North American companies operated with great profit. For instance, defense of the Santo Domingo Improvement Company precipitated the invasion of the Dominican Republic. Haiti was invaded to protect the investments of the City National Bank. When Mexico attempted to nationalize its petroleum industry, the marines were sent to protect the property and investments of U.S. oil companies there (174).

In summary, then, the example of Latin America during this period of colonialism illustrates how Third World countries were incorporated into the capitalist system early on.[2] The doctrine of Manifest Destiny supplied the moral basis for this. The Monroe Doctrine provided a quasi-legal (though completely arbitrary and unilateral) fig leaf covering the self-serving interventions that followed. Big Stick and Open Door policies gave practical expression to the incorporation. Such diplomacy was also invoked to prevent uncooperative countries from putting their own development goals ahead of those adopted by the industrial centers of the more developed North. All of this was justified by the claim that prosperity for U.S. business concerns in Latin America would bring great benefit to ordinary people there. Instead, however, great profits by the multinationals have never translated into prosperity for the overwhelming majority of Latin Americans. Rather, the economic gap between the United States and its neighbors to the south has grown steadily. In other words, the colonial period in Latin America provides yet another indication of how the Third World was disastrously integrated into the capitalist system during the nineteenth and early twentieth centuries.

The System's Crisis

Despite worker exploitation abroad and at home, the free market system still became starved for capital. Crisis signals had become abundantly apparent by the end of the nineteenth century. Depressions and recessions hit Europe with hammer-blow frequency. Worker unrest spread widely, giving birth to socialist movements throughout the world. The 1917 Workers Revolution in Russia further stimulated revolutionary activism. Then came the 1929 Stock Market Crash and the unprecedented worldwide depression that followed. In its wake, the attraction of socialism intensified for workers throughout the world. After many, often bloody struggles, it became apparent that the dominance of the industrial class might be sustained only with the support of their employees.

Toward securing that necessary alliance, the 1930s witnessed the rise of populist leaders such as U.S. President Franklin Delano Roosevelt (1933-45) who introduced his "New Deal" incorporating many elements of the traditional socialist agenda. F.D.R.'s program amounted to a kind of capitalist perestroika anticipating its socialist counterpart by more than half a century. The agreement promised workers a greater share in the benefits of capitalism in exchange for tying their economic destinies to those of their national employers and for political support of governments that, to an ever greater extent, served the interests of those business concerns. Now government bureaucracies functioned as intermediaries between business and labor in situations of conflict. The government not only accepted labor unions as legitimate, but it actually encouraged their formation. Thus, during the 1930s the labor movement in the United States grew in strength.

Following such directions, the New Deal gave workers shorter working days and weeks, child labor was severely restricted, a progressive income tax system was introduced, substantial inheritance taxes were imposed, the banking system was reorganized under stricter federal control, labor unions were recognized along with their right to strike and to bargain collectively with management, minimum wage laws were established, unemployment insurance was issued, disabled workers were assured of compensation, and social security was guaranteed. Previously all of these measures had been resisted by capitalists in the name of anti-communism.

Meanwhile, Latin America received its own version of the New Deal to head off socialist influences there as well. Roosevelt called his strategy the "Good Neighbor Policy." It was rhetorically based on principles of nonintervention, inter-American cooperation, reduction of trade barriers, and renunciation of force to collect debts or to defend North American private enterprise (186). Along these lines the United States renounced its "right" to intervene in Cuban affairs in 1934, and two years later "restored" Panamanian sovereignty. Earlier it had withdrawn its troops from Haiti (187). Beyond this, the United States floated loans and extended credit to Latin America. Additionally, something like "most favored nation" status was conferred on Haiti, Honduras, Guatemala, Nicaragua, Costa Rica, El Salvador, Cuba, Brazil, Colombia, Ecuador, and Venezuela. Such measures were directed toward the expansion of North American monopolies in the "chosen" countries -- again on the theory that the intensified presence of advanced capitalist entities would bring development to the "favored" countries.

At the rhetorical level, all of this was quite positive for countries designated by Franklin Roosevelt as "neighbors." But security measures against the Axis powers between 1939 and 1945, and similar concerns about the Soviets thereafter, caused Good Neighbor principles to be more honored in the breach than in the observance. In fact, most of the measures embraced under Good Neighbor rubrics were never implemented. According to Gallardo, they could not be, because the policy's limits were set by an overriding concern for the prosperity of U.S. business interests and for the maintenance of U.S. control in the Western Hemisphere (189). Such primary concerns routinely proved incompatible with Good Neighbor provisions. Whenever this became apparent, the provisions in question were set aside or violated. Nevertheless, Good Neighbor rhetoric continued to be used. So in the speeches of both North and South American presidents, concepts such as hemispheric defense and security, developmentalism, national sovereignty, democratization, and human rights played a central role.

Neo-Colonialism

The Second World War put people back to work in the developed countries. The huge "armies" of unemployed became armies indeed. Back home they were supported by factory workers (often women) who provided soldiers in the field with a supporting infrastructure. Afterwards the Marshall Plan for rebuilding a Europe devastated by the war provided continued economic stimulus for a revitalized U.S. economy.

Nevertheless, the war's end necessitated the arrangement of a New World Order. In the constitution of that framework, the United States found itself in an extraordinary position. Of all the industrial countries, it alone was left with its industrial system intact. As the free world's unquestioned leader, it could exert unparalleled influence over the shape of the post-World War II globe. That shape would find the Third World more hopelessly than ever on the underside of the capitalist system -- an integral part of it, but as always, subordinated to the needs of Western Europe and North America.

The 1944 Bretton Woods Conference proved momentous in establishing the basis for the new form of Third World subordination. The purpose of the conference was to avoid repetition of the conditions that brought the world to the prewar Great Depression. The vision that emerged was that of a great world market, which more tightly integrated the Third World. The market would be characterized by free enterprise, free trade, and free exchange of money. Taboo in all of this were protectionist measures and government interference in the market's wisdom (de Santa Ana 77).

The New World Order following the war brought four decades of unheard-of economic growth. Its chief stimulants were multinational corporations, which internationalized the world's labor force with a vengeance. But though capitalist activity intensified in the Third World, though production increased dramatically there, and though corporate profits rose proportionately, Third World citizens experienced a corresponding spread of poverty on an unprecedented scale. For instance, African countries produced more food than ever before; yet the greater part of the continent's population suffered from a hunger that Africans had rarely experienced previously (32).

Part of this poverty was due to the fact that the New International Order increasingly oriented Third World economies toward export. Another part was explainable by deteriorating terms of trade between the developed and underdeveloped worlds. Left to market determination, world prices of the First World's finished goods kept rising, while those of the Third World's raw materials kept falling. Thus, in 1960 four tons of Burmese cacao was enough to purchase a jeep. Ten years later the jeep's price rose to ten tons. This dynamic meant that Third World workers were constantly required to produce more (i.e., to work harder and longer) to acquire a fixed amount of First World manufactured products without which development and modernization were impossible (34).

This requirement caused underdeveloped countries to look for help from international lending agencies established at Bretton Woods. Two of these were destined to exert major impact on the Third World down to our own day -- the International Monetary Fund (IMF) and the International Reconstruction and Development Bank, popularly known as the World Bank. Both extended loans to developing countries. However, as conditions for debt extension, the banks gained increasing control over the economy and politics of the debtor countries. Early on that control became so massive that critics termed the system the banks administered, "neo-colonialism." Kwame Nkrumah, the former president of Ghana, offered a typical critique:

> Neo-colonialist politics is fundamentally intended to prevent newly independent countries from being able to consolidate their political independence, in order to keep them economically dependent and under the

control of the world capitalist system. In the case of pure neo-colonialism, the allocation of economic resources, investment power, the legal, ideological and other characteristics of the old (colonial) society persist without any change whatever, the only exception being the replacement of "formal colonialism" with "internal colonialism," exercised by dominant local classes rather than by the original colonial overlords. In this situation, independence has to be obtained on conditions which do not respond to the basic necessities of the society in question, and represents a partial denial of true sovereignty and a partial continuation of social disunion. Thus, the most important branch of neo-colonial theory is the theory of economic imperialism. (de Santa Ana 35)

Here Nkrumah's claim is that the postwar New World Order merely meant replacing undisguised colonialism with policies of *formal* "independence" and *formal* "democracy." But behind the window dressing, the reality remained basically unchanged. Local leaders friendly to the West were installed in positions of power. They were allowed to manage a system whose essentials greatly resembled the former colonial model. Monocultures continued mainly to the benefit of the developed world. Political control continued to originate from outside the country in question. If local leaders became unruly, and especially if they deviated from acceptable economic policy in terms of private property and income distribution, they were replaced by more obedient substitutes. These were usually installed through "democratic elections," but in times of crisis, outright dictatorships were regularly established in their place, often after the marines had been sent in to block a "communist" takeover. U.S. overthrow of the moderate, democratically elected Arbenz government in Guatemala provides an example. The purpose of the overthrow was to protect the interests of United Fruit. In the aftermath, a series of harsh dictatorships armed and supported by the U.S. government has controlled the country and terrorized the Guatemalan people (Kinzer 65-77).

The most frequent cause for such interventions and the resulting establishment of dictatorships were end-of-decade popular movements inspiring fear in business classes that they might lose control of their world system. Thus the Chinese revolution in 1949 led to "drawing the line" against communism in Korea and eventually in Vietnam. The 1959 establishment of a communist state in Cuba was countered by the installation of anti-communist dictatorships throughout Latin America during the 1960s beginning with Brazil in 1964. The success of Nicaragua's popular insurrection and of Iran's Muslim revolution in 1979 led to the "roll-back" policy of covert intervention of the Reagan-Bush years. Additionally, the 1989 popular uprisings throughout the USSR dethroned "historic socialism," thus giving the United States a freer hand in Third World intervention. The 1990 Gulf crisis and the 1991 Gulf War resulted.

The New World Order and "Cooperative Imperialism"

The end of historic socialism enabled historic capitalism to move definitively into its fifth Third World incarnation -- that of the "cooperative imperialism" which for UDC activists defines the New World Order. Referring to this stage as "ultra-imperialism," the Christian Conference of Asia: International Affairs, defines the term as "a configuration where imperialist powers cooperate to maintain optimum conditions of exploitation throughout the world, upon which their mutual interests depend" (1991, 4).

The key concept here is coordination (vs. rivalry) among Western powers. Under this arrangement, the world's rich nations continue to exploit the Third World, just as they have from the sixteenth century onward. Also the point of cooperative imperialism remains the relocation of capitalism's own problems abroad (6). But today the rich exploit more in concert with one another, than in simple colonial competition, which has traditionally provoked inter-imperialist wars.

Apart from alleviating the problems of the developed world, the effect of cooperative imperialist exploitation is to produce worldwide "harmonization downward," so that the traditional process of capital accumulation might proceed apace. "Harmonization downward" means basing the world's living standard on the least paid workers' wages and using this benchmark for wages and benefits of working people throughout the world. This is the latest incarnation of David Ricardo's "iron law of wages" and of Adam Smith's "invisible hand." It can operate today with new abandon since the global workforce has been internationalized to an unprecedented extent. For example, the North American Free Trade Agreement has placed employees in Berea, Kentucky, in direct competition with workers in Mexico City.

> Today's transnational corporations (TNCs) are able to outflank the structures created by national labour movements and put workers all over the world into competition with each other. TNCs can simply locate their facilities where costs for such things as wages, health and safety, worker benefits and environmental protection are lowest. They thus put workers, their communities, and even entire nations in competition with each other to see who can provide the cheapest conditions -- meaning for workers the worst conditions. The tendency, as in the days before labour organization, is for all workers to be forced toward the conditions of the most destitute -- now the most destitute in the world. (Brecher and Costello 73)

Obviously, this sort of transnational competition has linked the fates of First World working people with those of their Third World neighbors as never before. The principal tools for doing so have been the policies of the World Bank and the IMF. Under the assumption that free trade, privatization, and de-regulation (i.e., absence of protectionism) are self-evident goods, these impose "structural adjustments" on less developed countries in order to integrate them more securely into a world economy. In a reprise of theories long discredited, the "new" theory goes that all nations are able to compete on a free and equal basis. But of course, when the weak enter into competition with the strong in any field, the weak almost invariably lose. Unable to protect their own markets, enterprises, and profits, Third World countries are invaded by foreign concerns who routinely drive local producers out of business, while alienating resources and products, producing widespread unemployment, and often destroying the local environment in the process.

The "Uruguay Round" of discussions about the General Agreement on Tariffs and Trade (GATT) illustrates the way such multinational institutions and negotiations achieve control in this current stage of capitalism's development. According to GATT agreements sponsored by the world's richest nations, poor countries will soon be forced into commercializing their health care systems, opening their media to direct outside control, and removing from the hands of local government the regulation of environmental, occupational health, and other safety matters (Khor 1991, 24).

> The transnational service companies have lobbied the governments in the developed countries, particularly the United States, to expand the powers of GATT so that GATT becomes the policeman to ensure that the service companies will have freedom of operation in terms of their exports, imports and investments, particularly in Third World countries. They would like to see GATT eventually becoming a deregulator and a promoter of free trade and free investment in services. This includes banking, insurance, information and communication, media, professional services like lawyers and doctors, tour agencies, accountants and advertising -- the whole gamut of service industries which today form a greater proportion of the gross national product in industrialized countries and in the United States than does manufacturing or agriculture. (22)

This sort of deregulation will not only drive local companies out of business, destroy culturally specific ways of working, administering health care, and in general, viewing the world, it will also end up exporting yet more capital in the form of profit from the Third World to the First. The bottom line here is nothing short of disastrous for the victims of World War III.

In summary, the system of cooperative imperialism covered by thin veils of "low-intensity democracy," preserves the Third World's traditional function as a prime location for capital accumulation. As we have seen, low wages reign in UDCs. Unions are outlawed or extremely restricted. Radical (i.e., noncapitalist) parties are oftentimes declared illegal. Environmental protection is negligible or nonexistent. Frequently, opposition is eliminated by death squads, disappearances, threats, and intimidation. In other words, the Third World maintains its identity as an investment haven for the developed world's rich.

The principal newness of the New World Order is found in the sophisticated means developed nations now have at their disposal to control the Third World. Chief among these is the tool of international debt. Because of its importance, the debt crisis will be the focus of the second major section of this chapter. It graphically illustrates how the New World Order has long since (and disastrously) integrated the Third World into the international free market system.

THE DEBT SYSTEM
CAPITALISM'S DEVASTATION INCARNATE

The world oil crisis of the early 1970s brought capitalism's quarter-century boom to a screeching halt. The Arab Oil Embargo suddenly raised fourfold the price of capitalism's lifeblood. Prices of everything manufactured and/or transported by petroleum derivatives skyrocketed. The phenomenon of "stagflation" surfaced. This combination of severe economic slowdown joined with high rates of inflation occurred despite unprecedented rates of public spending in the United States.

Meanwhile in the Third World, signs of capitalism's inability to solve problems of widespread hunger and poverty were unmistakable. Despite increased private investments in the former colonies, the gap between the rich and poor countries was not only widening, but living standards for the vast majority in the Third World were plummeting from levels reached in the 1960s and early 1970s. In Brazil alone, between 1964 and 1984, monthly wages dropped from $127 to $40. As a result, fully two-thirds of Brazil's population was classified as malnourished -- and this while huge government spending projects caused the country's GNP to skyrocket in what was termed Brazil's economic "miracle." All of this gave rise to the wry comment that the country was prospering but the people were doing poorly.

Ironically, the major causes of such regression during the 1970s and 1980s was not merely the oil crisis with its attendant inflation, but the loans to Third World countries that the crisis made imperative. That is, demands by the Oil Producing and Exporting Countries (OPEC) squeezed surplus money and labor from consumers throughout the world, causing widespread decline in living standards. The money, however, was banked in Western institutions as "petro-dollars," causing in the process a capital surplus that had to be circulated. This imperative's result was a campaign to float loans throughout the world (George, *A Fate* 30-46).

To this campaign can be traced important aspects of the multi-billion dollar debts that today characterize Third World countries. The mere service of these financial obligations ends up siphoning off capital necessary for widespread economic development. As a result, between 1982 and 1986 alone, the transfer of money from the Third World to developed countries equaled one and a half Marshall Plans (Hinkelammert, *La deuda 19*). Moreover, the debt process has given First World creditors an *automatic* device for establishing a continuous flow of capital from the poor to the rich nations, and a new means of control over the economic and political destinies of the former colonies. The emergence of the debt system has also laid the groundwork for what Franz Hinkelammert calls the twentieth century's greatest holocaust (Hinkelammert, *Sacrificios* 49).

Hinkelammert's analysis of the problem not only exposes the links between international capitalism and Third World underdevelopment, it illustrates as well the human impossibility of the free market system as exposed by its impact on chronically poor populations. The system, of course, is basically one through which property owners use other people's money to acquire additional property. Capitalism is at heart a system of loaning, borrowing, and investing. Thus a person with sufficient credibility borrows money from a bank where largely local depositors have placed their money. With money thus acquired, the borrower buys property. He or she then derives income from that investment in the form of rent and/or product manufacture and sale. Part of this income repays the original loan. The borrower is left with property which, in effect, has cost nothing (Hinkelammert, *La deuda* 26).

All of this sounds quite normal and ingenious when theoretically described. It is the magic of the marketplace all over again. However, the description takes on more sinister overtones when the venue of the simple description happens to be the Third World. Take the case, for example, of a U.S. company investing in Latin America. Say it borrows money from a local bank and uses the money to build a factory as part of the local economy. The loaning bank's money, of course, represents savings deposits from the country's citizens. Typically, it comes as well from government deposits derived from "foreign aid" (usually in the form of loans, not gifts), for instance from the United States itself. So the foreign investor is, once again, using other people's money -- in this case that of local depositors and of developed world citizens -- to acquire additional property. So far, so good, it seems. The money is going to have a multiplier effect, we think, producing jobs, additional savings, more borrowing, more investment, more jobs, more savings, and so on.

When the factory is built and operating, and once original loans have been repaid, it comes time to share earnings with stockholders. This payment, however, can only be made in dollars, not in pesos, cordobas, cruzeiros, colones, quetzales, etc. The question becomes how to convert, for instance, Latin American earnings into U.S. currency (or foreign exchange). Beginning in the 1950s, multinational investors solved this problem by pressuring their own governments to extend foreign aid in the form of loans of dollars to the banks where the multinationals did their business. The companies then exchanged their local currencies for the loaned dollars and sent huge portions of their earnings home.

According to Hinkelammert, however, this whole process of foreign aid was nothing more than the transfer of money from one pocket of the capitalist system to the other after passing it through the hands of Latin American governments. Referring to the developed world's governments as "central states," he says, "The central state pays aid to the Latin American state, who hands it over to the multinational corporations in view of the profits they have made in the internal markets of Latin America" (33).

The bookkeeping connected with this process, Hinkelammert notes, reflects massive foreign investment and outright "aid." However, the actual net effect is a transfer of capital from Latin America to the developed world. The process has also meant that Latin American banks were left with huge debts to be repaid. In 1982, when it became apparent that the banks could not do so, the IMF insisted that the debts be nationalized. The money was to be acquired, the IMF insisted, by cutbacks in government social spending especially for the least well-off classes. Thus Third World countries in general and their poorest social strata in particular ended up footing the bill for the "free lunch" eaten by the investing multinationals. The meal was paid for by fictitious "aid," which created an equally fictitious "debt."

The understanding of this dynamic first dawned on Latin American analysts during the 1970s -- long before the current debt crisis emerged in its most virulent form -- when a series of studies, most notably in Chile, established the fact that direct foreign investment in Latin America represented the use of the continent's own resources, except for an initial 15 percent investment.

> Latin America financed direct foreign investment with its own resources, only to subsequently fall into absolute dependency as a result of this very investment. If the very states in question had made themselves responsible for corresponding investments, there would not have arisen the problem of the transfer of profits, much less that of the debt derived from it, and in this way, the development could have been exactly the same, and probably greater. (*La deuda*, 34)

Through the process just described, Latin America's debt has increased exponentially since the 1950s. Between 1974 and 1984 alone, the debt grew by 620 percent (17). Since 1982 the peoples of the subcontinent have paid $100 billion in interest. During that same period, their indebtedness has risen by an additional $100 billion. Meanwhile, they have received another $100 billion in additional "aid" to finance what they owe. Already such compounding has outrun Latin America's productive capacity. Fully 45 percent of Latin America's current export earnings must be applied to financing its debt (20). Nevertheless, the sum owed will reach a trillion dollars by the turn of the century (39).

Ostensibly to facilitate repayment of debts like these, the World Bank and the IMF necessitate a "structural adjustment" that lies at the heart of the New World Order and of the "financial low-intensity conflict" characterizing World War III. In itself, structural adjustment echoes demands long made by progressives in Latin America. But the adjustment of the World Bank and IMF means the opposite of what progressives originally intended. It now signifies the elimination of all development policies and a movement toward raw, antisocial and antistatist capitalism. The models for this type of restructuring are Chile, Argentina, and Uruguay, where the United States supported brutal dictatorships in the 1970s. Policies adopted include:

> • Changing the state's economic function to facilitating capital transfer to the already developed countries.
> • Orientation of underdeveloped political economies towards export.
> • Replacement of protectionist trade barriers aimed at national development with liberalization of all external markets.
> • Maximum privatization of state economic and social functions, especially education and health.
> • General weakening of the state's social functions.
> • Strengthening of the state's coercive functions so that the military and police become virtual forces of occupation within their own country.

• Weakening and discrediting of popular organizations such
as unions and cooperatives.
• Stimulation of foreign investment and of the participation
of foreign capital in all economic activities (*La deuda* 34).

In Hinkelammert's words, "Structural adjustment currently means: transformation of Latin America into a function of extreme capitalism capable of transferring to the countries of the center a maximum of surplus" (*La deuda* 32). Thus, the growing debt is international capitalism's latest and most effective mechanism for amassing capital at the expense of the Third World. The mechanism works automatically. Normally, no armies of occupation are needed to control recalcitrant governments. It is not even necessary to install puppet regimes (though it continues to help). And with the decline of historic socialism, and the extension of loans to the Soviet Union, the debt system extends eastward as well as to the south. The mechanism has also brought the United Nations to heel. There it works as both a stick and a carrot. As we saw in the case of the 1991 Gulf War, if governments refuse to support Western initiatives in the United Nations, the stick threatens denial of future loans; it promises difficulties in renegotiating existing debt terms. Alternatively, the carrot offers partial loan forgiveness or the easing of repayment schedules in exchange for cooperation with Western policy. Together all of this has maintained Latin America (and the Third World in general) as a huge field for what Hinkelammert terms "maximum surplus extraction" (34). The extraction continues the plunder that we have seen was characteristic of the sixteenth, nineteenth and early twentieth centuries (39).

In summary, then, the debt system provides another unmistakable illustration of the way international capitalism is linked to Third World underdevelopment. The exploitation represented in debt relationships also exposes the unviable nature of the capitalist system. To begin with, as we have already seen, the loans the system has generated are literally impossible to repay. In itself, this is bad enough. However, left to itself, the automated compound nature of interest calculations ends up siphoning off not only *all* the discretionary wealth produced by debtor nations, but also the natural and financial capital necessary for generating that wealth. Moreover, this capital transfer includes the very lives of Third World people, especially of children. Standards of living in the underdeveloped world inevitably plummet below survival level when the resources necessary for keeping people alive get transferred to the lending countries as part of basically fictitious debt payment schemes. In other words, the coin of debt payments is ultimately blood. The blood belongs to the very people who are responsible for producing the wealth of the system. Their deaths also represent destruction of the markets that growth-based capitalism requires for its survival. In other words, the debt dynamic reveals the self-destructive nature of the capitalist debt system itself. This self-destruction becomes even more apparent when examined in conjunction with the system's suicidal liquidation of its productive base in terms of the natural environment.

CAPITALISM'S DESTRUCTIVE EFFECTS
ON THE ENVIRONMENT

Environmental destruction (along with historical evidence and the facts of Third World debt) provides a third illustration of the Free Market system's lack of viability. Environmental degradation indicates another undeniable causal link between capitalism and the impoverished condition of Third World peoples. In fact, along with the exploitation of colonies, slaves, and underpaid workers, taking from the environment without putting back is one of the main sources of capital accumulation. "Free lunch" of this type is counted as profit and contributes to capital accumulation in the short term. In reality, however, as E. F. Schumacher pointed out in the mid-1970s, failure to conserve nonrenewable resources and to replace renewable ones is equivalent to capital destruction (13-15). In the end, it leads to the suicidal annihilation of capitalism itself.

Historically speaking, warnings about the industrial system's impending self-destruction have come in four stages. The first of these came from the New World's original peoples. Besides indigenous criticism of capitalism's essentially destructive effect on the environment, Fernando Mires has identified a second and third critique originating from bastions of colonialism itself. Here Mires refers to observations by Karl Marx in *Das Kapital* -- criticisms later extended by authors such as Herbert Marcuse and Erich Fromm. In *Das Kapital* Marx wrote:

> All progress realized in modern agriculture is not only progress in the art of swindling the worker but also in the art of swindling the earth. During a determined period of time, every step which leads to the intensification of [the earth's] fertility is at the same time a step towards the exhaustion of the perennial fonts which give rise to that fertility. The process of destruction is all the more rapid insofar as a country like the United States, for example, supports itself on big industry as the basis of its development. Thus, capitalist production knows how to develop technique in combination with the social process of production only by undermining at the same time the two original fonts of all wealth: the earth and man. (Hinkelammert, *"Capitalismo sin alternativas"* 15)

The third critique of capitalism in terms of its environmental impact came in the early 1970s with the publication of *Limits to Growth* (referred to as *LTG*). It widened the scope of criticism to include not only capitalism, but the Western industrial system itself. Moreover, the source of dissent this time was not some declared enemy of capitalism. Instead the critique originated from within the industrial community itself. Thus, the Club of Rome's publication marked what Mires calls "the crisis of industrialist consensus" (*El Discurso* 18, 20). It profoundly questioned the whole ideology and practice of economic growth. According to *LTG*, the modern industrial system needed control as its cumulative effect since the eighteenth century had been to overload the natural environment to the extent that population pressures were threatening to suffocate the human race; nonrenewable energy sources were diminishing toward the point of exhaustion; the atmosphere, the earth, the seas, drinking water, were approaching the saturation point relative to toxic waste (Meadows et al. passim).

Limits to Growth generated a whole genre of supporting literature (e.g., Mancur and Landsberg). One of the most important contributions was E. F. Schumacher's already mentioned *Small Is Beautiful* . This book too represented a break in the industrial consensus. A committed businessman, Schumacher accepted the basic "limits to growth" thesis. Economies of the capitalist type, he said, could be preserved only by a radical rejection of the growth ideology and by the introduction of new forms of technology and especially of new ways of thinking. Schumacher went further still, attempting to criticize the very foundations of Western civilization (1973, 50-58). Without accepting that basic critique, the Carter administration endorsed and elaborated the *Limits to Growth* directions in its *Global 2000 Report* published during the final year of its tenure (Barney vii).

Almost from the outset, apologists of economic growth questioned the various expressions of the *LTG* thesis. It was not, they said, correct in many of its assumptions and in still fewer of its predictions (Mesarovic and Pestal 37-39). In particular, critics attacked the position that resources are limited. The Bariloche Document, an Argentine study, provided a case in point. It denied the problem of resource depletion (Mires, *El discurso* 17). Other responses to *LTG* held that the worldwide crises predicted by the Club of Rome would not be global but regional in character. They indicated that prospects for economic growth remained especially propitious in the Third World.

It was this rejection of the *LTG* thesis that indirectly sparked the fourth environmental critique of capitalism. It arose during the 1980s and early 1990s when the Reagan and Bush administrations embraced the anti-Club of Rome thesis and repudiated the supporting literature *LTG* had generated. In doing so, both administrations advocated policies of unrestricted growth, not only in the already industrialized countries, but particularly in the Third World. The unspoken assumption guiding this policy was that all countries of the world could attain consumption levels approaching those of the developed world if only the free market were allowed to work its magic. The guiding image here was something like an expanding pie of which everyone would eventually get a similar slice. This, of course, took no account of the clear nonuniversalizability of the developed world's way of life. If the United States, with a mere 6 percent of the world's population consumes 40 percent of the earth's product, the "American Way" could not nearly be approximated by the 70 percent of humankind now living in the Third World.

Of course, the "Reagan Revolution" ignored such facts. Its denial and a whole series of related events led to heightened concern about the environment. The events in question included increasing alarm about hundreds of toxic-waste dumps like that uncovered in New York State's Love Canal; the nuclear contamination at Three Mile Island; the Chernobyl disaster; the thousands of deaths caused by the release of chemicals into the atmosphere in Bopal, India; the increasing number of oil spills, most notably that of the Exxon Valdez; the discovery of holes in the earth's ozone layer with its resulting connection to widespread skin cancer; the disastrous loss of topsoil worldwide; contamination of drinking water caused by agricultural insecticides and fertilizers; problems of medical waste washed ashore on beaches throughout the world; publicity surrounding nuclear refuse generated by the military; the phenomenon of global warming linked to destruction of tropical rain forests; heightened consciousness about widespread extinctions of plant and animal species; connections made between war and intentional destruction of the environment -- for instance through the use of Agents Orange and Blue in Vietnam, in the deliberate release of oil into the Persian Gulf during the war with Iraq, and in the oil fires caused by arson and bombing in the same war.

All these events gave edge to the fourth wave of environmental criticism, which picked up where the third had left off. In the spirit of E. F. Schumacher, the new critics found the root of ecocide not only in industrial expression of the Western tradition but more generally in that cultural inheritance itself. It was not so much scientific thought, they said, but "scientism" or the quantification of all reality that lay at the heart of the problems created by industrialism. Such pure calculation transferred to economics the method of mathematical abstraction that seemed to work so well in the physical sciences. Thus scientism insisted on quantifying the essentially unquantifiable, including natural life forms and even human life itself (Mires, *El discurso* 43). Marxism exhibited a similar defect in limiting all reality to the historical thus shifting emphasis from "the seasonal rhythms of the universe and from the transcendent liberation experiences to a shaping of the time process toward some ultimate fulfillment within the historical order" (27).

To counter the modernist tradition, the fourth wave of environmentalists often looked to nonWestern sources of the requisite new social radicalism. These would refocus the importance of the ritual celebrations, codes of conduct, and interior discipline needed to complement and correct the West's emphasis on the material and purely historical. Thomas Berry names the insights required including those of "the sages, rishis, yogis, gurus, priests, philosophers, prophets, heroes, and divine kings of antiquity: Confucius, Buddha, Ignathon, Moses, Isaiah, Darius, Ch'in Shih Huang Ti, Asoka, Plato, Christ, and later Mohammed" (26). Such vision often sees the earth as a living organism (19). Both Berry and José Hinajosa find suggestions in the Christian tradition that would accord subjectivity to the earth itself. According to Hinajosa, the rights to be respected and protected and to be considered a sacrament are inherent consequences of the earth's subjectivity (10-11).

> Considering the sacraments from a philosophical point of view leads us to discover the sacred in the material, not as an intent -- valid for Christians -- to encounter the presence of God in everything, but as the necessity to value things themselves and to discover their capacity to communicate something more and different from what appears on the surface. A sacrament thus understood is a sign of something else. As Leonardo Boff puts it: "The human world, even the material and technical is never only material and technical; it is symbolic and loaded with meaning." (11)

At a less esoteric level, this fourth approach seeks corrective insight from those traditionally marginated from the industrial decision-making processes, namely, the victims of modernization. Mires identifies them in the following way:

> Without doubt, the victims of the process of industrial development have been peasants robbed of their property in Europe's process of "original accumulation," but equally the freed servants, the enslaved Blacks, the Indians killed in their own lands, the women expropriated of their female wisdom by means of witch hunts and the Inquisition, until we come to our own day and situations such as Hiroshima, Nagasaki and Chernobyl which have converted the entire population of the earth into potential victims. (*El discurso* 42)

Indigenous Spokespersons

Typically, those articulating the fourth critique of industrialism looked to those who spoke the first criticism -- the Western Hemisphere's first people -- as the marginated group offering the best hope of salvific perspective in the face of the West's dominant vision. The New World's first peoples typically organized their ways of life around ecological considerations that considered the earth as meriting veneration and love (100). Nevertheless, indigenous attitudes were by no means romantic but utilitarian in the sense that they sought to preserve the fonts of production, rather than to ignore their destruction as was the practice among European settlers (101). In fact, practical scientific and technological knowledge among first peoples often surpassed that of their European conquerors, whose colonial processes systematically destroyed indigenous ecosystems. Because of its small scale and energy efficiency, "primitive" technique today frequently provides examples of the "appropriate technology" sought by Schumacher (Schumacher 161-179).

Additionally, first peoples fostered agricultural diversity suited to micro-environments recognized as distinct ecological systems (Mires, *El discurso* 86). The Incas, for example, located corn fields near sources of light, water, and fertilizer. They selected disease-resistant strains of seed and cultivated them in relatively sophisticated ways (90). Together such practices, knowledge, and technical advance produced grain surpluses that were stored in anticipation of drought years.

Finally, indigenous approaches to work judged productivity not in terms of "growth," "development," "gain," "accumulation," and "exploitation," but relative to personal happiness -- working to live instead of living to work. Both poverty and overabundance were considered evils to be avoided (106). In fact, the goal of human endeavor was to *underutilize* human work. Thus as Soza points out, members of the New World's original nations were often mystified by work practices their European masters imposed on them.

> The indigenous complained because workers can't stop to chat with their companions because the boss yells at them or views them negatively for conversing and for losing time. He doesn't like it when the workers lose time. By way of contrast, the "human" work day is a one of chatting and of

joy, because it's (during the workday) that one joins most other members of the community and, apart from the work that's accomplished, each one shares knowledge and life experiences. That is, far from just working, workers learn (during the workday) by means of interchange with everyone else. (Mires, *El discurso* 111)

Consequences of the New Environmental Consciousness

The fourth wave of criticism just noted heightened environmental consciousness especially in the First World. The new critique made citizens there less willing to accept industry's environmentally destructive policies -- at least close to home. Resultant political pressures led multinationals to shift their industrial operations and disposal activities to the Third World, where environmental consciousness was much lower, and where controls had been kept lax (59). In this situation, there surfaced at least two additional specific links between international capitalism and the deteriorating conditions of the Third World.

In the first place, Third World forests -- including the environmentally precious rain forest of the Amazon region -- were cleared on an unprecedented scale. More than anything else, clear cutting served developed world timber industries whose patterns of deforestation were meeting with increasing resistance at home. Relocation to the Third World largely conserved what was left of First World forests. In addition, governments in the underdeveloped world offered the advantage of not requiring reforestation, so timber could be "harvested" without concern for resulting erosion and desertification and their inevitable effects on water tables and weather patterns (60). Critics, it seemed, were correct. The environmental movement was becoming a First World luxury. Hedström writes: "If current practices continue in the Third World, the physically accessible forests there will disappear in about 40 years. By the year 2000 the land mass covered by forests will be reduced by 40% in the countries of the Third World, compared to barely 0.5% in the industrialized countries of the North" (3).

Deforestation was also connected with North American eating habits, which radically altered those of their neighbors to the south. With the introduction of fast food hamburger chains in the mid-1950s, it became imperative to secure large quantities of beef at low prices. Again as Hedström writes, cheap hamburgers demanded cheap meat. Thus, with greater frequency, cattle herds were located on cleared Central American land because of the region's comparatively low production costs. From 1960 to 1980 alone, Central American beef production went up 160 percent and the region's 400 square kilometers of tropical forest was cut in half (Hedström 47). In this way, Central America was transformed from a constellation of "banana republics" to a collection of "hamburgerized" nations. Meanwhile, though beef production increased exponentially, local consumption of red meat typically dropped (46). Increased hunger resulted as land formerly used to produce beans, rice, and corn for local consumption was transformed into pasture (44).

Another environmental problem caused by transnational activity was the dumping of banned products and the disposal of waste in the Third World. Perhaps the most devastating evidence of the predatory mentality behind such practices appears in an internal memo written on December 12, 1991, by Lawrence Summers, then one of the World Bank's top officials -- later advanced by the Clinton administration to undersecretary for international affairs. Summers' former employer, the World Bank, we recall, is one of the lending agencies ostensibly fostering development in the Third World. His memo was made public by the Greenpeace organization of environmental activists:

Just between you and me, shouldn't the World Bank be encouraging more migration of the dirty industries to the LDCs? I can think of three reasons:

1) The measurement of the costs of the health impairing pollution depends on the foregone earnings from increased morbidity and mortality. From this point of view a given amount of health impairing pollution should be done in the country with the lowest cost, which will be the country with the lowest wages. I think the economic logic behind dumping a load of toxic waste in the lowest wage country is impeccable and we should face up to that.

2) The costs of pollution are likely to be non-linear as the initial increments of pollution probably have very low cost. I've always thought that underpopulated countries in Africa are vastly under polluted. Their air quality is probably vastly inefficiently low (*sic*) compared to Los Angeles or Mexico City. Only the lamentable facts that so much pollution is generated by non-tradable industries (transport, electrical generation) and that the unit transport costs of solid waste are so high prevent world welfare enhancing trade in air pollution and waste.

3) The demand for a clean environment for aesthetic and health reasons is likely to have very high income elasticity. The concern over an agent that causes a one in a million change in the odds of prostrate (*sic*) cancer is obviously going to be much higher in a country where people survive to get prostrate (*sic*) cancer than in a country where under 5 mortality is 200 per thousand. Also, much of the concern over industrial atmospheric discharge is about visibility impairing particulates. These discharges may have very little direct health impact. Clearly trade in goods that embody aesthetic pollution concerns could be welfare enhancing. While production is mobile the consumption of pretty air is a non-tradable. (Avrigan 2)

CONCLUSION
THE BANKER'S TESTIMONY

Summers' memo is valuable because it represents "reluctant testimony" supporting some of the five principal contentions of this chapter. First of all, the World Bank official's recommendation shows the less developed world's unmistakable integration into the capitalist system. That integration, we have seen, was evident from the very beginning of Europe's "discovery" of the New World. It continues today under the celebrated New World Order which, among other things, uses the less developed world to dispose of First World wastes.

The transnational companies with their often highly contaminating industries have free entry into the majority of Third World countries, who guarantee them economic profitability and security in their operations. Already by the end of the last decade, these companies controlled almost half of world industrial production, and half the foreign trade of the Third World. These companies in no way respond to the basic conditions which could bring real economic development to these countries. On the contrary, the multinationals constitute a threat to the economic and political sovereignty of the countries where they operate. Rarely do they adjust their operations to legislation controlling foreign investment. Often they block efforts which [Third World] countries make in some cases to gain more effective control over their own natural resources. (Hedström 2)

Secondly, precisely as issuing from a World Bank official, Summers' comments provide a reminder of how the custodians of Third World debt can use those impossible obligations to coerce compliance with a New World Order that inevitably impoverishes those who resentfully find themselves under its sway. The underdeveloped world's external debt becomes a point of leverage to persuade less developed countries to make their lands available to activities that have been outlawed or which are politically unacceptable in the developed world. In exchange for such concessions, debts are renegotiated or forgiven, or further loans are secured -- all with the further devastating consequences earlier noted.

Thirdly and most shockingly, Summers' memo illustrates complete disregard for the rights and concerns of the people being dumped on. Thus it demonstrates capitalism's impossibility in virtue of the system's tendency to destroy the workers and consumers on which it depends for its own survival. Notice how Summers' analysis takes place exclusively from above -- from the viewpoint of waste producers. In adopting this vision, the World Bank official gives expression to a profoundly classist and equally destructive view of the world's marginated. He recommends that nations with the lowest wages supply waste sites, apparently because it costs industries less when workers get sick in places where wage earners are poorly paid. Besides, he says, life-threatening health problems such as cancer require long periods to develop. They go largely undetected and matter less where mortality from hunger and other diseases is high. African countries are especially attractive places for dumping, Summers argues. In a reversal of typical developed world thinking about Third World contribution to global problems, countries of Africa are identified as "underpopulated." Because they are not doing their part in contaminating the world, they should be persuaded to accept waste from those who are shouldering a new "White Man's Burden" by producing greater quantities of hazardous waste.

Fourthly, Summers' position completely ignores anything like the rights of the environment itself. In this failure, it evidences capitalism's relentless march toward the inevitable destruction of the natural productive base on which it depends for its continued existence. The logic here is that of pure market reasoning. Clean air and clean environment are seen as commodities tradable for industrial goods that are "world welfare enhancing." This is another example of capitalist thinking that has traditionally seen activities destructive of the environment billed as nonetheless productive (Dierckxsens 9). Reasoning of this type led the coordinator of the *LTG* project, Dennis Meadow to comment: "I've tried long enough to be a global evangelist, and I've come to learn that I can't change the world. Besides, the human race is acting like a suicide, and there's no sense in arguing with a suicide once he's already jumped from the window" (Interview in *Der Spiegel* quoted by Hinkelammert "Nuestro proyecto," *Pasos* 33, 15).

Finally, Summers' memo indirectly issues a challenge to First World inhabitants like ourselves to expand horizons beyond what we can immediately perceive and beyond the limits of perception imposed by our Western tradition of "scientism." To some extent (though it is ever decreasing), we have our lakes, mountains, and forests, our relatively clean air, our comparatively safe products. Meanwhile, nearly 80 percent of the earth's population (thought of as "inferior peoples") live second-class lives of shorter duration that have more illness, are more dangerous, and have much poverty by comparison to the other 20 percent of the population. Ingemar Hedström refers to our need to inform ourselves of the global effects of overconsumption:

> Ecology has become a critic and even a denouncer of the functioning of modern societies. Among the things which have been denounced is the superexploitation of the Southern hemisphere, that is of the so-called Third World, on the parts of the comparatively rich countries of the North, of the so-called First and Second Worlds. In this sense, consciousness of the global ecological problem must mean acquiring awareness of the socioeconomic, political and cultural situation of our societies. This in turn implies knowing the situation of exploitation of the countries of the South by the industrialized countries of the North. (12)

In fact, Hedström has well expressed the challenge facing peace activists in the face of a world war waged not only against the world's poor but against nature itself.

NOTES

1. As a sixteenth-century historian, Clemens Sender, noted:

> The names of Jacob Fugger and his cousins are known in every kingdom and territory, even among the pagans. Emperors, kings, princes and lords have dealt with him. The Pope has acknowledged and embraced him as a beloved son, and cardinals have risen to their feet when he has entered the room. All the business men of the world refer to him as an enlightened man, and all the pagans have marvelled at him. He is the glory of all Germany. (Mires, *En Nombre* 19)

2. The incorporation encompassed:

> a vast spectrum of actions from mere threats to the establishment of protectorates, to armed interventions including the drawing of frontiers and the creation of new republics, the occupation and administration of

ports and customs, the annexation of Puerto Rico and the purchase of the
Virgin Islands, the financial annexation of Central America and Cuba, the
destruction of three independent governments, the promotion of
subversion in Panamá, Honduras and México, and the non-recognition of
independent governments and the support of titular and semi-titular
governments, the acquisition of naval bases in Guantánamo, Samana
Bay, Corn Islands, the Gulf of Fonseca and St. Thomas, the organization
of militarized police forces (National Guards) under North American
control, interferences and diplomatic pressures intended to obtain
economic advantages over Europe, the securing of privileges for North
American banks and, in general, the power to distort or impede any
process of national development. (Gallardo, *Elementos* 175)

WORKS CITED

Avrigan, Tony. "Should We Bank on the World Bank?" *The Tico Times* (21 Feb.
    1992): 2.
Barney, Gerald O. (Study Director). *The Global 2000 Report to the President:
    Entering the Twenty-First Century,* vol. 1. Washington: U.S. GPO, 1980.
Berry, Thomas. *The Dream of the Earth.* San Francisco: Sierra Club Books, 1988.
Brecher, Jeremy and Tim Costello. "People's Transnational Coalition." *Third World
    War.* Hong Kong: CCA - International Affairs, 1991, 73-78.
Christian Conference of Asia, International Affairs. *Third World War.* Hong Kong:
    CCA - International Affairs, 1991.
de Santa Ana. *La práctica económica como religion.* San José, Costa Rica: Editorial
    DEI, 1991.
Dierckxsens, Wim.   "Hacia el desarrollo sostenible? Después de la Perestroika y la guerra
    del Golfo Pérsico." *Pasos* (Numero Especial Jan. 1991): 5-17.
Galeano, Eduardo. *Las Venas Abiertas de América Latina.*   México: Siglo Veintiuno
    editores, 1980.
Gallardo, Helio. *Crisis del socialismo historico: ideologías y desafíos.* San José,
    Costa Rica: Editorial DEI, 1991.
_____. *Elementos de politica en América Latina.* San José, Costa Rica: Editorial
    DEI, 1989.
George, Susan. *A Fate Worse than Debt: The World Financial Crisis and the Poor.*
    New York: Grove Wedenfeld, 1988.
Girardi, Giulio. *La conquista de América: con qué derecho?* San José, Costa Rica:
    Editorial DEI, 1989.
Hedström, Ingemar. *Somos parte de un gran equilibrio.* San José, Costa Rica:
    Editorial DEI, 1988.
Hinajosa, Jose Francisco G. "Esta Viva La Naturaleza?"*Pasos* 38, (Nov./Dec.1991):
    1-12.
Hinkelammert, Franz J. "Capitalismo sin alternativas?" *Pasos* 37, (Sept./Oct.1991):
    11-23.
_____. *Dialetica del desarrollo desigual.*   San José, Costa Rica: Editorial
    Universitaria Centroamericana, 1983.
_____. *La deuda externa de América Latina: el automatismo de la deuda.* San José,
    Costa Rica: Editorial DEI, 1988.

_____. "Nuestro proyecto de nueva sociedad en América Latina: el papel regulador del Estado y los problemas de la auto-regulación del mercado." *Pasos* 33, (Jan./Feb.1991): 6-23.

_____. *Sacrificios humanos y sociedad occidental: lucifer y la bestia.* San José, Costa Rica: Editorial DEI, 1991.

Khor, Martin. "The Recolonisation of the Third World." *Third World War.* Hong Kong: CCA - International Affairs, 1991, 21-24.

Kinzer, Stephen. *Bitter Fruit: the Untold Story of the American Coup in Guatemala.* Garden City, N.Y.: Doubleday, 1982.

Meadows, Donella H., Meadows, Dennis L., Randers, Jorgen, and Behrens, William W. lll. *The Limits to Growth.* New York: New American Library, 1972.

Mesarovic, Mihajlo, and Eduard Pestal. *Mankind at the Turning Point: The Second Report to the Club of Rome.* New York: E.P. Dutton and Co., Inc., 1974.

Mires, Fernando. *El discurso de la naturaleza: ecologia y política en América Latina.* San José, Costa Rica: Editorial DEI, 1988.

_____. *En nombre de la cruz.* San José, Costa Rica: Editorial DEI, 1989.

Mora, Arnoldo. "Los protagonistas de la conquista de América."*Pasos* 3 6 (July/Aug.1991): 12-16.

Olson, Mancur and Hans H. Landsberg. *The No-Growth Society.* New York: W.W. Norton & Co., Inc., 1973.

Schumacher, E. F. *Small Is Beautiful: Economics As If People Mattered.* New York: Harper and Row, 1973.

4

Illusion: Ideology Is Dead

Destructive practices like those reviewed in Chapter 3 demand a supporting theory. Hinkelammert identifies this theory as the "Western tradition" so prized and celebrated in our schools.[1] It supports what he terms a global "totalitarian system" whose emergence process he describes in terms of establishing "market totalitarianism." These phrases refer to the growing unwillingness of the dominant entrepreneurial class to either recognize or tolerate any alternatives to a worldwide society governed by the mechanism of free market capitalism.[2]

A review of Western intellectual history supports the allegation of totalitarianism within the "free world." In fact, the 500-year process of business class ascendency has gradually extended entrepreneurial sway over one key institution after another as well as over the natural environment itself. This chapter will focus on the growth of business control over three institutions: church, state, and market. This last institution eventually swallows up nearly all other relationships until private property, the business contract, and the laws of supply and demand become the final arbiters of everything including decisions about which humans and which natural species shall live or die, about what is morally right and what is wrong.

To recognize the establishment of such "market totalitarianism" it is not necessary to espouse any "conspiracy theory." One need not imagine capitalists plotting at any point to initiate, advance, or complete their project of capital accumulation and total control. The logic of the market itself and historical events dictated capitalist goals and suggested the means to achieve them. Additionally, as we shall see below, ideological needs arose at each epochal juncture -- the drive to change theological understandings, political philosophies, and economic theories. Here too it is completely unnecessary to imagine smoke-filled rooms where the rising middle class concocted theories or paid lackey intellectuals to do so. Instead, a process analogous to Darwin's "natural selection" took place in the realm of ideas. The emerging dominant class needed justifying theory, and from the welter of conflicting thought any age produces, its members selected the ideas that advanced their cause. These they characterized as "Great Ideas." Our children still study them as the apex of human intellectual achievement if they are among the elite still required to study the "great books."

BOURGEOIS CONQUEST OF THE CHURCH

In the process of establishing the complete control its market exercises in today's world, the emerging middle-class directorate has had to overcome the formidable obstacles posed by the Judeo-Christian tradition and by the very bourgeois humanism that originally justified the middle-class project intent on distancing itself from the medieval forms of church and state. Both the Judeo-Christian and the humanist traditions emphasized human dignity and personal responsibility for individual actions and for the welfare of others. Strong currents within the biblical tradition also rejected accumulation of wealth and the practice of usury as sinful. Evidently, Roman Catholic doctrine on such matters had to be circumvented if the bourgeois approach to the world were to prevail. The entrepreneurial system centralized accumulation of capital; its bankers survived by lending money at high interest. The human casualties inevitably resulting from the processes of accumulation and lending had to somehow achieve moral justification.

The Roman Catholic Church, however, represented an obstacle that could not easily be surmounted. It embodied all the residual "regressive" tendencies of the medieval era so distasteful to the merchants, bankers, craftsmen, and others included in the rising middle class. "The Romanists," as Martin Luther called them, were not only the continent's most extensive landowners but they also reinforced their position with a religious doctrine and political might that was clerical, patriarchal, authoritarian, hierarchical, classist, and centralized. It took a long time therefore to remove ecclesiastical obstacles to the ascent of the entrepreneurial class. In fact, the removal took place in three main stages. It is true, the new middle class was the protagonist of the second and third of these stages. But the pivotal agents of the first were the nobles of Europe's emergent nation-states. This is the story peacemakers must understand to place their political positions in historical perspective.

The Nobility Undermine Papal Authority

The Reformation was the instrument that most powerfully undermined ecclesiastical roadblocks to business class progress. The reform movement's most direct beneficiaries were European princes, who, before the sixteenth century, had been locked in a death struggle with the papacy. The issue here was not predominantly theological but economic as well as one of authority. As we saw in the previous chapter, a gradual shift in the basis of Europe's wealth from land to money caused tensions among all of the continent's social forces from the pope and the emperor to the noble, middle, and peasant classes. European princes needed cash to finance their wars and to sponsor their voyages of exploration. These projects ran directly counter to projects of capital accumulation sponsored by the Roman papacy. Popes exacted taxes from Europe's royalty. All of this was intolerable to continental princes.

The problem of papal taxation was not a small one. It found royal families casting about for ways to avoid it. But how could they escape? The church's ideological safeguards (or "protecting walls" as Luther was eventually to call them) seemed unassailable. The pope was the acknowledged deputy of Christ himself. The pope's word was law, and his law was absolute. It bore the authority of God. Moreover, the pope had the power of opening and closing the very gates of heaven to all souls, no matter how royal. Disobedience might bring the offending prince excommunication forbidding him access to confession and to the forgiveness of sin necessary for entering heaven. Even an unbelieving prince felt himself bound. Refusal to honor the pope's authority could place the unfaithful one's people under interdict until the prince relented. This meant that no one in the offender's realm could receive the sacraments as long as the interdict remained in place. Even before the age of democracy, few royal families could withstand the pressure of a citizenry whose eternal salvation was jeopardized by their leader's stubbornness or greed.

Clearly, exit from the royal dilemma would require a change in religious understanding that would invalidate the theory consolidating papal power. But from what quarter was the change to come? It is here that Martin Luther and the other Protestant reformers assumed center stage. These religious innovators provided the new thought required to strip the pope of his absolutist claims. Of course, Luther was interested only in reforming the Roman Catholic Church. But his invocation of the Gospels to do so allowed the royal classes to disobey papal directives. In effect, Luther said, the bluebloods were popes and bishops. If the pope failed to reform the church, such reformation became the nobles' responsibility. This was the thrust of the Great Reformer's Address to the Christian Nobility written in 1520.

Luther's theology was interpreted as a godsend by royal families across Europe. So while aristocrats in places like France, Spain, Portugal, and Italy largely kept faith, others reformed their churches in various ways. All the reformed states denied the pope's central authority. The priesthood and religious orders were abolished. Church lands and treasuries were confiscated. The result was relief from papal taxation and authority, new lands for Europe's crowns, hard cash for royal treasuries, and "religious wars" until the middle of the seventeenth century, when the bloody Thirty Years' War concluded with the Peace of Westphalia in 1648. Papal power had been royally undermined. It remained for a class of new scientists to complete the excavation.

Galileo

In the year 1610, Galileo Galilei published his *Starry Messenger*. Galileo's book contradicted the understanding of the heavens, which the church had accepted on a par with divine revelation for well over a thousand years. That understanding had been based on the theories of Aristotle and of the second-century Egyptian astronomer, Ptolemy. By contrast, Galileo's findings seemed to confirm the speculations of the Polish cleric, Nicolaus Copernicus, who in 1543 theorized that the sun, not the earth was the center of the universe. Coming on the heels of the Reformation, the discoveries could not be endured by the Catholic Church -- so threatening appeared the second challenge to its authority. So in 1616 the Roman inquisition condemned Copernican theory as "absurd in philosophy and formally heretical, because expressly contrary to Scripture." By doing so, the Roman Catholic Church attempted to reassert its authority and in the process placed the Bible itself as an obstacle to modern understandings of truth.

Such objections were not new to Galileo. He had been confronted with them for six years (Drake 153-54). The book of Josuah, it was pointed out, had the Jewish general stopping the sun during battle, so that his armies might have more time to defeat their enemies (Joshua 10: 12-14). Clearly this represented infallible testimony that the sun moved. Similarly, the author of the Book of Psalms referred to the sun arising like a strong man and running his course across the heavens (Psalm 19:4-6). What further testimony was needed biblically to discredit Galileo's conclusions? So in 1615 Galileo made his response. He did so to the Grand Duchess Christina in a landmark letter that was not made public until 1635. The letter is significant because it further weakened ecclesiastical authority by carving out a realm immune from church tutelage even for Catholics -- the realm of science.

In his letter Galileo argued that God is revealed in two ways, in sacred Scripture and in nature. Sacred Scripture was written for simple folk, he said (Galileo,"Letter to the Grand Duchess" 199). Its statements are often ambiguous and metaphorical. These cannot be taken literally in every case. Even St. Jerome, Thomas Aquinas, and other master theologians recognized this (200-201). Since it is so difficult to ascertain the exact meaning of biblical passages, one must often resort to God's revelation in nature to determine the truth. When God's written word conflicts with natural revelation, the latter is to prevail, because it is clearer and less ambiguous (182-83). By making this distinction, Galileo in effect exempted scientific findings from biblical criticism. Once this exemption had been made, the bourgeois program of liberation from medieval authority needed only to extend the notion of "science" to realms of life beyond physics. This, of course, is exactly what happened over the next 300 years.

Deism Lays the Foundation for Market Totalitarianism

The final step in eliminating church and theological obstacles from the establishment of market totalitarianism was to come in the eighteenth century with the establishment of Deism as the quasi-official business class understanding of God. Significantly, Deism was the form of religion adopted by most of the founding fathers of the United States as well as by economists such as Adam Smith. It is to Deism's God that Jefferson referred when he confessed that all are "endowed by their creator with certain unalienable rights."

Deism envisioned the precise type of God the bourgeois needed to establish the quasi-divine character of a market. The idea was to defend the divine in the face of challenges presented by the eighteenth-century scientific mind. The scientific laws of physics and reason apparently left decreasing room for a God presented in the Bible as intervening in history, especially by way of miracles. The parting of the Red Sea and Jesus' healing wonders, for example, seemed a priori excluded by laws of nature which, by the way, also seemed capable of explaining away such interventions. Galileo's observation to the Grand Duchess (supported by his references to Augustine) seemed apt: the Bible was written for simple people of prescientific orientation. What could it possibly mean for "the enlightened"?

The response was to set the Bible aside as the final word of revelation. Galileo and Newton had implied as much. There are two "books" of revelation, sacred Scripture and nature. When conflict arises between the two, nature's disclosures are more authoritative. Did this mean that science had taken the place of God? Were scientists, then, the new priestly class? And what sort of God did they preach?

Perhaps the best answer to this last question was given by Deist minister William Paley and his image of the "Watchmaker God." Following something like Thomas Aquinas' proof from causality for the existence of God, Paley imagined the universe as a huge watch. If one found a timepiece lying on the beach, Paley said, there would be no problem in concluding that the mechanism must have a watchmaker. The intricate interplay of springs, cogs, and wheels issuing in regular movements simply could not have happened by chance. One would have to see a creative mind behind it all. Paley asked, how much more is this true of the "watch" we call the universe? It is infinitely more complicated than any timepiece found on the sand. The universe has its wheels and cogs, its springs and regular movements. Its design is more wondrous than any human artifact. The universe too must have its "Watchmaker" -- a God who created it and set it spinning and whose laws can be discerned by careful examination of the Great Machine (Paley 22, 53, 70).

Once again, Paley's God was just what the bourgeois needed to divinize or at least give a theological stamp of approval to the emerging social configuration they directed -- especially (as we shall see below) to their central institution, the capitalist market. Since the market was understood as directed by laws of nature, its norms were God-authored too. Following Galileo, Deists then were able to assert that such laws took precedence over "prescientific" understandings of economics expressed in sacred Scripture. In this way, as we will see, it became unscientific and, therefore, theologically unsound to follow Scripture's letter by objecting to usurious practices or even to take care of the poor in any way interfering with the natural outworkings of market laws of supply and demand.

To summarize, with the establishment of Deism, the business class conquest of church was rendered complete. With that key institution out of the way or at least sufficiently domesticated, the establishment of bourgeois totalitarianism could proceed.

BOURGEOIS CONQUEST OF POLITICS

Proceeding, however, made it imperative that the field of politics also fall under business class control. Here on the European front, at least, the group blocking access to public power was Europe's royalty. In the colonies, the problem was the prior existence of native peoples claiming sovereignty over the lands European businessmen wished to exploit.

Power Wrested from Europe's Royalty

After the Reformation, with papal authority less an obstacle, at least in the Protestant countries, royal classes asserted their dominance with new abandon. Their need for cash, however, continued unabated. It caused them to increase tax pressure on the decidedly unroyal, including the often richer bankers and merchants. Taxes were also increased for colonial representatives in the New World. The Spanish crown pressured their *encomienderos*; similarly, the British royal family harassed "settlers" on the North American continent. Such taxation more than anything else made these middle classes seek their own means for invalidating royal privilege. Once again, a change in spirituality was needed -- this one powerful enough to level royal classes just as their ecclesiastical counterparts had been debased by the Reformation.

The Enlightenment thinkers of the eighteenth century met the need. Following Galileo and Newton, they found it necessary to rethink the whole corpus of human learning and experience from the ground up. Thus the eighteenth century witnessed the publication of ground-breaking encyclopedias and dictionaries. These embodied the rejection of traditional learning and attempted to rethink and re-present the entire world from undeniable first principles analogous to the laws of physics found in Sir Isaac Newton's *Principia* .

In terms of establishing bourgeois political control, a revealing attempt to perform this monumental task had already been made by René Descartes in 1637. His question, like that of later Enlightenment scholars, was, "After Copernicus, what do human beings know for certain? From what unquestionable point can one start 'enlightened' thinking?" His answer: "What I know for certain is that I am thinking about this problem. And if I am thinking, I must exist"(29, 30). In other words, Descartes' "still point" for launching the post-Copernican process of rebuilding the edifice of knowledge was his own individual rational process and existence. *"Cogito; ergo sum."*

Though unintended and unforeseen by Descartes himself, significant political consequences followed from his celebrated point of departure. For if the individual is primary, explaining the existence of human community became a problem. Why did individuals come together in the first place in political formations such as towns, provinces, and nations? Enter Thomas Hobbes and John Locke. Hobbes theorized that individual human beings formed political communities for protection of their lives and property. Without such mutual aid formations characterized by known laws and police forces, individuals would be prey to others among them who happened to be the strongest. There is safety in numbers, Locke added. Even the strongest individuals or groups can be defeated if the body politic faces them down in large enough numbers and with good enough organization (Locke 374-77). The origin of human community, then, could be explained to the satisfaction of the ever more powerful business classes by invoking the two great realities characterizing the lives of such "self-made" men of commerce -- self-interest and the contract.[3] Self-interest was primary; it was the form that rationality took in everyday life. It meant that each individual acting rationally in a situation of relative scarcity would attempt to accumulate as large a share as possible of the available resources.

Hobbes states explicitly that humans are motivated by the desire for gain, and Locke comes close to identifying rationality with the desire for unlimited accumulation. It is noteworthy that he regards the propensity to unlimited accumulation as rational not just in the prudential sense but also in the moral sense of being in accord with the law of nature or reason. (Jagger 30)

In other words, the self-made men of the seventeenth and eighteenth centuries universalized their own psychological disposition as "natural." Society too was "self-made," they asserted. Rugged individualists, like busines men, came together and, in effect, formed a corporation. They set policy and elected a board of directors. When either party broke the "social contract," the agreement might be considered null and void. Revolution would be justified.

It was through this kind of essentially business class reasoning that the "divine rights" claims of the royalty were finally delegitimized. Kings sat on their thrones, well-to-do commoners theorized, not because of divine privilege, but because the body politic accorded them power. When their wielding of power ceased to serve the common good, the royalty could be judged unfaithful to the contract and, with impunity, might be dethroned.

Thinking like this led directly to Thomas Jefferson's formulation of the Declaration of Independence in 1776. Jefferson borrowed heavily from Locke. The French Revolution's Declaration of the Rights of Man followed suit thirteen years later. Over the next two centuries, the forces thus set in motion swept the world, absolutely invalidating medieval royalist spirituality. Irresistably, the business classes took charge of the modern world. Their own spirituality became sacralized as the thought that made "the ascent of man" possible. In reality it marked the ascent of the propertied classes.

Power Wrested from Non-Europeans

All of this had political consequences for the non-European world as well. It laid the groundwork for European imperialism precisely as a totalitarian project. Enrique Dussel makes this point. He observes that Descartes' essentially self-referential starting point unintentionally predetermined that the political and economic configurations that followed would inevitably be imperialistic. As numerous commentators have observed, the employment of self-consciousness as philosophy's baseline created the problem of escaping such self-inflicted limitation. Strictly speaking, it merely established the fact of subjective experience, but the cost of this dubious accomplishment was problematizing the real existence of "the other" and of the external world. In this way, the question became, Do others really exist? The only answer possible was that if they do, their experience must be like the questioner's own.

In other words, Descartes' point of entry enclosed those who followed him in a totality, shutting out the possibility that the "other's" experience of self-consciousness might be significantly different from his own. It thus represented the thin side of the spiritual wedge justifying the cultural annihilation of those outside the European totality.

Dussel goes on to explain. Descartes' *cogito* directed subsequent thinking to privilege the specifically European way of *thinking* which then became synonymous not only with rational processes altogether, but (joined to the *ergo sum*) with life itself. This had at least two effects. For one, in line with the whole history of Western philosophy, it succeeded in reiterating thought (vs. practice) as the primary focus of philosophy (*Ethica* 33). Thus for Westerners, logical consistency or orthodoxy continued to be more important than justice understood most fundamentally as ensuring each individual's access to prerequisites for keeping body and soul together. Thus ethics too, which had been philosophy's traditional end point, was further deemphasized.

In addition, Descartes' *cogito* prepared Western philosophy to establish specifically *European* thought as the measure of thinking and of life itself. This becomes especially clear in relation to the ongoing invasion (vs. the "discovery") of the New World. In that setting, the point of heated debate in the drawing rooms of Europe from the sixteenth century on became whether or not the New World's original nations possessed true rationality and humanity, since they apparently did not share the self-interested thought processes of their various *conquistadores*. In particular the New World's first peoples exhibited little understanding of their invaders' insatiable hunger for gold and silver (15, 16). In the face of such obtuse insensitivity, the general conclusion of the European intellectual community was negative: no rationality here.

This conclusion found its genocidal fruit justified by Descartes' *ergo sum* -- the most loaded of the words comprising his fateful redefinition of modern philosophy's starting point. Conjoined as they were with the specifically European *cogito*, they not only identified *being* with a particular way of thinking, they ended by philosophically relegating those not participating in North Atlantic rationality to the sphere of non-being. For if European self-consciousness reflected in the *cogito* was a guarantee of one's being, those without such self-awareness had that guarantee removed. In this way, millions of Native American lives could be expended. They were effectively marginalized, designated as "primitive," and thus as fair game for slavery and slaughter.

In other words, by virtue of his brief conjugation, Descartes' *Ego cogito* unforeseeably transmuted into *Ego conquiro*, and the process of the non-European world's exploitation could proceed apace, but now with the official blessing of Europe's mainstream philosophers. That endorsement was completed in the work of Friedrich Hegel whose philosophy of religion Dussel signals as the most coherent expression of European imperial ontology (63). Following Descartes' lead, Hegel identified thought and being. But he progressed further still down the path of idealism by designating as divine, the Absolute Idea he understood as the pattern for everything that exists in the created world. In this way, European self-consciousness became participation in the life of the Absolute Spirit, and consequently itself became divinized. Thus the groundwork was laid for justifying theologically, as well as philosophically, the political totalization of European experience in relation to the rest of the world (Dussel 35-40).[4]

BOURGEOIS CONQUEST OF ECONOMICS:
THE VINDICATION OF SELF-SEEKING
AND LIBERATION FROM FELLOW-FEELING

The business class conquest of economics faced obstacles even more formidable than those necessary to gain control of either church or state. In the case of economics, the barriers were presented not by rival ecclesiastical or noble classes but by deeply rooted moral values. Here the challenge to bourgeois theorists was to justify pursuit of unrestrained self-interest, the incorporation of unwilling subjects into the bourgeois system, and to surmount formidable obstacles of fellow-feeling and responsibility for others. Each of these requirements was problematic; opposition to them was centralized in both the Judeo-Christian tradition and by bourgeois humanism itself. As already noted, the New Testament generally saw self-centered pursuit of wealth as an obstacle to salvation. Old Testament law demanded special state economic provision for those unable to meet their own needs -- including widows, orphans, resident aliens, and the incapacitated. For its part, bourgeois humanism not only advocated a universalist ethic recognizing the responsibility of each for all, but also its increasing tendency (at least in theory) was to oppose the imposition of conditions (economic or otherwise) on others without their consent.

Nevertheless, as the philosophers of the propertied classes themselves admitted, the market could not operate freely and with maximum efficiency if its activity was limited by medieval moral constraints condemning self-seeking. Much less could the bourgeois order function if it observed "dark age" prohibitions against the lending of money. Additionally, if capitalism's basic mechanism recognized alternatives, its inherent tendency toward unlimited growth would be frustrated. Finally, if the market were required to serve the fundamental needs of all society's members by, for example, providing full employment, it could never survive as a specifically free institution operating without government regulation.

On the contrary, what market efficiency sought was a rationale enabling capitalists to pursue their own interests across the globe while somehow discounting the needy with good conscience. To this end, capitalists required a broadening of the concept of "science" to include economics. This would accord their theories "value freedom." Additionally, within the category of science, the new directors needed natural laws that would delegitimate opposition to their order. Economics' achievement of scientific status would enable the discipline to invoke Galileo's exceptionalist principle in order to relativize Biblical teaching on social justice as "prescientific" and therefore as inapplicable even for believers.

In the late eighteenth and early nineteenth centuries, Adam Smith, Thomas Malthus, David Ricardo, and others supplied the rationale capitalists either wittingly or unwittingly sought. Smith's theories and formulations of "natural laws" justified self-seeking and the inevitability of an entrepreneurial order which afterward became sinful to oppose. As we shall see presently, Malthus discovered a powerful mechanism for absolving capitalists of responsibility for their system's alleged victims. Ricardo applied Malthus' insights in a way that made neglect of the poor seem an ethical act of love and responsibility. The basic insights of these giants of capitalist theory were gradually attenuated over the next hundred years -- largely as a result of pressure from the working classes who emphatically experienced the market as something less than efficient and beneficial. However, in more recent times, the triumph of neoliberal thought has returned earlier theories to relevance under the aegis of free trade agreements and the New World Order. These points are worth pursuing one by one. Once again, they illustrate the totalitarian nature of free market capitalism and its triumph over basic fellow-feeling.

Economic Liberalism: Smith, Malthus, Ricardo, and the Invisible Hand

Adam Smith's first contribution was to establish (against biblical precedent) the general beneficence of self-seeking. On Smith's theory, self-interested human activities of production, selling, and buying automatically engage market laws as inevitable as Newton's principles of gravity and inertia. When market laws are allowed to function without interference, he theorized, the resulting dynamic facilitates the nearest approximation human beings can make to utopia here on earth. That is, the tendency of the free market is toward harmony of interests. Self-seeking thus becomes the most efficient expression of humanitarian benevolence. In this vein, Smith writes against mercantilist laws requiring promotion of "the public interest."

> [E]very individual necessarily labours to render the annual revenue of the society as great as he can. He generally, indeed, neither intends to promote the public interest, nor knows how much he is promoting it. By preferring the support of domestic to that of foreign industry, he intends only his own security; and by directing that industry in such manner as its produce may be of the greatest value, he intends only his own gain; and he is in this, as in many other cases, led by an invisible hand to promote the end which was no part of his intention. Nor is it always the worse for society that it was no part of it. By pursuing his own interest, he frequently promotes that of society more effectively than when he really intends to promote it. (167)

Here Smith's focus is on the unintentional effects of intentional market activities. The entrepreneur's intention is only to augment his own wealth. But by pursuing that end, he often promotes the public interest. Put otherwise, with his discovery of the specifically automatic nature of the market mechanism, Smith had achieved the great synthesis between private and public interest, which moralists had sought throughout the ages. And he had done so without controversial appeal to "values" or religious principles. After Smith, economists become less circumspect in recognizing unintended benefits for unfettered economic activity. With the passage of time, they increasingly drop the qualifier "frequently" from Smith's assertion about self-interested activity automatically coinciding with public good. Eventually almost every act of production, buying, and selling falls under the umbrella of a publicly beneficial endeavor -- even what was considered specifically sinful by medieval standards. Years before Smith, Mandeville had put it this way: "private vices lead to public good" (Hinkelammert, 1992, 59).

This brings us to Adam Smith's second great contribution toward establishing market totalitarianism. According to Smith (still emphasizing the unintentional), every economic interchange with Europeans implicitly affirms the market order; it causes one to be irrevocably incorporated into the system. Consequently, for instance, when a group of Native Americans sold Manhattan for $24 in beads and whiskey, the trade brought them not only trinkets and drugs, but by implication, the indigenous also purchased all the presuppositions of the new European order. In fact, Smith considered as aggressive any attempts to revoke such consent or to otherwise resist the inevitability of the system he explained. He qualifies as "despotic" (and hence as illegitimate) societies that refuse to submit to market law (Hinkelammert, *Sacrificios* 31). Along these lines, Locke deemed culpable not only the direct Native American resistance to European settlers, but also the Native American systems of property distribution which were in themselves hostile and aggressive. On account of these systems, the New World's original peoples supposedly merited punishment even to the point of extermination.

> Locke placed property above everything. In this way, considering private property as a natural law, a law of God and of the human race, he imaginarily transforms all resistance against such relations of production into acts of aggression against the human race and against God himself. Locke's imagination is such that any act of conquest of expansion or of colonization is transformed into an act of legitimate defense of the human race, represented by private property. Now every bourgeois aggression appears as a legitimately defensive action against aggressors who do not have even the least aggressive intent. The conquest of the entire world is transformed into an act of self-defense and of just war. The whole world, even in the case where it does not recognize private property, is transformed into an aggressor. (Hinkelammert, *Democrácia 143*)

To reiterate our central point: attitudes like these reveal the tendencies toward totalitarianism inherent in the market system itself.

Overcoming Fellow-Feeling

Still, however, for all its claims to general beneficence, the activation of the bourgeois market was accompanied by a legendary misery that even the most persuasive apologists for the system could not deny. Why were so many in the new industrial centers living in unprecedented widespread squalor? Influenced by the residual medieval tradition and by Renaissance humanism, many raised a call for public programs to alleviate poverty. Taking the form of primitive social welfare programs, the resulting "poor laws" tended to interfere with the natural outworking of market laws of supply and demand, relative to the labor pool. This raised general alarm among owners of capital. If people were not driven by the spectre of hunger to accept jobs for subsistence pay, employers would be forced to attract workers by "unnaturally" high wages that would, of course, cut into profit margins and generally upset the "natural" order of things. But on the other hand, how could inheritors of the biblical tradition deny their responsibilities to the poor?

In 1798, a British parson, Thomas Malthus, planted a seed that would eventually come to fruition in the thought of David Ricardo. Malthus discovered an economic law that has remained pivotal to business class thinking ever since. What some have called his "utterly dismal theorem" blamed the poor themselves for the poverty and misery that accompanied the development of free market capitalism. This theory emerged from the parson's meditation on the burgeoning and correspondingly miserable populations of English industrial cities such as Manchester, London, Birmingham, and Liverpool. His analysis located the cause of the growing misery in the poor's procreative irresponsibility. Lacking discipline, the working class insisted on raising large families despite the hunger the insistence produced. This diagnosis, of course, ignored historic causes of late eighteenth century urban population growth. Malthus gave scant notice, for example, to the laws of enclosure that drove subsistence farmers from former medieval manors in the countryside, when it became more profitable for landlords to raise sheep in place of basic crops. Such laws stimulated a massive peasant migration to the cities where the sheep's wool would be processed in the textile mills dominating the great urban centers. Ignoring the effects of enclosure, Malthus asserted that the poor were their own worst enemies. Their situation might be alleviated only if workers took account of the fact that unrestrained procreation inevitably outruns food supply, "that population, when unchecked, goes on doubling itself every twenty-five years, or increases in a geometrical ratio [1, 2, 4, 8, 16, etc]. Meanwhile subsistence goods, under circumstances most favorable to human industry, could not possibly be made to increase faster than in an arithmetical ratio [1, 2, 3, 4, 5, etc.]" (Malthus 8, 12).

With words like these, Malthus became industrial culture's first harbinger of the population explosion theory. Of course this held that the cause of hunger and misery is a numerical disproportion between the number of mouths the world has to feed and the amount of food the planet produces. Once again, the hungry themselves were responsible for their condition of want. This analysis is as current today as it was at the end of the eighteenth century. But it was Malthus who had planted the seed in 1798.

Death as Lubrication and Lesson

Nineteen years later David Ricardo reaped Malthus' harvest. He seconded Malthus' point about population, using it in a theory that has also proven central both to classic laissez-faire economic theory as well as to its New World Order revival. Ricardo formulated a Newtonian "Iron Law of Wages," which "scientifically" explained away any need to care for those rendered jobless by the outworking of the era's New Economic Order. Ricardo's law had been anticipated in its basic thrust by Smith himself nearly half a century before. Then Smith had classified as "natural" a labor market dynamic that condemned surplus population to death. Smith not only saw these deaths as natural, he dispassionately considered them as a type of "lubrication" that kept the market functioning smoothly (Hinkelammert,"El mercado como" 65).

Along these same lines, Ricardo observed that wages are determined by supply and demand just like the value of any other commodity. In fact, like artisans and men of commerce, workers have a product to sell -- the work of their hands. But on entering the market, they find that other laborers have nearly identical products to offer. Hence workers must determine their comparative advantages or competitive edges. Their options include working harder than others; working cheaper; or doing both. According to Ricardo, worker competition naturally results in their receiving wages as close as possible to what is necessary to keep their bodies and souls together. If they will not work for such a wage, someone else will. It was as simple as that. In more technical language, Ricardo said: "Labour, like all other things which are purchased and sold, and which may be increased or diminished in quantity, has its natural price. The natural price of labour is that price which is necessary to enable the laborers, one with another, to subsist and to perpetuate their race, without either increase or diminution" (93).

This being the case, providing income for workers independent of the market (for example through England's "poor laws," or by union negotiation) is always counterproductive. Citing Malthus, Ricardo pointed out how such attempts at helping the poor rob them of the necessary stimulus they need to make them work (Heilbroner 87). Ricardo put it this way:

> These then are the laws by which wages are regulated, and by which the happiness of far the greatest part of every community is governed. Like all other contracts, wages should be left to the fair and free competition of the market, and should never be controlled by the interference of the legislature. The clear and direct tendency of the poor laws is in direct opposition to these obvious principles. This pernicious tendency of these laws is no longer a mystery since it has been fully developed by the able hand of Mr. Malthus; and every friend of the poor must ardently wish for their abolition. It is a truth which admits not a doubt that the comforts and well-being of the poor cannot be permanently secured without some regard on their part, or some effort on the part of the legislature to regulate the increase of their numbers, and to render less frequent among them early and improvident marriages. The operation of the poor laws has been directly contrary to this. They have rendered restraint superfluous, and have invited imprudence by offering of the wages of prudence and industry. (105-7)

Clearly, then, Malthus and Ricardo fathered the ideas which have become central to modern thinking about poverty and hunger. The main cause of hunger is overpopulation. As long as the poor continue having so many children, many deaths are inevitable. But only the poor can do anything about this unfortunate fact. To help them by interference in the market is counterproductive; it rewards destructive behavior, removes incentive and finishes by making the problem worse. Moreover, well-intentioned interference in the marketplace is even unchristian. Ricardo's citation of Parson Malthus to support his theory indicates this, as does the above citation's reference to "every friend of the poor" ardently wishing the abolition of public welfare. For Ricardo it is concern for the poor that prompts elimination of social programs to help them. With Ricardo, then, the business classes had completed assembly of the arsenal they needed to defend their system against value claims to the contrary. Calling on Ricardo, Smith, and Malthus, property owners were subsequently enabled to effectively set aside biblical, medieval, and humanist values contradicting the self-seeking and neglect of others endemic to their system.[5]

BOURGEOIS CONQUEST OF NATURE

Closely related to the bourgeois triumph over fellow-feeling was business class success in overcoming human sympathy for the natural environment. After all, the industrial project, as conceived since the mid-nineteenth century, could not succeed without reducing nature to nearly absolute submission. Ideologically speaking, the need here was to legitimate exploitation of nature as thoroughly as feasible, and with as little guilt as possible. As in the case of fellow-feeling, success in this area was deeply indebted to ideological application of Darwin's theory of evolution. Here, however, the specifically self-serving usage of Darwin was more subtle. The natural world is, after all, the legitimate field of the life sciences.

Nonetheless, use of evolution to establish human dominance over nature was not difficult. Doing so entailed reiterating that by decree of nature (and/or God) all life forms are in competition. Secondly, came the reminder that in life's competition, the strongest quite naturally survive. Thirdly, science and its evident power over nature has clearly enthroned human beings as the strongest of all species. Consequently, "man" has a legitimate right to dominate nature in all its life forms, using it for his own benefit. To subordinate human prosperity, then, to concern for the rain forests, ozone layers, spotted owls, snail darters, or any other species is patently irrational.

That such reasoning is ideological, self-serving and arbitrary becomes evident by contrasting its legitimating narrative with another possible approach to the relationship between human beings, their natural environment, and one another. This approach is equally based on the theory of evolution but it leads to radically different conclusions. The second narrative is ideological too; that is, it arises from commitment. But that very origin illustrates the point of this chapter: ideology (or what Gallardo calls "conceptual spirituality") is by no means dead.

The second approach begins from the position that all life forms, including human beings, are part of a great web of life. The web is self-regulating in a delicately balanced way. Its powerful processes must therefore be respected by all without domination. Human beings represent the evolutionary process "coming to itself" in the act of self-consciousness (Berry 128). Thus they are capable of understanding the evolutionary process, can admire and celebrate it. They can even use it for their own benefit. However, in doing so, they must never eliminate life forms that represent their very own forbears, brothers, and sisters. Much less may humans kill or otherwise harm their human sisters and brothers who are united to them by bonds which precede those of nation, culture, language, religion, or family. In sum, all humans must care for the planet and for each other. They must resist the ill-perceived "freedom" of individuals and groups to destroy the heritage they share.

Of course, this second account did not even occur to most in the nineteenth or twentieth century West. There it continues to find only small niche in the "marketplace of ideas."

Marxism, the Tradition of Dissent and the Neoclassical Response

Nevertheless, capitalism's pretensions to benign totality were not accepted as self-evident by everyone. They especially did not sit well with the colonized, with the working class, and with those who identified with them. Chief among the latter, of course, was Karl Marx, the philosopher par excellence of capitalism's victims. The objections raised by these critical thinkers eventually brought changes in capitalist theory and practice.

Marxism

Karl Marx represents the counterpoint to Adam Smith. In fact, Marx's point of departure was Smith himself. But it is not the case that Marx disagreed with Smith absolutely. On the contrary, the philosopher of the working class gave assent to virtually all of Smith's theory about the way the market works. Marx recognized, for instance, the laws of supply and demand, the labor theory of value, the iron law of wages. He also accepted Smith's and Ricardo's accounts of the origins of rent, profit, and interest. Above all, Marx affirmed the theory that the intentional acts of market participants often have unintended effects, which frequently end up being more important than those that were intended. In other words, he too accepted a theory of an "invisible hand." This much, he said, was indeed scientific, measurable, undeniable. To this point, Smith had done his job well.

However, where Marx differed from Smith and the other patriarchs comprising the first group of "worldly philosophers," was in his characterization of the unintended effects of intended actions, and in his indication of the direction toward which the fingers of the "invisible hand" were pointing. Smith, of course, had said the market dynamism leads toward general social good. In Marx's eyes, such claims were naively utopian. In contrast, he claimed that market activity had overwhelmingly destructive effects. Marx's thesis was that the market's fingers were pointing towards chaos rather than toward the general happiness of society.

Marx drew his conclusion by paying attention to the claims and living conditions of the working-class people of his day. These gave testimony that sharply contradicted the bourgeois understanding of Malthus, Ricardo, and of Smith himself. Against Malthus, Marx was able to see that the laws of enclosure, mentioned earlier, better explained industrial center population explosions than did lust and lack of discipline on the part of workers. Marx also perceived that low wages and on-the-job accidents made large working-class families imperative. In places like Manchester and Birmingham, for example, entire families sweated out long days in front of power looms and industrial presses to earn enough money to keep them alive. Besides, it was often the case that children were able to get jobs when their parents could not. So it made perfect economic sense to have many offspring. Against Ricardo, Marx saw that workers were not predominantly lazy, needing the spectre of hunger to make them work. On the contrary, their working days stretched over seemingly endless 14 -18 hour periods and followed a frenetic pace dictated by the unvarying rhythm of the machines their human appendages attended. And finally, against Smith, Marx was able to see that the unintended negative effects of the market not only eclipsed the good outcomes Smith myopically celebrated; but also that the negative effects shaped the lives of innumerably more people than the system's beneficiaries. Moreover, the negative effects were cumulative; they caused progressive immiseration promising to eventually destroy the key elements on which the market depended for its very sustenance -- the working-class itself as well as the natural environment. In other words, working class deaths were not the oil market machinery needed to run efficiently; they were the grains of sand that would cause the mechanism to grind to a screeching halt.

> In agriculture as in manufacturing, the transformation of production under the sway of capital, means, at the same time, the martyrdom of the producer; the instrument of labour becomes the means of enslaving, exploiting, and impoverishing the labourer; the social combination of and organization of labour-processes is turned into an organised mode of crushing out the workman's individual vitality, freedom, and independence. In modern agriculture, as in the urban industires, the increased productiveness and quantity of the labour is set in motion and bought at the cost of laying waste and consuming by disease labour-power itself. Moreover, all progress in capitalistic agriculture is a progress in the art, not only of robbing the labourer, but of robbing the soil; all progress in increasing the fertility of the soil for a given time, is a progress towards ruining the lasting sources of that fertility. The more a country starts its development on the foundation of modern industry, like the United States, for example, the more rapid is this process of destruction. Capitalist production, therefore, developes technology, and the combining together of various processes into a social whole, only by sapping the original sources of all wealth--the soil and the labourer. (Marx, *Capital* 555-56)

The Wider Tradition of Dissent

Marx reached his conclusions about destruction of the labor force by analyzing data routinely excluded from bourgeois theory. Such information was reflected in the transcripts of Great Britain's Saddler and Ashley Committees, whose parliamentary investigations preceded by more than a decade the publication of *The Communist Manifesto* in 1848. These inquests supply more compelling evidence of the unintended negative effects of market activity than do either the novels of Charles Dickens or the reflections of Marx and Engels about surplus value. In their responses to questions of blue-ribbon panelists, workers described a virtual slavery in the work place: extremely low wages, unpaid overtime, exploitation of children and women, health-threatening work conditions, physical abuse, arbitrarily unstable employment, and resulting destruction of family life and values.[6]

Q. At what time in the morning, in the brisk time, did those girls go to the mills?
A. In the brisk time, for about six weeks they have gone at 3 o'clock in the morning, and ended at 10, or nearly half-past at night.
Q. What was the length of time they could be in bed during those long hours?
A. It was near 11 o'clock before we could get them into bed after getting a little victuals, and then at morning my mistress used to stop up all night, for fear we could not get them ready for the time; sometimes we have gone to bed, and one of us generally awoke.
Q. What time did you get them up in the morning?
A. In general me or my mistress got up at 2 o'clock to dress them.
Q. So that they had not above four hours sleep at this time?
A. No, they had not.
Q. The common hours of labor were from 6 in the morning till half-past eight at night?
A. Yes.
Q. Did this excessive term of labor occasion much cruelty also?
A. Yes, with being so much fatigued the strap was very frequently used.
Q. Have any of your children been strapped?
A. Yes, every one; the eldest daughter; I was up in Lancashire a fortnight, and when I got home I saw her shoulders, and I said, "Ann, what is the matter?" She said, "The overlooker has strapped me; but," she said, "do not go to the overlooker, for if you do we shall lose our work." Her back was beat nearly to a jelly.
Q. What were the wages in the short hours?
A. Three shillings a week each.
Q. When they wrought those very long hours what did they get?
A. Three shillings and sevenpence halfpenny.
Q. For all that additional labor they had only 7 1/2 pence a week?
A. No more
("Report of Committee" 192-94).

Data like these not only provided the specifically human basis for Marx's analysis, they reflect as well the fact that by far he was not alone in describing the disutopian nature of the industrial order. Already in 1729 Jonathan Swift had mercilessly indicted the unreason of market rationality in his scathing *Modest Proposal*. There he offered a satirical market solution for Ireland's problem of surplus population. Sell infants as meat in fine restaurants, he suggested. After all, there's a market for such delicacies as proven by landlords' insatiable appetites for devouring parents. Moreover, the "victims" of Swift's proposal, he points out, might find their lot as a market food commodity preferable to what they have to endure as market labor commodities. Anticipating critiques of the market for its genocidal tendencies, as well as Ricardo's self-absolution of responsibility for the economically marginated, Swift advises:

Some persons of a desponding spirit are in great concern about that vast number of poor people, who are aged, diseased, or maimed, and I have been desired to employ my thoughts what course may be taken to ease the nation of so grievous an encumbrance. But I am not in the least pain upon that matter, because it is very well known that they are every day dying and rotting by cold and famine, and filth and vermin, as fast as can be reasonably expected. And as to the young laborers, they are now in as hopeful a condition; they cannot get work, and consequently pine away for want of nourishment, to a degree that if at any time they are accidentally hired to common labour, they have not strength to perform it; and thus the country and themselves are happily delivered from the evils to come. (506)

In a similar vein, though less satirically, Charles Dickens popularized insights into working-class life and consciousness in books such as *Hard Times*. The trade union movement of the 1830s and 1840s, and the experiments in planned societies undertaken by Saint-Simon and Fourier in Europe and by Robert Owen in North America registered other dissenting voices. In his own way William Jennings Bryan also refused to be swept along by the cult of a market which took no responsibility for its victims. One of the main reasons Bryan rejected Darwin's theory of evolution was that the theory's ideological use (as distinct from its employment as an hypothesis within the life sciences) would reinforce a more general acceptance of the very "survival of the fittest" mentality that the writings of Smith, Malthus, and Ricardo reflected so clearly:

Darwin reveals the barbarous sentiment that runs through evolution and dwarfs the moral nature of those who become obsessed with it. Darwin speaks with approval of the savage custom of eliminating the weak so that only the strong will survive and complains that "we civilized men do our utmost to check the process of elimination." How inhuman such a doctrine as this! He thinks it injurious to "build asylums for the imbecile, the maimed, and the sick," and to care for the poor. All of the sympathetic activities of civilized society are condemned because they enable "the weak members to propagate their kind." (Bryan 335)

During the Second World War, Dietrich Bonhoeffer called the bourgeois order's religious underpinnings into question. Afterward, the Frankfurt School of critical thought updated Marxist criticism to address the changed situation of postwar Europe and the United States.

Perhaps, however, the most cogent voices dissenting from the market's pretensions to totality spoke with nonbourgeois, nonwhite, nonmale, and non-Western accents. During the colonial period, these belonged to defenders of Native American rights such as Bartolomé de las Casas and Antonio Valdivieso (Todorov 151-167). Among Abya Yala's original peoples, Black Elk and Chief Seattle evidenced a wisdom absent from mainstream Eurocentric thought (Carroll and Noble 1988, 236-37). Similarly, the words and actions of slaves and defenders of slaves and their descendents cried out for attention (Zinn 1980, 23-38). These questioned classist and sexist interpretations of the ideals expressed in the U.S. Declaration of Independence and in the French Declaration of the Rights of Man. Spokespersons for slaves and former slaves such as Nat Turner,

John Brown, Frederick Douglass, Harriet Tubman, W.E.B. Dubois, Malcolm X, Martin Luther King Jr., and Stokeley Carmichael demanded that understandings of the 1776 declaration be broadened to truly embrace *all* men -- and all women as well. Women including Mary Wallstonecraft, Sojourner Truth, and Simone de Beauvoir assumed critical standpoints derived from specifically female experience (102-123). And (of special interest here) Third World thinkers, including theologians of liberation rounded out the chorus of dissenters.

The Neoclassical Response

Such voices have not been without their effects. The most important of these occurred during the Great Depression. As indicated earlier, this was the era of capitalism's perestroika, when the system's dysfunctions became so generally apparent that its directors feared that the dissenting voices indicated above might prevail. Accordingly, as was seen earlier, the very recommendations Marx had made at the end of The *Communist Manifesto* were co-opted into the capitalist system.

However, changes in capitalism were not limited to desperately self-defensive practice; they also reached to the level of theory. Theoretical reforms were nothing new, of course; they had been anticipated since the days of John Stuart Mill and the utilitarians. For once again, under pressure from the bourgeois humanitarian tradition and from those marginated by capitalism, the openly sacrificial rationales of Smith, Malthus, and Ricardo became less defensible. As a result, Smith's profoundly classist theory of the "invisible hand," which accepted and even affirmed the deaths of some at society's base so that others at the top might live, was replaced by "equilibrium theory" in mainstream economics (Heilbroner 188-91). Here instead of acknowledging that not all can have a slice of the market's pie, this form of capitalist revisionism discovered an opposite inclusive tendency in the market. All those could be included who were willing to take the practical steps to achieve inclusion. In other words, as opposed to the convictions of Smith and Ricardo, the market's inertia moved in the direction of full employment; it excluded no one, nor did it demand that anyone sacrifice his or her life. Smith's concept of the market had been static -- an approach rendered obsolete by quantum leaps in technology realized especially following World War II. Now the idea was that technological advance would expand the world's economic pie. In the process economic growth would ensure better products, better salaries, and a better future for all -- without poverty.

Though this was the long-term, natural tendency of the market, equilibrium theorists pointed out that some were too shortsighted or impatient to see light at the end of the tunnel. These tended to be overwhelmed by short-term "frictions" in the forms of unemployment, poor health care, lack of housing, inadequate education, absence of retirement provisions, or of Third World underdevelopment. Those lacking patience needed concessions, while the rest of society awaited the market's long-term tendencies to activate. In other words, what was envisioned after the depression, and especially during the postwar period of euphoria over technological progress and expanding economies was a universal welfare state. However, between 1945 and 1970, welfare concessions were understood as simply anticipating the market's automatic tendencies toward equilibrium. Hence the concessions were to work with the market's natural tendencies, never against them.

Socialism's Response to Neo-Classicism

Initially socialists responded to changes in capitalist practice and theory with a jubilant celebration. Socialism had triumphed over capitalism. The "end of history" had dawned. This was especially the tenor of thought at the 1934 "Congress of Victory" celebrated by Russia's Communist Party led by Joseph Stalin (Hinkelammert, "Capitalismo sin alternativas?" 11). But thereafter socialist theorists in Iron Curtain countries wrote less about capitalism's inevitable demise due to its necessary destruction of the labor force and of the environment on which it depended for its continued existence. They criticized capitalism less in terms of Marx's central point about the system's inevitable automated tendencies toward self-destruction. They spoke less of a future qualitatively different from that of advanced capitalism. Instead, communists boasted that socialism was a more efficient path toward the common horizon sought by the competing systems. Guided by this vision, historic socialism in the East often mimicked the West's imperialism and joined its capitalist opponents in their onslaught against the natural environment. As Hinkelammert notes, in the midst of theoretic celebration, all of this amounted to an admission of defeat by historic socialism. The United States was acknowledged to determine both the direction and the pace of industrial development (11). The Soviets envisioned themselves in hot pursuit.

NEO-LIBERALISM AND THE RETURN OF THE INVISIBLE HAND

By the end of the 1970s, the events recounted in the previous chapter led directly to a general loss of faith in the welfare state and in the processes of international development. It will be recalled that chief among the occurrences were the Arab Oil Embargo, stagflation in capitalist economies, the widespread realization of environmental limits to economic growth, and a persistent and growing gap between rich and poor classes within the developed countries and between developed and underdeveloped countries themselves.

All of these factors made it clear that poverty was a more difficult problem to solve than was generally thought in the heyday of post World War II euphoria. After the war, a whole series of new programs were launched to eliminate poverty in both developed and underdeveloped nations. In the United States, for example, Kennedy's "New Frontier" and Johnson's "Great Society" continued along the lines marked out by Roosevelt's "New Deal." In the Third World, the directions indicated by the "Good Neighbor Policy" were followed by UN proclamations of the first and second "Development Decades." But each of these trajectories was contradicted by developments signaled earlier. These made it clear to economists on the left that attempts to eliminate poverty would have to run counter to the market's natural tendencies, which were not in the direction of equilibrium, but toward greater concentration of wealth and toward widening gaps between rich and poor. In the light of these realities, economists on the right concluded that the welfare state idea was a failure. It represented an institutional solution to a personal problem. Apart from individual moral decision, poverty was basically incurable.

With these later conclusions, neoliberalism, the offspring of Nietzschean postmodernism, was born. It was "neoliberal" to distinguish it from classic nineteenth-century economic theory, which, as we saw, was "liberal" in the free enterprise sense championed by Smith, Malthus, and Ricardo. During the 1970s and 1980s liberalism in that sense (ironically self-styled as "neoconservatism") enjoyed a resurgence in the form of "Reaganomics" and of policies espoused by Great Britain's Margaret Thatcher. These approaches characterized the welfare state's political economy as a huge mistake. According to neo-liberals, welfare state policy interfered with the "magic of the market place." It mistakenly introduced socialistic policies with the resulting and entirely predictable results of inflated government bureaucracies, inefficiency, inflation, trade imbalances, and loss of personal freedom.

In this context, "market place magic" was a significant phrase. The term "magic," of course, refers to actions that occur automatically and mysteriously when certain preconditions are met. In the case of the market, those preconditions comprise the actions of buying and selling. These activities engage laws of supply and demand along with other principles related to employment, wages, rent, interest, and so forth. According to the proponents of market place magic, when such laws are allowed to function without interference (with the government "off the backs" of producers, as President Reagan put it), the resulting dynamic historicizes the nearest approach to utopia that human beings can make on earth. Everything works out for the best. Market participants seek only their own enrichment, but in doing so, they not only benefit themselves but the "greatest number" possible in the process. In other words, references to the "magic of the market place" were a reprise of Adam Smith's "invisible hand."

According to this classical theory revisited, the free market could cure all the problems capable of remediation within a given society, if only marketplace magic were left to operate without restraint. This was not to say, however, that all of the world's ills fell into the "remediable" category. Such universalism was utopian and utopias were by definition unrealistic. In the light of the failures of historic socialism and of the welfare state, a new realism took center stage for neo-liberals. Poverty at home and underdevelopment in the Third World were cruel facts of life which would have to be endured, since, once again, they might be cured only by change of attitude and by individual choice.[7] Accordingly, neoliberalism's new realism demanded that hard choices be made -- ultimately on the basis of what Nobel Prize laureate Friedrich Hayeck termed the "calculus of lives":

> A free society requires certain moral standards which finally can be reduced
> to the maintenance of lives: not the maintenance of all lives, because it

could be necessary to sacrifice individual lives in order to preserve a greater
number of other lives. This is why the only moral rules are those which
contribute to the calculus of lives: property and the contract.
(Hinkelammert, *Sacrificios Humanos* 32-33)

The implications of neoliberal "calculus of lives" is most evident in the
Third World. There Hinkelammert and other Latin American analysts use the
term "neoliberal" to refer to the theory undergirding the policies of "structural
readjustment" which over the last dozen years or so the IMF has standardly
imposed on Third World debtor countries. As seen earlier, the "international
lending organization of last resort," the IMF, has required such readjustment
measures in exchange for the refinancing of existing Third World debts and as a
precondition for further loans. Here the theory is that state involvement in the
economy is the root of the problems experienced by economically
underdeveloped nations. So the cure for their ills is "free enterprise" -- or as
Hinkelammert puts it, "more market." For Hinkelammert, this prescription is
the latest expression of "market totalitarianism."[8]

After the fall of historic socialism the market system was left without rival
or alternative. It thus became increasingly possible for countries of the center
(especially the "group of seven") to dictate the destinies and internal politics of
virtually every country in the world. The means for doing so were called the
New World Order and specifically centralized market mechanisms connected to
external debts and the structural adjustments required to repay them. Such
instruments were augmented by bourgeois totalization of communications media
that all but excluded discourse about alternative arrangements of political
economy.

> [N]either are there means of communication capable of criticizing the
> system. Nor does short wave radio have news from outside, for now there
> really is no outside. Freedom of opinion in the means of communication
> has lost its meaning, insofar as the media suppose that we live in a society
> which has no alternative. Today control of opinion is planetary --
> something we experienced for the first time with information about the war
> against Iraq. There was no alternative information in the entire world; all
> the means of communication repeated the same story. (Hinkelammert,
> *"Capitalismo sin alternativas?"* 21)

That the director class realizes it has achieved total control is revealed in its
various proclamations of the "end of history" (Gallardo 1). By this, Francis
Fukuyama, for example, means that the future will simply be more of the same.
This implies that no change is possible in the condition of the world's starving.
Meanwhile, up to 40,000,000 people die of preventable, hunger-related causes
annually (Nelson-Pallmeyer, *War against the Poor* 10). That's like the death
toll from 300 jumbo jets crashing each day for a year, with no survivors, and
with most of the victims children. But none of that constitutes proof that the
world's "traffic control" system, its free market economy, does not work. No one
is to blame. No one is responsible. The market, after all, is in charge.
Politicians and economists are simply technicians who adjust public life to the
market's optimal performance. In other words, the market's laws are beyond

challenge. It decrees; the rest of us obey. There is simply no alternative. Put otherwise still, the entrepreneurial utopia of a world without utopias has been realized.

CONCLUSION

Hopefully, the foregoing chapter has made it clear that what is commonly presented in our schools as "the ascent of man" reflects in reality a severely restricted spirituality belonging to a particular class. This celebrated way of thinking is partial not only in the sense that it falsely presents one class' viewpoint as universally true and as the destiny of humankind. It is also partial in that step by step it has relativized and in the end denied its own foundations -- namely, the Judeo-Christian tradition and Western humanism itself.

The key to entrepreneurial ideology, we have seen, is its reductionism -- something which, again, Hinkelammert reminds us lies at the heart of every totalitarian system. Under capitalism, human relations tend to be reduced to simple market functions.[9] Thus, in the Third World, for instance, people are urged to cooperate with campaigns against tuberculosis because limiting the disease will increase exports of foodstuffs. This suggests that if eradicating tuberculosis had little or no economic benefit, it might just as well be ignored.[10] In our own country cost/benefit analysis directs debate about the feasibility of social programs. This mode of reasoning quantifies human life in terms of earning power over a normal lifespan. When the cost of saving human lives so calculated becomes greater than the anticipated benefit (in terms of countervailing profit opportunities), saving human life becomes "irrational." In other words, concepts of human transcendence and of the incalculable have been all but entirely lost to late twentieth-century capitalism. Nowhere is this clearer than in relation to issues of environmental protection (Berry 13ff).

Another key to business class spirituality is its systematic denial of public responsibility for the poor. Solutions for the unintended effects of the free market economy are sought in voluntary charitable acts rather than in political action to remediate the market's automatically destructive tendencies in terms, for example, of unemployment and environmental devastation. Such charity, of course, remains totally disproportionate to the market's self-regulated effects. The result is that human and natural life goes on being destroyed in the name of nature itself and of "natural law." This amounts to yet another denial of the Judeo-Christian tradition that condemns human sacrifice and that stands ready to relativize the provision of any law, even God's own, in order to save human life. As we will see in the chapter that follows denying this anarchic character of the biblical tradition required a rather complete inversion of the Western understanding of the Bible.

NOTES

1. In a scathing indictment of Western civilization, Franz Hinkelammert contradicts the Western intellectual tradition so celebrated in the mainstream's "war

education" underlying World War III. Instead of perceiving Western thought as guiding "the ascent of man," he describes it forthrightly as the destructive ideology of the particular group that over the last 500 years has achieved control of the world -- the business classes. Their interpretation of history is an "ideology," he says. We would say it constitutes the "spirituality" of the New World Order. It represents a partial, historically conditioned consciousness that pretends to be universal, eternal, and inevitable. In reality, however, dominant categories of thought are white, male, Eurocentric, racist, and sexist. The categories normalize the most destructive history the world has known.

> [F]rom the 15th century on (bourgeois society) transformed itself into the society which dominates the entire world and which colonized the rest of the continents.
>
> It transformed Africa into a hunting ground for slaves and set up in America the most wide-ranging empire of forced slave labor in human history; that empire lasted for more than four centuries. Western society conquered Asia and transformed it into a simple producer of raw materials for its centers and destroyed traditional production. Western society developed a racism previously unknown in any human society.
>
> Today Western society dominates a world where fully one quarter of the population lives in subhuman conditions, without any hope of escape. It is a society where hunger has struck the majority, while some countries live in sumptuous abundance.
>
> Western society has produced wars the like of which humanity has never before seen. Western society has produced systems of domination so extreme that they are without precedent in any previous historical period or in any other part of the world. Here it is a question of systems which have exterminated entire populations. Western society has also invented black holes of secret services, where human beings are dehumanized to insuperable levels.
>
> Western society has developed productive forces never before seen. But it has developed them with such destructiveness that it has placed itself at the limits of its own existence and has endangered the continuity of the human subject itself.
>
> This development of productive forces has destroyed the capacity for life on the part of the world's majority. [The West] has developed systems of torture of high sophistication, overseen by doctors and psychologists capable of completely destroying the human personality. It has developed arms which if used would destroy the very earth itself. It has created a technology so irrational that it alone, even without wars, tends to eliminate the earth's life systems.
>
> The twentieth-century witnesses the society of the West *in extremis.* From the great concentration camps of the totalitarianisms of the first half of this century, it has passed to the Gulags of the Free World. These extend throughout the whole Third World in the form of great fields of misery supervised by the secret services and the black holes capable of swallowing up all who resist. Nature itself is debased and nuclear arms symbolize the apocalyptic threat which hangs over the earth.
>
> Western society has done all of this in the name of service to humanity, in the name of love of neighbor and of salvation, democracy and freedom. Western society believes it is the only free society in the history of the human race. No one has escaped this illusion, not the churches, not other saviors, not the ideologies, not any social group.
>
> Today Western society presents itself as the solution to the great problems which it has created itself. In the last decade, this offer has been presented

through a fatal mystique of its dominant social mechanisms, in a market mystique. It has thrown a party on the eve of the plague, a great celebration before the deluge. It is a party which begins with the resigned song of postmodernity; it is an ideology of dance on the volcano's edge when it is already known it is about to erupt. It is the funeral dirge.

Western society has arrived at its end. What is unknown is whether it will succeed in taking humanity and the earth along with it as it disappears into the black hole it has created. (Hinkelamamert, *La Fe* 9-10)

2. Consequently, the market is seen as the remedy for nearly all human ills. Mention any problem: underdevelopment, hunger, education, racial, or political problems; in nearly every instance, the dominant ideology proposes "more market" as the solution. Thus Hinkelammert refers to the social configuration that eventually took charge of the modern world as "market totalitarianism." In this context, he follows Hannah Arendt in describing "totalitarianism"

as a movement which radically polarizes the world starting from the imagination of a perfect institutionality, and which passes from the social technique derived from this perfect institutionality to social terror. Totalitarianism reduces the subject to a single social relationship and isolates it in order to make the perfect institutionality appear as uniquely necessary. Within the socialist society, Stalinist totalitarianism originated from a concept of perfect planning derived from socialist relations of production. Its perfect institutionality therefore was the planning mechanism. In capitalist society, the first totalitarian movement arose in German nazism which derived its perfect institutionality from the imagination of a racial purity constituting its totalitarian society as a society of war. In the contemporary totalitarian movement, perfect institutionality comes to be the market projected as total market isolating subjects and reducing them exclusively to market relationships. (Hinkelammert, *Democrácia*. 205)

Here Hinkelammert identifies three recent historical expressions of totalitarianism. We are accustomed to think of the first two, Stalinism and Nazism, as meriting the term's application. The third, -- contemporary free market capitalism -- less comfortably fits the category for most. Hinkelammert, however, explains the connection. In his analysis, totalitarian systems are essentially rooted in institutions considered somehow perfect by their proponents. These institutions centralize devices that dictate a proper technique to guarantee a utopian, best possible world. In all cases, the technique is basically reductionist; it isolates a key social relationship as synonymous with being human, excluding all others.

On the socialist side, Stalinists saw centralized economic planning in these terms. Elite planners were the privileged knowers, setting production goals and, in the process, largely determining social relationships. Meanwhile, as the first expression of capitalist totalitarianism, German Nazism cultivated racial purity to achieve social perfection. It would eliminate the impure by mililtary technique. For its part, the latest form of capitalist totalitarianism envisions the free market as the mechanism that is capable of automatically interpreting and solving human dilemmas of all types. The remedy reduces human problems to technical matters of adjusting personal activity to market dictates. Historically speaking, however, Hinkelammert indicates, totalitarian relationships of all three kinds have always necessitated terroristic tactics for their successful imposition.

3. Philosophers of the nonroyal property-owning classes accorded abstract theorizing of this kind the highest degree of explanatory value, despite the fact, of course, that it was by no means demonstrable, self-evident, or in any way historical. Such characteristics make the ideological nature of the new thought stand out. As Jagger indicates:

> As soon as one takes into account the facts of human biology, especially reproductive biology, it becomes obvious that the assumption of individual self-sufficiency is impossible. Human infants resemble the young of many species in being born helpless, but they differ from all other species in requiring a uniquely long period of dependence on adult care. This care could not be provided by a single adult; in order to raise enough children to continue the species, humans must live in social groups where individuals share resources with the young and the temporarily disabled. Instead of community and cooperation being taken as phenomena whose existence and even possibility is puzzling, and sometimes even regarded as impossible, the existence of egoism, competitiveness and conflict as endemic to the human condition, would themselves become puzzling and problematic. (41)

4. Hegel's theological justification is worth pause, since on Dussel's analysis, it accounts for what he sees as the sacralization of the European system. It begins with the Cartesian premise identifying thought and being. From there it goes on to posit God as the Absolute Spirit, the fullest expression of being itself, always identified with the Absolute Idea. Next, Hegel cites religion as the path to fullness of life, again understood in terms of thinking and knowing. All religions, Hegel says, have worth, although the most primitive, like those found among African tribes, are little more than magical superstitions. However, the religions of spiritual individuality, especially as practiced by the Greeks and Romans, gradually removed those elements and in a real sense prepared for the fulfillment of all religion expressed in Christianity (Dussel 38).

In Hegel's understanding, Christianity manifested the supreme reality of the Spirit (42). In practice, this meant that nothing essential to the human spirit was missing from the European experience. Nothing requisite to the human condition could be learned from those outside the continent. From the theological viewpoint, then, as well as the philosophical, Europe was a self-sufficient, self-referential totality, that had now widened its net to encompass God. It thus enjoyed the divine right to impose itself on other less perfect cultures -- in the name of the Absolute Idea that it represented.

This, of course, it had been doing since the time of the crusades, and more aggressively still, with the onset of the invasion of the New World at the conclusion of the fifteenth century. But Hegel's contribution was to provide ideological justification for such practice. Subsequently, Dussel says, this form of thinking undergirded not only the second wave of Europe's colonization of the Third World in the nineteenth century; it also provided underpinning for the policy of Manifest Destiny, for the Monroe Doctrine, and for CIA actions of counterinsurgency and counterrevolution carried out in defense of "the security of the Western Hemisphere" whose tradition must be protected against the forces of godlessness (44,45). This line of thought also bears close relationship to the West's justification of the nuclear arms race and of the low-intensity conflict so characteristic of World War III.

5. It is worth indicating that such discounting of contradictory traditions in the name of science was reinforced in the late nineteenth and during the twentieth century with the ideological application of Darwinian biology, Freudian psychology, and

even of contemporary chaos theory. Herbert Spencer, for instance, applied the Darwinian biological concept, survival of the fittest, to the realm of economics to justify neglect of society's weaker members. Freud's theories about innate aggression were similarly employed to denigrate as "irrational" the biblical concept of love of neighbor (55-63). Contemporary chaos theory has been invoked by neoliberal theorists to reintroduce Adam Smith's "invisible hand" which, like chaos theory, imagines disorder producing order (Hinkelammert, "Capitalismo sin alternativas?" 18).

6. It is interesting to note how the testimony that follows is parallelled by workers interviewed in Mexico, for instance, in connection with the North American Free Trade Agreement. Here a young worker describes her experience in an automobile seat belt factory.

"I am 22 years old and I've been working in the maquiladoras (factories) for six years. I have lasted longer than the others," she tells us as she shows us her hands -- deformed fingers and with an enormous, tannish-yellowish corn on each of her thumbs which extends from the tip down to the palm."This is the cost of working here. I get minimum wage and I do what appears to be very simple. The strap comes to me on a conveyor belt, I must stretch it out, placing the pieces on each end, and then I must hold it with a hot iron for 20 seconds, lift up the iron, take away the belt, and begin the operation again. As you see, it doesn't seem like much, but when you have to do five operations, like I do, in 30 seconds, with a hot machine, and 1,800 times a day, the results are this." And she shows us her hands again. "I repeat, I am not old. I'm 22; nevertheless, I know that I'm not going to last long because my hands hurt more and more. There was a time when they were only deformed, they didn't hurt. Now the pain gets worse and worse, and furthermore, my movements are not as fast as they used to be. Therefore, in a short while they will lay me off, or, more likely, they won't renew my contract. Here one gets used to being terminated in December and in January they do new contracts, and, of course, those who are no longer useful don't get new contracts. That's the way it goes every year, and we know it. But what can you do? They won't pay for my hands. When I've gone to the social security to ask the doctor for sick leave, or some kind of proof that the machine is hurting my hands, they have told me that the problem is hereditary, or that it is rheumatism, or that it was caused by my own negligence." (Arenal 66-7)

7. In this way, neoliberal doctrine seemed to involve itself in the contradiction of advocating changes of mind and intention to remediate problems, which by definition were unintentionally caused. Thus for example, neoliberal governments preferred basically utopian, voluntary programs bolstered by ad campaigns to curb pollution and resource waste. Meanwhile, the unregulated market's essentially fragmentary decision-making modus operandi, neoliberal government's advocacy of economic growth, and the lower costs associated with waste and pollution ensured that such unintended consequences would continue virtually unabated.

8. As previously indicated, establishing market domination along these lines includes several standard steps: (1) The removal of import tariffs protecting local industry from imported goods. According to neoliberal theory, this "levels the playing field" for the free competition of manufactured goods. Such competition results in lower consumer costs, stimulates local economy, and increases employment. (2) The privatization of state-run businesses and services. Private ownership, the theory holds, reduces government bureaucracy and inefficiency. It

also cuts government expenditures, since few state-run enterprises turn a profit. Thus money is saved to service the country's debt. (3) Lay-offs of government employees. This is a direct result of privatization and saves the government from paying thousands of salaries each month. To reiterate, the money saved from salaries not paid can be directed toward service of the national debt. (Not incidentally, this as well as other IMF measures generally cause widespread unemployment. But this, the theory says, has the good effect of reducing the amount of money in circulation, thus drying up inflation, a major problem in debtor countries.) (4) General direction of the Third World economy towards export. In this instance, the goal is the earning of "foreign exchange" (money, principally dollars, which can be used to repay bank loans). (5) Devaluation of local currency. Devaluation makes Third World goods cheaper to buy on the international market. The measure makes it possible for foreigners to buy more goods with fewer dollars, marks, yen, etc. The resulting boom in export brings more "foreign exchange" into the less developed country and creates employment along with increased local profits. Once again, all of this facilitates the return of that currency to the lending countries in the form of interest payments.

9. This is ironic at least, since during the Cold War capitalism's traditional indictment of Marxism was that it reduced all of life to economic relations.

10. Recently Helio Gallardo has predicted that within the next few years, we will see such market-directed evaluation of human life played out on an unprecedented scale relative to the worldwide AIDS epidemic. It is predicted, for example, that within the next five to ten years, Brazil alone will have five to ten million AIDS cases. Gallardo observes that even if a cure for the disease is discovered, its general application in the Third World is highly unlikely. The cure will be costly and complicated to apply, and in any case, the majority of lives in the underdeveloped world are considered surplus and therefore expendable. Besides this, the Malthusian spirituality of overpopulation provides a convenient disclaimer of responsibility for those who might possess the cure.

WORKS CITED

Arenal, Sandra. "They Won't Pay for My Hands." *Trading Freedom: How Free Trade Affects Our Lives, Work and Environment.* John Cavanaugh, John Gershman, Karen Baker, and Gretchen Helmke, ed. San Francisco: The Institute for Food and Development Policy, 1992: 66-67.

Berry, Thomas. *The Dream of the Earth.* San Francisco: Sierra Club Books, 1988.

Bryan, William Jennings. *The World's Most Famous Court Trial. Tennessee Evolution Case.* Cincinnati: National Book Company, 1925.

Carroll, Peter N., and David W. Noble. *The Free and the Unfree: A New History of the United States.* New York: Penguin Books, 1988.

Descartes, René. *Descartes Selections.* Ralph M. Eaten, ed. New York: Charles Scribner's Sons, 1927.

Drake, Stillman. *Discoveries and Opinions of Galileo.* Translated with an introduction and notes by Stillman Drake. New York: Doubleday Anchor Books, 1957.

Dussel, Enrique. *Para Uma Ética Da Libertação Latino-Americana.* São Paulo, Brazil: Edições Loyola, 1980.

Galilei, Galileo. "The Letter to the Grand Duchess Christina."*Discoveries and Opinions of Galileo.* Translated by Stillman Drake. Garden City, New York: Doubleday Anchor Books, 1957: 175-216.

_____. "The Starry Messenger." *Discoveries and Opinions of Galileo*. Translated by Stillman Drake. Garden City, New York: Doubleday Anchor Books, 1957: 27-58.

Gallardo, Helio. "Francis Fukuyama: el final de la historia y el tercer mundo" *Pasos* 28, (March/April 1990): 1-9.

Heilbroner, Robert L. *The Worldly Philosophers*. New York: Simon and Schuster, 1969.

Hinkelammert, Franz J. "Capitalismo sin alternativas?" *Pasos* 37, (Sept./Oct. 1991): 11-23.

_____. *Democracia y totalitarismo*. San José, Costa Rica: Editorial DEI, 1987.

_____. *La fe de Abraham y el Edipo occidental*. San José, Costa Rica: Editorial DEI, 1991.

_____. "El Mercado como sistema autoregulado y la critica de Marx." (Manuscript made available to "invited researchers," March 1992, DEI, San José, Costa Rica.)

_____. *Sacrificios humanos y sociedad occidental: lucifer y la bestia*. San José, Costa Rica: Editorial DEI, 1991.

Jagger, Alison. *Feminist Politics and Human Nature*. Sussex: Rowman and Littlefield Publishers, Inc., 1988.

Locke, John. *Two Treatises of Government*. New York: New American Library, 1960.

Malthus, T. R., and A.M. Malthus. *An Essay on the Principle of Population; or a View of Its Past and Present Effects on Human Happiness,* vol. 1. London: T. Bensley, 1807.

Marx, Karl, and Friedrich Engels. *Capital,* Trans. by Samuel Moore and Edward Aveling. New York: Modern Library, 1906.

_____. *The Manifesto of the Communist Party*, Trans. by Samuel Moore. Moscow: Foreign Languages Publishing House, n.d.

Nelson-Pallmeyer, Jack. *War against the Poor: Low-Intensity Conflict and Christian Faith*. New York: Orbis Books, 1989.

Paley, William, D.D. *Natural Theology; or, Evidences of the Existence and Attributes of the Deity*. London: Baldyn and Co., 1819.

"Report of Committee on Factory Children's Labour." *Parliamentary Papers*, 1831-1832, vol. 15, 95-97, 192-194

Ricardo, David. *The Works of David Ricardo*. Piero Sraffa, ed. Cambridge: Cambridge University Press, 1951.

Smith, Adam. *An Inquiry into the Nature and Causes of the Wealth of Nations*. Edinburgh, 1806.

Swift, Jonathan. "A Modest Proposal." *The Writings of Jonathan Swift*. Robert A. Greenberg and William Piper, eds. New York: W.W. Norton and Company, 1973.

Todorov, Tzevetan. *The Conquest of America*. New York: Harper and Row, 1984.

Zinn, Howard. *A People's History of the United States*. New York: Harper and Row, 1980.

5

Illusion: God Requires Human Sacrifice

The prevailing interpretation of the Judeo-Christian tradition forms a key part of the spirituality of oppression reviewed in Chapter 4. It was not despite that interpretation, but under its very influence that some of the most heinous crimes of the West have been committed: the crusades with their looting and slaughter; the Inquisition and its legendary torture and executions; the conquest of the Americas with its unprecedented genocide and plunder; the suppression of free thought imaged in the Galileo trial; the burning of witches and intolerance of women's spirituality, so much a part of U.S. history; the slavery of Blacks and the practice of apartheid in South Africa; the Vatican's turning a blind eye to the Jewish holocaust; the persecution of homosexuals and others considered "deviant" and nonpersons; the wholesale killing of Christians by National Security States and by low-intensity conflict throughout the Third World; enthusiastic support of capitalism, which annually causes up to 40,000,000 preventable deaths from hunger-related causes; in short, the crimes of empire -- all of these and more have found their inspiration in the Bible. There since the fifth century, Christian "princes" have discovered a legitimating story that gives divine authority to their own laws, which demands the payment of the unpayable debts it imposes, which extorts sacrifice of the innocent for a promised future salvation that never arrives, and which imposes a religious totalitarian worldview which the West has secularized in its New World Order.

Yet an examination of biblical sources with moral imagination (i.e., from the viewpoint of empire's victims) shows that the story justifying Western crimes represents a 180-degree inversion of the Judeo-Christian tradition. As we shall see, that inversion has most modern Christians, in effect, identifying "God" with empire -- which early followers of Jesus described as "the Beast" of the Apocalypse. The distortion of biblical revelation has today's believers confusing Jesus with Lucifer and Lucifer with Jesus.

This thesis is not at all unimportant for peacemakers regardless of whether or not they consider themselves believers. Waging World War III has become a profoundly theological exercise despite the general secularization of the West. If peace activists doubt this, the prosecutors of the war against the world's poor do not. Recall the already-mentioned Santa Fe Document, which in 1979 advised the incoming Reagan administration to mount a theological offensive of its own to counteract the "dangers" of Third World theology (Duchrow et al. 186). Similarly in 1987, the confidential documents of the Seventeenth Conference of American Armies held in Mar del Plata, Argentina, devoted fully fifteen pages to theological analysis (125-40). Two years later, during a major World War III battle in El Salvador, the U.S.-supported Salvadoran Army brutally assassinated a team of Third World theologians, whose reflection specifically assisted liberation struggles of poor people in underdeveloped countries. Pablo Richard relates the incident to the theological dimensions of the ongoing war of the rich against the poor:

> Many people, horrified, condemned these crimes, but very few have reflected upon the meaning of these deaths. In fact, they condemned the crime while simultaneously giving political support to the president of El Salvador. The six priests formed a team that reflected, taught, wrote from within the process of liberation of the Salvadoran people. They were friends, they prayed together, they thought together about the future of the people, they created pastoral strategies and policies of liberation. In a strict sense of the word, they were a team which practiced the Theology of Liberation on a day to day basis. The death of the Jesuits was a terrorist act against the Theology of Liberation. They were killed precisely because they did liberating theology in a concrete process of popular liberation. Witnesses told us that, after murdering these priests, they took out their brains -- they "de-brained" them, to be very sure that their intelligence was really dead. Within this team, too much holiness and intelligence had been accumulated and that had become unbearable to the powerful. With the death of the Jesuits and of the Theology of Liberation, an effort is made to take from the poor their voice, their hope, their awareness, their faith, their spiritual power. (Durchrow et al. 202)

Robbing the poor of their spiritual power, then, is part of World War III. That is because increasingly, people of faith in the Third World find that the Judeo-Christian tradition can be subversive of empire. It can undermine precisely at key points in the spirituality of the New World Order -- its absolutization of market law, its requiring the payment of an unpayable debt in the name of justice, its willingness to sacrifice the innocent to bring about a "utopian" future devoid of utopias, and its imposition of totalitarianism. We would add that the entire Judeo-Christian tradition can reveal a God who exercises moral imagination, one who not only adopts the viewpoint and cause of the poor, but who ultimately becomes a poor person, persecuted, tortured, and killed by empire. This is moral imagination in its most exalted and concrete form.

This chapter will attempt to elaborate all of this. It will show how the God of the Bible personifies moral imagination. Yahweh is, in fact, the God whose chief characteristic is identification with the poor and those victimized by empire and its laws. As such, the biblical God is immanent in history and undercuts empire at its legal, economic, and religious roots. This God, however, was largely co-opted by empire from the fifth century on. The co-option transformed the immanent God of the Bible into the divine underwriter of an other-worldly, totalitarian system that made possible the crimes reviewed in Chapter 3.

THE IMAGINATION OF GOD:
IMMANENCE IN ACTION

The idea of "moral imagination" should not be strange to inheritors of the Judeo-Christian tradition. It might be said that the faculty constitutes the very essence of the biblical God, whom the tradition reveals as immanent, a God who acts in history, not above it. The divine exercise of moral imagination in this sense is evident in the Old Testament, in the person of Jesus, and in the early church.

God's Imagination in the Old Testament

Clearly, the most basic Old Testament faith concerns an immanent God who gives a particular piece of land to a particular nation of escaped slaves at a particular moment in time. Thus the most ancient scriptural texts are not about the creation of the world. Even less are they about reward and punishment in some afterlife. As we will see, centralization of the Genesis texts and focus on afterlife are part of a later inversion of Old Testament faith. Instead, the Bible's earliest summaries of belief tell of a subversive God who, by hearing and responding to the cry of a well-defined group of poor and enslaved people embodies moral imagination:

> A wandering Aramean was my ancestor; he went down into Egypt and lived there as an alien, few in number, and there he became a great nation, mighty and populous. When the Egyptians treated us harshly and afflicted us, by imposing hard labor on us, we cried to the LORD, the God of our ancestors; the LORD heard our voice and saw our affliction, our toil and our oppression. The LORD brought us out of Egypt with a mighty hand and an outstretched arm, with a terrifying display of power, and with signs and wonders; and he brought us into this place and gave us this land, a land flowing with milk and honey. (Deut. 26: 5-9)

Here the basis of Israelite faith is the Exodus from Egypt. In a real sense, everything else in the Bible is commentary on that event, meant to illuminate that experience and to reinterpret it in various historical circumstances. Again and again, those circumstances were those of imperial oppression and colonialism -- by the Assyrians (in the eighth century), the Babylonians in the sixth, the Persians in the fifth, the Greeks in the second and by the Romans during the time of Jesus. In every case, the people of Israel hoped for a repetition of the Exodus event and a restoration of their God-given land. They wanted it to be God's land once again. Some of their prophets (including most prominently Jesus of Nazareth) spoke of a future for Israel in which Yahweh (not the Greeks or Romans) would reign. They referred to that future as the "kingdom of God." In the Old Testament, there is nothing that can be unambiguously interpreted as associating that phrase with a life after death.

The Imagination of God in the New Testament

The most unmistakable exercise of imagination as we have been explaining it is found in the New Testament. In fact what emerged as the central doctrine of Christianity specifically holds that Jesus of Nazareth, as the fullest expression of God's revelation, personally identifies with "the other," who turns out to be the lowliest of the low -- the slave and the executed criminal. Paul encourages Jesus' followers to similarly exercise "moral imagination:"

> Let the same mind be in you that was in Christ Jesus, who, though he was in the form of God, did not regard equality with God as something to be exploited, but emptied himself, taking the form of a slave, being born in human likeness. And being found in human form, he humbled himself and became obedient to the point of death -- even death on a cross (Phil. 2:5-8).

Even more directly related to the issues we have been exploring here, Matthew's narrative of Jesus' words and deeds highlights the divine act of moral imagination in terms of a final judgment. The surprising revelation there is that Jesus so identifies with the hungry, thirsty, homeless, naked, imprisoned, and sick that he considers done to himself whatever is done to others in such conditions of want. Jesus' words call believers to radically commit themselves to the socially marginated. In a sense God "materializes" in intersubjective relationships with the poor and oppressed in this world.

> "Lord, when was it that we saw you hungry and gave you food, or thirsty and gave you something to drink? And when was it that we saw you a stranger and welcomed you, or naked and gave you clothing? And when was it that we saw you sick or in prison and visited you?" And the king will answer them, "Truly I tell you, just as you did it to one of the least of these who are members of my family, you did it to me." (Matt. 25:37-40)

What is important to note in all of this is that even in the New Testament, little unambiguously refers to the afterlife. Of course, the early Christians believed firmly in the resurrection of Jesus. But they clearly expected his imminent return to earth, where he would finally establish God's kingdom. To reiterate, biblical emphasis is on possession of the "holy land," on community fidelity to a "covenant," and on eviction of hated foreign imperialists.

The Subversion of Moral Imagination
The Loss of Immanence

A key transformation of Christianity took place after Jesus' death, when non-Jews (Gentiles) became dominant in the community of Jesus People. Up until that time, Jesus' followers apparently thought they would remain a sect within Judaism. As the Acts of the Apostles indicates, they continued to remain true to the synagogue practices. But with the influx of Gentiles, it became necessary to distance Christianity from its Jewish roots. Converted Gentiles wanted no part of circumcision, of Jewish dietary restrictions, of temple and synagogue worship, and of identification with Roman provinces like Galilee and Judea. So early church leaders came to the conclusion that the Jewish law could no longer bind anyone (Acts 15). Paul even claimed that the Jewish law was cursed, since it was responsible for the condemnation and execution of Jesus (Gal. 3:13).

Part of Christianity's distancing from Judaism involved its disidentification from the land of Israel. Several factors contributed here. Once again, Gentiles found it virtually impossible to identify their new faith and God with an out-of-the-way Roman province inhabited by ethnically marginal people. Secondly, after the destruction of Jerusalem in A.D. 70, Jews themselves were driven from their homeland. (They were not to return to "repossess" it until after 1948.) And there seemed little hope of their ever regaining it. Nonetheless, Jews continued to promise themselves that "next year" they would celebrate Passover in Jerusalem. Meanwhile (following trends in Roman "mystery cults" heavily influenced by Persian thought) Christians increasingly spiritualized biblical references to the "Promised Land," to "land flowing with milk and honey," and to the "Kingdom of God," so that they referred to an ever more well-defined afterlife, which (as we will see in detail below) came to include a purgatory and limbo, as well as a heaven and hell.

All of this required a shift of direction in terms of the basic Bible story explaining the fundamental human condition. As we saw earlier, that story, for the Israelites, was the Exodus. It emphasized liberation from slavery, Yahweh's gift of land to Israel, and a covenant law ensuring the honoring of Yahweh that involved more than anything the practice of justice in Israel -- especially regarding the poor, widows, orphans, slaves, and resident aliens. As Native American scholar Vine Deloria argues, Israel's faith and its resistance to imperialism resembled the typical outlook of Abya Yala's First Peoples (191).

However, for Gentiles in an international church, Israel's story was too national, too ethnic, too particular. So its primacy of importance was replaced by the Genesis stories. These gave Christianity a universal cast. The stories of the creation and fall connected the whole human race to a set of "first parents." It explained human misery, not in terms of oppression by foreign imperialists, but as the result of an "original sin," which infected not only the first man and woman, but all of their descendants wherever they might be found.

As developed by St. Augustine in the fifth century, the universalization of the biblical tradition was elaborated into a theory expressing a world vision that was truly totalitarian (Johnson 115). All the Bible was now understood as a commentary on the Genesis rather than the Exodus stories. With Adam and Eve's sin, human beings merited God's anger and punishment. Creation itself became loathsome in his eyes. God slammed closed the gates of heaven. They were not reopened again until the death of his son, Jesus, partially satisfied God's vengeance. Afterward he allowed a chosen and predestined few to enter heaven; the rest were justly condemned to an eternity of punishment in hell. This sort of universal, other-worldly faith made Christianity attractive to the Roman Empire. In 383, it adopted Christianity as its own. As a result, Christians who had been enemies of empire became its allies.

Further Alienation from Immanence
In the Medieval and Modern Periods

Though focus on the afterlife was attractive to their betters, it was not so easily accepted by peasants, craftspeople, laborers, and menial workers. These were the heart and soul of the feudal system of production that emerged after the fall of the Roman Empire in the early fifth century. So despite resistance by its hierarchy, feudalism at the grassroots level continued to link the experience of God to land and earth. For instance, though "lords" technically owned the land and though they extracted from peasants whatever was produced above subsistence requirements, the wealthy were prevented by feudalism's complex of interlocking rights and responsibilities from disposing of their possessions without regard for peasant rights considered God-given at the time. To think otherwise was tantamount to atheism (Starhawk 191). Disbelief of this type was reflected in the Robin Hood tales of lower class resistance to infringement of hunting and wood gathering rights by royal "owners" of England's forests (196).

All of this began to change in the late feudal and Renaissance periods when markets came to dominate Western Europe and when peasant theological outlooks, customs, and claims against authority gradually came to be viewed as superstitious expressions of the "dark ages." As we saw in Chapter 3, a contrasting "enlightened" market mentality was stimulated by navigational breakthroughs and by the sixteenth century influx of gold from the Americas. Newly far-flung internationalized markets and technological innovations (chiefly in the textile industry) made it more profitable to produce grain and other products such as wool and lumber for market exchange, rather than for immediate consumption. Thus, as we saw, ideas of property ownership changed; fields were enclosed, peasant rights were denied, and subsistence farmers were driven off to flood the increasingly industrialized cities -- their places on the land taken by sheep producing wool for capitalism's first major industry. In this way, theological focus in the upper classes shifted to reinforce the rights of property owners rather than those of peasants. Continued peasant resistance was overridden by Luther and later by Deist theologists. Thus land grabbing and monied class appropriation of forests, wastelands, and swamps were justified in terms of the increased production and profitability associated with the protestant work ethic. Puritan leader Richard Baxter had earlier given clear expression to the revised theory:

> If God show you a way in which you may lawfully get more than in another way (without wrong to your soul or to any other), if you refuse this, and choose the less gainful way, you cross one of the ends of your calling, and you refuse to be God's steward, and to accept His gifts and use them for Him when He requireth it: you may labour to be rich for God, though not for the flesh and sin. (Weber 162)

Meanwhile, Christian hope -- at least for the poor -- was ever more detached from this world.

In the emerging property-owners' world, those who spoke for an immanent God, for a God of the oppressed and propertyless, for a God who gifted a living earth to the poor were increasingly anathematized. The wars against sixteenth century radical reformers were largely wars against immanence usually associated with the politics of resistance (Starhawk 205). Such demonization largely stood behind the persecution of witches who insisted on the vitality of the earth and nature as the experience of a living God accessible to ordinary people. Denigration of "this-worldly" theological focus also found expression in the persecution of religious radicals of the time by both Catholics and Protestants.

> Radical sects, like Witches, preached immanence (God manifest in the world). Familists, one of the earliest sects, were followers of Henry Niclaes, born in 1502, who taught that heaven and hell were to be found in this world. A related sect, the Family of the Mount, "questioned whether any heaven or hell existed apart from this life: heaven was when men laugh and are merry, hell was sorrow, grief and pain." Christ, they held, was within every believer. (209)

In the wake of the Reformation and witch hunts, "pagan" or pseudo-Christian festivals, feasts, and folk customs -- traditional community-builders among the poor -- were deemphasized or rooted out. Sacred meeting grounds, holy wells, groves, forests, and glens were abandoned and their (largely oral) traditions lost. In all of this, the immanent God of the Bible became increasingly distanced from history.

The colonial process spread the property-owning mentality throughout the world, even among people whose religious traditions connected them to the earth and history more closely than did the already-alienated medieval Christianity. Thus New World settlers

> brought the ethic of private property and the absolute right of ownership to the New World; they imposed it on Africa, India, and the Far East, and they extended it to the ownership of people. Slaves were viewed as subhuman -- savages and devil worshippers, without inherent value except potential profitability. This property ethic supported a ruthless slave-trade, just as it justified expropriation of land from the Native Americans. (198)

In summary, what Starhawk terms the sixteenth century "war on immanence" anticipated and spiritually prepared for the New World Order and its attendant World War III against the Bible's original beneficiaries. To repeat Pablo Richard's analysis, the new order takes "from the poor their voice, their hope, their awareness, their faith, their spiritual power." It transforms the God of moral imagination into an ally of the rich, the powerful, the oppressor who indefinitely postpones human happiness.

MORAL IMAGINATION
THE SUBVERSION OF LEGAL ORDERS

Part of turning the Bible against the poor involved inverting what might be termed a tradition of "biblical anarchy." Anarchy of this type relativized legal systems oppressive of those without recourse to anyone but God -- those whom the Bible defined as "poor." The tradition is central to both Old and New Testaments. Like the tradition of immanence, biblical anarchy receded after the fifth century, and especially with the onset of the modern era.

Old Testament Relativization of Legal Orders

The biblical tradition of siding with the poor found legal expression in the Mosaic Law. Unlike the laws of empire, which protect the interests of the male, the rich, and powerful, the Law of Moses shielded the poor from their exploiters. Despite its patriarchal nature, the law's overriding purpose remained, ensuring that Israelites would not return to the slavery and oppression from which they had escaped at such great cost. Accordingly, both the practices and beliefs that traditionally prepare the way for slavery's return were forbidden. So the laws regulated land ownership, debt, sacrifice, and slavery itself. And since it is the poor who are predominantly threatened by such tools of oppression, protective statutes made them its primary beneficiaries. Widows, orphans, resident aliens, poor farmers, and slaves themselves: these enjoyed the special protection of the law. Such groups represent precisely the ones for whom the biblical God revealed particular concern in the primordial and defining act of liberation.

> You shall not wrong or oppress a resident alien, for you were aliens in the land of Egypt. You shall not abuse any widow or orphan. If you abuse them, when they cry out to me, I will surely heed their cry; my wrath will burn, and I will kill you with the sword, and your wives shall become widows and your children orphans. (Exod. 22:21-24)

New Testament Relativization of Legal Orders

The practice of moral imagination consistently led its biblical practitioners, especially the prophets, to relativize laws that pretended to be absolute. The traditions about Jesus describe him as appearing in the prophetic line. This vocation called him to practice what we would describe today as civil disobedience (Meyers 130). Repeatedly, Gospel narratives depict Jesus as calling attention to oppressive laws and then deliberately breaking them in the presence of authorities to unmask the basic injustice of the legal system (e.g., Mark. 2:1-12; 3:1-6). That injustice became crystallized in Mosaic prescriptions governing the Jewish Sabbath. Jesus' pronouncement that "The Sabbath was made for humankind, and not humankind for the Sabbath" had the effect of relativizing the whole corpus of Jewish law in terms of human welfare (Mark. 2:27). If any law, including God's own, contradicted human well-being, Jesus' pronouncement made clear that the law was to be disobeyed. Put succinctly, a central aspect of the Good News preached by Jesus was that human beings were free to disobey the law.

Subversive Imagination in Paul

The apostle, Paul, followed directly in Jesus' subversive line. Paul's position in Roman society especially equipped him for the exercise of moral imagination. As a Jew and a worker, Paul himself personally experienced a social alienation that played an important role in shaping his theology of law. Most importantly, however, in terms of his marginalization, Paul was a prisoner -- an outlaw who was himself unjustly treated by the Roman law. (Tamez 52ff.)

This last condition is inseparably linked to Paul's reflection on the destructive power of law. He experienced Rome's "justice system" precisely as injustice. Similarly, the people to whom he wrote, largely slaves, workers, and the poor, found themselves victims of a system supported by a well-defined set of laws (1 Cor. 1:26-31). Even more centrally, Paul understood Jesus of Nazareth as one unjustly condemned by the law. The Jewish high priests had him executed, not in contravention of their legal system but precisely in obedience to it. As a result Paul ended up explicitly rejecting the entire Mosaic corpus as invalid. True, it had prepared the way for the fullness of revelation in Jesus. But with that function fulfilled, it could no longer bind anyone. Neither could any other law obligate in any final sense. In other words, following the logic of Jesus himself, Paul's position was that if God's most sacred law governing the Sabbath was made for human beings and not the reverse, so is every other law. No law is valid that condemns the innocent. Once again, this insight highlights the legally subversive effect of viewing reality from the victim's standpoint.[1]

The Death of Divine Imagination

In the fourth century, following generations of persecution, apocalyptic resistance to Roman law and order was finally reversed. This happened in 313 with the Edict of Milan, under Constantine I (306-337). The decree made the cult of Jesus legal in the empire. Sixty-seven years later, under Theodosius I, Christianity became the official imperial religion. By these steps, the faith of Moses, Amos, Jesus, and Paul became largely identified with a law and order which John of Patmos, in Revelation, had vilified as bestial and idolatrous. The liberating *Logos* of John the Evangelist became associated intimately with the essentially conservative stoic *Logos* of the emperor, Marcus Aurelius. From then on, the biblical God was transformed into the supporter of law and order in the Roman sense. Put otherwise, the Christian God, in many cases at least, became the Beast of the Apocalypse.

In the medieval period, the tendency corresponding to the exaltation of law and order is the displacement of Christian hope into the afterlife. This tendency was indelibly engraved on the Western mind through Dante's *Divine Comedy*. It is from this source that most in our culture derive their strongest images of heaven, hell, purgatory, and Satan. Significantly in terms of Christianity's wedding to the Roman Empire, Dante places Brutus and Cassius in the uttermost depths of hell along with Judas Iscariot. Thus the crime of "treachery to their master," Julius Caesar, is placed on a par with the betrayal of God himself

(Dante 282-87). Put otherwise, by the early fourteenth century, the meaning of Christianity had become so inverted that rebellion against empire's law and order was understood as the most unspeakable offense against God.

Reformation Inversions

The Lutheran and Calvinist versions of the Reformation continued the medieval trend domesticating the anarchistic thrust of the Judeo-Christian tradition expressing the hope of the poor in an anarchic God opposing any and all legalized orders of oppression. True, Luther began by centralizing an interpretation of law that annulled its power when legal observance proved harmful to the community. Thus, he invoked the Gospel to allow the royal classes to disobey papal directives. But in its dominant form, Reformation reinterpretation stopped well short of extending the privilege of disobedience to the dispossessed centralized in the Mosaic Covenant, in the preaching of Jesus, and in the letters of Paul. In fact, it made the binding force of the law stronger, by demanding that believers obey it with enthusiasm. In his commentary on Romans, Luther writes: "To fulfill the law, we must meet its requirements gladly and lovingly; live virtuous and upright lives without the constraint of the law, and as if neither the law nor its penalties existed. But this joy, this unconstrained love, is put into our hearts by the Holy Spirit, as St. Paul says in Chapter 5. But the Holy Spirit is given only in, with and through faith in Jesus Christ." (21)

Theology like this not only robbed those without public power of their right to disobey laws in conflict with human welfare, it also turned freedom to disobey the law into "freedom" to obey it. The elite implications of this understanding were illustrated during the peasant rebellions of 1524-25, when in the name of law and order, Luther opposed the German peasantry's rejection of the feudal and manorial burdens placed upon them by the noble classes. In effect, then, Luther helped transfer the seat of absolute authority in Europe from the Vatican in Rome to royal palaces scattered throughout Europe.

Even more to the point, by the time John Calvin systematized Reformation thought in 1536, he specifically denied the right of disobedience to those oppressed by their overlords. In fact, he renders governing authority virtually inviolable. In *Institutes of the Christian Religion*, Calvin writes:

> But we must, in the meantime, be very careful not to despise or violate that authority of magistrates, full of venerable majesty, which God has established by the weightiest decrees, even though it may reside with the most unworthy men, who defile it as much as they can with their own wickedness. For, if the correction of unbridled despotism is the Lord's to avenge, let us not at once think that it is entrusted to us to whom no command has been given except to obey and suffer. (1960; Book 4, Chap. 20, no. 29)

Enlightenment Inversions

The command (for those without wealth or public power!) to suffer and obey was linked to market law by the time the business classes established their dominance toward the end of the eighteenth century. As we saw in Chapter 4, Deist thinking played an important part in this development. Deists understood the laws of the market in ways analogous to Marcus Aurelius' *Logos* . Laws of supply and demand, wages and rent were the guiding ordering principles of the universe. They had to be obeyed at all costs, even if it meant the deaths of millions who might otherwise be saved. By death's discipline, the poor would be taught valuable lessons in thrift, hard work, and continence. Moreover, (following Galileo's maxim) "scientific" market laws took precedence over seemingly contradictory mandates in sacred Scripture. In this way, then, the market law, which controlled the world order of the business classes, was established as the very law of God. It demanded both the payment of debt and human sacrifice.

MORAL IMAGINATION
AND THE INVERSION OF EMPIRE'S DEBT ECONOMY

Empires thrive on debt. That is the whole point of imperial systems in the first place. Their economies invariably exact wealth transfer from colonies on the supposition that the tribute is somehow "owed" to the "mother country" because of alleged benefits conferred on colonial peoples by their conquerors. Thus the legendarily oppressive taxes of the Roman Empire weighed heavily on the descendants of Abraham in Jesus' day. New World conquistadors even held that the original nations of Abya Yala owed debts to the Spanish crown. These had to be paid in gold by meeting quotas of the precious metal or by slaving in the gold mines themselves (Todorov 134). As we saw in Chapter 3, cooperative imperialism uses the law and spirituality of debt to virtually hold the entire Third World in a kind of debt slavery and to gain effective control of its internal politics and national economies.

Debt in the Old Testament

As the personification of moral imagination, the God of the Poor fundamentally subverts the debt-based economies of empires ordering worlds new or old. In fact the Old Testament portrays Yahweh as decreeing the Mosaic Law precisely to protect former slaves from conditions like debt servitude, which would reintroduce imperial bondage. Debts are to be paid, the law said, unless payment costs the life or even a relatively minor inconvenience for the debtor. Exacting interest from the poor, however, is always against the law.

> "If you lend money to my people, to the poor among you, you shall not deal
> with them as a creditor; you shall not exact interest from them. If you take
> your neighbor's cloak in pawn, you shall restore it before the sun goes

down; for it may be your neighbor's only clothing to use as cover; in what
else shall that person sleep? And if your neighbor cries out to me, I will
listen, for I am compassionate." (Exod. 22:25--27)

In addition, an institutional provision directly benefiting the poor was
established to further control debt along with other elements (land tenure and
slavery) that commonly threaten the independence of the law's main
beneficiaries. The "Jubilee Year" provided that every fifty years land that had in
any way been lost by its original owners should be returned to them. At the
same time, slaves should be freed and all debts canceled. The Book of Leviticus
expressed the Jubilee spirit in this way:

> If any of your kin fall into difficulty and become dependent on you, you
> shall support them; they shall live with you as though resident aliens. Do
> not take interest in advance or otherwise make a profit from them, but fear
> your God; let them live with you. You shall not lend them your money at
> interest taken in advance, or provide them food at a profit. I am the LORD
> your God, who brought you out of the land of Egypt, to give you the land of
> Canaan, to be your God . (Lev. 25:35-38)

There is no evidence that the Jubilee Year was ever actually honored in
ancient Israel. Nevertheless the institutionalization of debt forgiveness, land
reform, and emancipation of slaves reveals ancient Israel's perception of God's
attitude on such matters. Yahweh, they implied, recognized that the "natural"
processes of borrowing and lending, of selling and buying, of employing and
being employed tend toward unjust accumulation on the part of the few at the
expense of the many. The unjust accumulation occurs cyclically; so twice each
century things must be set straight.

Debt in the New Testament

We pick up the connection between Jesus' proclamation and the Mosaic
Law's provisions about debt from the description Luke gives of Jesus' project at
the beginning of the third Gospel:

> "The Spirit of the Lord is upon me, because he has anointed me to bring
> good news to the poor. He has sent me to proclaim release to the captives
> and recovery of sight to the blind, to let the oppressed go free, to proclaim
> the year of the Lord's favor." (Luke 4:18)

These words about proclaiming the year of the Lord's favor reaffirm
Yahweh's traditional option for the poor in words already spoken by Isaiah to the
Israelite exiles in Babylon (Isa. 61:2-3, 6-9). With his own reaffirmation, Jesus
links the kingdom to the institutionalization of Isaiah's "year of grace." As we
have already seen, this is a reference to the year of Jubilee first announced in
Leviticus 25. In this context, Jesus' words in the "Our Father," "Forgive us our
debts as we forgive our debtors," can be understood as a prayer begging Yahweh

to bring in the Year of Jubilee, with its forgiveness of debts, land reform, and freeing of slaves (Yoder 66-7).

> The prayer was raised in the context of a struggle for the institutionalization of a Jubilee Year. The Jesus movement, with its messianic identity, was committed to bring about this reality in which sharing held priority over anxiety about possessions. (de Santa Ana *"Sacralizaciones y sacrificios"* 19)

In other words, the Lord's Prayer, with its petition for the arrival of God's reign, centralized the theme of debt forgiveness. Remission of this-worldly indebtedness was the way to secure forgiveness of the unpayable debt sinners owe God.

The Anti-Debt Community of Acts

If Jesus proclaimed a Jubilee Year to usher in the Kingdom of God, the first community of Christians as reflected in the Acts of the Apostles should be considered a Jubilee community. It adopted practices reflected in Leviticus 25. The community implemented permanent land reform. There was no debt among them. In fact according to the idealized portrait in Acts, there were no poor among them at all.

> Now the whole group of those who believed were of one heart and soul, and no one claimed private ownership of any possessions, but everything they owned was held in common. With great power the apostles gave their testimony to the resurrection of the Lord Jesus, and great grace was upon them all. There was not a needy person among them, for as many as owned lands or houses sold them and brought the proceeds of what was sold. They laid it at the apostles' feet, and it was distributed to each as any had need. (Acts 4:32-35)

Here the connection between the practices of the early Christian community and Jesus' proclamation of Jubilee or the year of "grace" is hard to miss. The reference to no "needy person among them" refers directly to ideals connected with the God of the poor as expressed in the text from Deuteronomy cited above in connection with the Old Testament tradition about law and debt.[2]

Debt in Christendom

The modern displacement of the biblical tradition of debt forgiveness began with Tertullian. (Hinkelammert, *Sacrificios humanos* 70). For the first time, he expresses an authoritative understanding of redemption as the payment of a ransom due to God. This ran contrary to the theology, for example, of Origen who expressly denied that redemptive payment was due to God. Similarly, Chrysostom identified the devil, not God, as the one exacting a ransom payment. Jesus' death invalidated the devil's (legalistic) claim and thus brought about liberation from demonic bondage. This was the understanding that prevailed in Christian circles throughout the entire first millennium of Christianity (69).

    The definitive turning point came in the eleventh century with Anselm of
Canterbury. According to Anselm, human sinfulness offended God's sense of
justice. Only the blood sacrifice of a divine equal was capable of appeasing the
resulting wrath of God. Jesus' death, then, represented sacrificial payment (vs.
forgiveness) of the otherwise unpayable debt incurred by human sinfulness.
From Anselm on, justice was found in the fulfillment of debt law (72). He thus
set the stage for inverting the Gospel teaching that justice demands *pardon* of
debts to the belief that justice exacts debts' *payment* even when, strictly
speaking, the debts are unpayable (86).[3]

    Anselm's interpretation was taken up by Reformation thinkers. They began
in a biblically accurate way understanding the basic relationship between God and
sinners in terms of debtors burdened with an unpayable debt. With the same
accuracy, Jesus was seen as a redeemer whose death eliminated human debt with
God by manifesting God's forgiveness. However, for the Reformers, the debt
cancellation was not due to forgiveness, but to *payment;* Jesus *paid* the
unpayable debt. This effectively reversed the meaning of the debt petition in the
Lord's Prayer. For the Father's acceptance of Jesus' payment made God one who
places observance of debt obligations above forgiveness. In this way, it became
theologically correct to expect that even unpayable fiscal debts be paid in some
way. The way, of course, is the one imputed to Jesus, namely by personal
blood sacrifice. Put otherwise, since Jesus perfectly well enables humans to pay
their debts with God, human beings should honor their debts with one another --
even if attempts to pay cost human lives. After the sixteenth century, the real
offense becomes refusing to imitate Jesus' payment of debts whatever the cost.
And the meaning of the debt petition of the Lord's Prayer becomes inverted to
mean, "Forgive us our debts in the measure we pay the debts we owe others."
(Hinkelammert, 64) [4]

MORAL IMAGINATION
AND THE SUBVERSION OF SACRIFICIAL SYSTEMS

    Like debt , the requirement of sacrifice is central to the maintenance of all
empires new or old. It is central to war and to its more subtle forms in World
War III. The literature of "structural adjustments," of "debt repayment," and of
"modernization" is full of references to "high social costs," "austerity," and
specifically to "sacrifices." In times of war, the innocent are the ones usually
offered up, as for instance in the carpet bombing of cities. In biblical terms,
those actually sacrificed are society's least (especially children) -- the very ones
championed by the God of the Bible.

    Nevertheless, a central tenet of Western spirituality is that God is pleased by
the sacrifice of the innocent. It is the way to greater good, to preserving social
order, to achieving fullness of life, forgiveness -- "salvation." Greek tragedy
fostered this spirituality. Creon's sacrifice of his niece, Antigone, is meant to
prevent chaos from erupting in Thebes. Agamemnon's ritual offering of his
daughter, Iphigenia, makes it possible for the Greeks to conquer the Trojans.

Even those who are unaware of these myths are influenced by them, their lessons are part of Western social fabric. We take them in with our mothers' milk.

More powerfully still, biblical stories are used to support the Western conviction that life comes from death, specifically from the death of innocent children. In particular, the culture employs the stories of Abraham and Isaac and that of Jesus himself to reinforce the notion that parents must be prepared to sacrifice their children to empire's higher good (e.g., by generously sending them off to war, even if it means their death). After all, we are told that is God's way; as God He was pleased by His own son's death.

However, once again, closer examination of the biblical tradition contradicts this nearly universal conviction. The God of the Bible is the God of life, not of death. The thrust of the Abraham myth is exactly the opposite of what the West believes -- God does not require human sacrifice. Moreover, the Bible never presents Jesus' death as exacted by his father, but in terms of an assassination offensive to God and calling for radical repentance. What pleased God was not Jesus' death, but his life, which led his contemporaries to assassinate him to preserve the status quo Jesus challenged.

The Myth of Abraham and Isaac

The Abraham story illustrates Yahweh's rejection of innocent death as leading to fullness of life. The myth is about Israel's founding father, and about his faith, which differed radically from the beliefs of the tribes that neighbored ancient Israel. They practiced child sacrifice routinely. In contrast, Abraham came to believe that Yahweh, the God of life, did not require human sacrifice. That belief would have scandalized his contemporaries. It is emphasized in this Genesis account.

> God tested Abraham. He said to him, "Take your son, your only son Isaac, whom you love, and go to the land of Moriah, and offer him there as a burnt offering on one of the mountains that I shall show you." So Abraham rose early in the morning, saddled his donkey, and took two of his young men with him, and his son Isaac. Abraham took the wood of the burnt offering and laid it on his son Isaac, and he himself carried the fire and the knife. Isaac said to his father Abraham ,"The fire and the wood are here, but where is the lamb for a burnt offering?" Abraham said, "God himself will provide the lamb for a burnt offering, my son." When they came to the place that God had shown him, Abraham built an altar there and laid the wood in order. He bound his son Isaac, and laid him on the altar, on top of the wood. Then Abraham reached out his hand and took the knife to kill his son. But the angel of the LORD called to him from heaven, and said "Do not lay your hand on the boy or do anything to him; *for now I know that you fear God, since you have not withheld your son, your only son, from me."* And Abraham looked up and saw a ram, caught in a thicket by its horns. Abraham went and took the ram and offered it up as a burnt offering instead of his son. (Gen. 22:1-13 Emphasis added)

This story attributes the elimination of sacrifice to a revelation made to the founding father of the people of Israel. According to this myth, Abraham's original perception was that Yahweh, like other gods, operated according to the logic of child sacrifice. Prepared to fulfill a sacrificial law, he receives a special revelation contradicting the sacrificial legalism of his day. The story, then, reveals the God of Israel once again as a subversive God for whom life brings life. In terms of human sacrifice, it roots Israelite faith in a nonsacrificial tradition.

Nonetheless, the text itself indicates editorial attempts to obscure its subversive character. Subsequently, these efforts at domestication enable our culture to turn the myth's meaning on its head. In other words, Genesis 22:1-13 reflects a "battle of the Gods" within the Bible itself. This is indicated within the quotations we have printed in italic. According to Hinkelammert, they are later additions that have caused the text to be remembered as immortalizing an Israelite patriarch whose virtue was found in his willingness to sacrifice his first born son, rather than as a person embracing a faith that enabled him to *refuse* human sacrifice. But of course, Hinkelammert notes, there would have been nothing heroic in a father's willingness to sacrifice his son. In effect, all of Abraham's contemporaries shared such "heroism." The noteworthy was the opposite behavior.

Hinkelammert traces the additions to temple priests who during the period of Davidic dynasty were, like all ruling classes, anxious to establish the necessity of sacrificing children to the existing social order.

> [W]e know who made the insertions which invert the text's meaning. It was the temple priests who had to affirm the new law of Sinai. Child sacrifice in all human myths represents affirmation of law. In order to link this law with the history of Abraham, they had to reinterpret that tradition so Abraham would end up affirming the law's binding force. To fulfill the law he was prepared to kill his own son. The law, any law, says: we must be similarly prepared. (*La Fe de Abraham* 19) [5]

The Assassination of Jesus

The earliest traditions about Jesus' death contradict common interpretations in terms of a sacrifice exacted by an angry God who could be appeased only by the blood of an equal. The following three points show the difficulty of supporting such readings from the biblical texts:

(1) The high priest of Jesus' day, not Yahweh, was the one who understood Jesus' death in terms of a human sacrifice necessary to save the entire Jewish community. His reasoning is expressed clearly in the Gospel of John.

> [T]he chief priests and the Pharisees called a meeting of the council and said "What are we to do? This man is performing many signs. If we let him go on like this, everyone will believe in him, and the Romans will come and destroy both our holy place and our nation." But one of them, Caiaphas, who was high priest that year, said to them, "You know nothing at all! You do not understand that it is better for you to have one man die for the people

than to have the whole nation destroyed." He did not say this on his own, but being high priest that year he prophesied that Jesus was about to die for the nation, and not for the nation only, but to gather into one the dispersed children of God. (John. 11:47-52)

The reference here to the high priest's prophecy clearly identifies Jesus' death with benefit for the world. But there is no assertion here of God's intending Jesus' death as a sacrifice to appease God's anger.

(2) The earliest Christian traditions understood Jesus' death in terms of an assassination calling for repentance, not as a sacrifice exacted by God. Thus words attributed to Peter say:

Jesus of Nazareth, a man attested to you by God with deeds of power, wonders, and signs that God did through him among you, as you yourselves know -- this man, handed over to you according to the definite plan and foreknowledge of God, you crucified and killed by the hands of those outside the law. Now when they heard this, they were cut to the heart and said to Peter and to the other apostles, "Brothers, what should we do?" Peter said to them, "Repent, and be baptized every one of you in the name of Jesus Christ so that your sins may be forgiven." (Acts 2:22-38)

The call to repentance makes it clear that the responsibility for Jesus' death lay with those who crucified him, not with God. Jesus' resurrection from the dead offers his murderers another chance at repentance (Pixley, 1991a, 126). The reference to "plan and foreknowledge of God" does not support the dangerous (and counterbiblical) claim that Jesus' death was exacted by a God whose anger could be satisfied alone by the blood sacrifice of his son (Pixley, 1991a, 130). Instead, the statements about God's foreknowledge were intended to mitigate the "scandal" the cross represented for Jews. It was nearly impossible for them to accept the idea of a crucified "messiah." So the early Christians had to establish the position that Jesus' death could be harmonized with God's will. The harmony can best be understood in terms of a "prophetic script" that ensured that those who vigorously oppose "this world" in the name of God's order or kingdom typically suffer assassination. God's will was not the murder of Jesus but his proclamation of the Kingdom. Jesus' death was not predestined in any other sense any more than were the predictable murders of John the Baptist, Gandhi, Martin Luther King Jr., Malcolm X, Ernesto Guevara, or Monsignor Oscar Romero (de Santa Ana "*Sacralizaciones y sacrificios*" 18).

(3) Even the specifically sacrificial (i.e., ritual) interpretations of Jesus' death do not justify it in terms of God's will nullifying the criminal aspect of the murder. Ritual interpretations are found, for example in 1 John. 1:7; Rom. 3:25; Rev. 1:5; 1 Pet. 1:2; Rom. 5:9; Heb. 9:13-14. None of these attributes responsibility for Jesus' assassination to God; the murderers designated in Peter's sermon remain assassins. Similarly, the Gospel of John connects Jesus' sacrifice with the slaughter of Pascal lambs (John 19: 31-37). And the portrayals of the Last Supper by the synoptics have Jesus identifying the wine he blesses with "my blood of the covenant, which is poured out for many for the forgiveness of sins." Both references are allusions to ritual surrounding the Mosaic Covenant. There half the blood from sacrifices connected with the pact

was poured on the altar, while the other half was sprinkled on the people (Exod. 24:6). Blood in this case signified communion between Yahweh and the people of Israel. The synoptics' references to "forgiveness of sin" is thus associated with commitment to solidarity with God's people as stipulated in the Covenant.

In summary then, though Jesus' death is often interpreted in sacrificial terms, the ones offering the sacrifice are the temple priests who commit a crime in doing so. Alternatively, Jesus' acceptance of death as a consequence of his commitment to Yahweh's kingdom is viewed self-sacrificially in the face of the unjust order he opposed. Jesus' blood has redemptive value in the sense that it buys back from slavery. It has the power to purify consciences and to cement unity with God. However, Yahweh is never portrayed as an angry God exacting a son's death to appease divine anger. In the New Testament, Yahweh continues to be as much against human sacrifice as in the Abraham / Isaac story.

Post-Biblical Traditions on Sacrifice

For the New Testament tradition, the death of Jesus signified the end of the sacrificial order; the assassination of Jesus at the hands of the temple priesthood represented a sacrifice to end all sacrifices. According to common interpretation, this makes Christianity antisacrificial. But already this understanding represents a significant departure from biblical tradition, for from the Abraham myth on, Judeo-Christianity is not antisacrificial, but nonsacrificial relative to human offerings.

The distinction is an important one. Nonsacrificiality means that the tradition denies all forms of subordinating human welfare to legal requirements epitomized in statutes requiring ritual blood sacrifice. Antisacrificiality means interpreting Jesus' definitive sacrifice as expressing a divine law, which in extreme cases confers on Christians the right to oppose violently whatever is interpreted as human sacrifice wherever it is found. The justifying rationale runs as follows: (1) if Jesus' sacrifice ends all sacrifices, then (2) sacrifices are forbidden by divine law; (3) therefore, wherever sacrifices are performed, (4) killing is justified to stop the sacrifice, (5) which denies the efficacy of Jesus' sacrificial death.

This is basically a war-making mythology that peacemakers must understand. Following its line, all that is necessary to justify the slaughter is to interpret the actions of designated enemies in terms of sacrifice. In this way, every war becomes a war to end war -- a sacrifice to end sacrifices. This was the case with the Crusades, where Arabs were seen as aggressors against European Christians. Above all, the antisacrificial line of thinking applied to the conquest of the Americas. The practice of human sacrifice among the Aztecs conferred on the Spanish and Portuguese the right to kill the indigenous if they refused to stop their sacrificial practices and convert to Christianity (Todorov 154). Similarly, the nineteenth Century British colonization of India was justified in terms of gentlemen stopping the practice of burning widows on the funeral pyres of their husbands. Even the Nazis used the discovery of mass graves in Katyn, Poland, to justify their World War II campaign against Russian communists. The point was to end the sacrifices and human rights violations of the brutal

Soviets (Hinkelammert, *Sacrificios Humanos* 145). Finally, fabricated tales of innocent babies mercilessly torn from the incubators by Iraqi soldiers gave reason for unprecedented mass bombings of Baghdad in 1991.

The point is that the idea of sacrifices to end all sacrifices is central to Western spirituality. Whether it is specifically connected to Christianity or not, antisacrificial (vs. nonsacrificial) thinking is part of the inversion of Christianity. It has Christians enthusiastically serving the interests of empire. But the effect of the service has them offering incense at the altar of the Beast, rather than at the altar of Yahweh.

FORECLOSURE OF BIBLICAL MORAL IMAGINATION: THE ESTABLISHMENT OF WESTERN TOTALITARIANISM

Christian theology's war on immanence led to a totalitarianism which we see as endemic to Western conceptual spirituality. Medieval Christianity's framework of ideas and especially its exclusive doctrine of "no salvation outside the church" was utilized to justify genocide as the ultimate sacrifice required by God. In this way, the persecution of Jews, the Crusades against Islam, the slaughter of the First Nations of Abya Yala, the slavery of Africans, and the burning of witches were rendered nearly inevitable.

Christianity's totality of perception crystallized in the Middle Ages. It became a system complete unto itself and pushed to the extreme the religious inversions reviewed so far - the otherworldliness, the insistence on debt repayment, the necessity of human sacrifice. Our argument in this and the following chapter is that the basic medieval framework survives in our own era in secularized form. It is almost as if medievalists tapped into archetypes which, though repressed in the secular world since the Enlightenment, make their inevitable return in the New World Order. There dogma has it that there can be "no salvation outside the market."[6]

The purpose of this final section, then, is to expose the theological foundations of modern Western genocidal reasoning and to set up understanding of the NWO worldvision which we will examine in our final chapter. Figure 5 begins to illustrate our meaning. It finds complementary illustrations in our final chapter's Figures 6 and 7.

In the medieval system, the meaningful world was seen in terms of spiritual organization so total that it reached from heaven to earth, to the realms of hell below the earth. According to this schema, the destiny of all human beings was accounted for in terms of a "communion of saints" with a unitary world vision. Worthy human beings belonged either to the church triumphant, the church militant, or to the church suffering. Otherwise, sinners were consigned to the realm of lost souls in limbo or hell.

Medieval Heaven

According to the vision depicted in Figure 5, heaven and the life of the Holy Trinity represented the perfect community -- fullness of life. In heaven, the saved

FIGURE 5
THE COMMUNION OF SAINTS

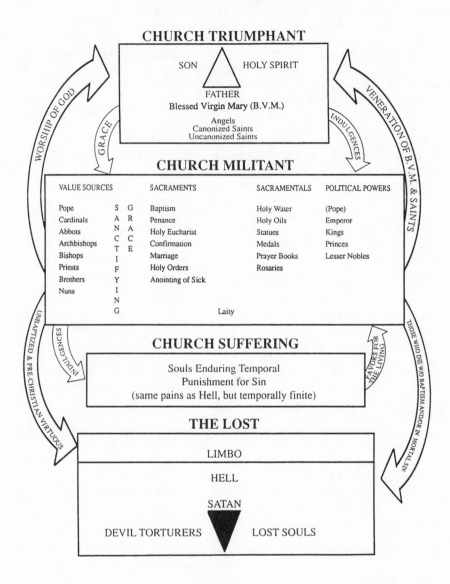

worshipped the Father, Son and Holy Spirit who shared a dynamic love explained expressly in terms of perfect community. In company with the mother of Jesus, the holiest of all human beings, the triumphant joined as well the seven choirs of God's special servants, the angels and archangels, and with the saints both canonized and uncanonized. Canonized saints were those enrolled on the list of souls infallibly proclaimed by the church as having been saved and as constituting role models for the faithful on earth. Following the examples of the saints was the way to get to heaven. Uncanonized saints were the millions of unheralded virtuous Christians who had entered God's presence for all eternity. All of these triumphant souls passed into eternity in what medieval theology saw as the best conceivable life -- constant worship of the triune God. They also helped the faithful on earth by interceding on their behalf.

The Church Militant

The second division of the Communion of Saints belonged to the church militant just mentioned. These were Christians on earth still fighting the "good fight" against the world, the flesh, and the devil. The faithful were enabled to wage their battle only because of membership within the organization uniquely efficacious in this struggle, the Holy Catholic Church. With all its faults, it too was thought a perfect community in that its mission was to represent the "best possible" approximation of heavenly life within the confines of a corrupt world. Its worship anticipated the life of heaven perfectly. But the challenge of the rest of life in both church and society at large was to progress continually toward the heavenly ideals.

This paradoxically perfect but flawed community was presided over by a divinely established hierarchy that provided spiritual vision and moral guidance. In these terms, the hierarchy's function was to articulate the largely utopian ideals derived from the heavenly realm. The hierarchical chain of command ran from the pope to cardinals, to abbots, archbishops and bishops, to priests, unordained "religious" (men and women), and to the laity. Besides offering utopian challenge, the services of this clerical class provided access to sanctifying grace -- a share in the life of God without which it was thought impossible to either please God or to enter the realm of God's life, heaven. Medievalists believed that a soul without grace could no more live in God's presence than a fish without gills could live in water.

Sanctifying grace was extended to the faithful on earth through the sacramental system. The seven sacraments not only communicated, restored, or increased shares in the life of God (sanctifying grace), they also supernaturalized key moments in the human life cycle that otherwise would remain merely natural: birth (baptism), forgiveness after sin (penance), eating (eucharist), transition to adulthood (confirmation), marriage (matrimony), exercise of leadership within the church (holy orders), sickness and death (extreme unction). Medieval Christians understood that one's share of sanctifying grace might also be increased by virtuous acts such as fasting, pilgrimages, prayers and penances. The impulse to perform such acts was understood as "actual grace." This "passing help from God to do acts of virtue" could be stimulated by "sacramentals" sanctioned by the Catholic Church. Sacramentals included blessed items such as holy water, oil, rosaries, statues, crucifixes, "holy pictures," prayer books, scapulars, and medals struck in honor of the saints.

All sectors of earthly life were subject to the discipline and piety of the Roman Catholic Church. Emperors and kings, princes, dukes, and earls as well as commoners took their turns humbly confessing their sins to the priest. And though the pope and emperor we often at odds over limits of authority, the pope prevailed more often than not. Papal power was enhanced after 1302 when Boniface VIII declared the authority of the pope supreme even in temporal affairs. However, even before that declaration, popes were able to bring emperors to their knees through the exercise of excommunication and interdict, as we have already explained in Chapter 4.

The Church Suffering

The church suffering constituted the third level of the Communion of Saints. These inhabited purgatory-- a condition of soul for deceased Christians not yet worthy of heaven. Their unworthiness stemmed from abiding attachments to sin and the world and from the need to make reparation for damage done to God's majesty and to neighbor by their sins. Amends were made by purgatorial suffering that included all the torments of hell understood especially as a purifying fire. Purgatory's punishments, however, differed from those of hell since the former were "temporal" and destined to end once the soul had achieved the state of purification requisite for entry into heaven. In a sense, purgatory represented the medieval understanding of the worst world possible for those who still had hope of saving their immortal souls.

According to medieval spirituality, one's stay in purgatory might also be shortened by means of indulgences gained by members of the church militant on behalf of the church suffering. "Indulgences" canceled one's liability to punishment in purgatory still owed on sins forgiven but for which God's majesty required greater "satisfaction." Indulgences were granted for recitation of prayers, for fastings, pilgrimages, and other pious actions. The amount of time in purgatory remitted by each act was stipulated by church authority in terms of years and days. The faithful could even gain "plenary indulgences" or complete remission of punishment in purgatory for all sins committed in their lives. Indulgences, both partial and plenary, might also be gained by the church militant on behalf of souls suffering in purgatory. Of course the sale of such writs of forgiveness was one of the main issues of the Protestant Reformation.

The Lost

The final realm in the totality represented by Figure 5 indicates the fate of all outside the Communion of Saints. Adults who died in sin were consigned to an eternal hell where they were subject to the punishment most commonly described as burning in eternal flames. This was indeed the "worst conceivable" world. Hell was the abode not only of lost souls outside the system of grace but also of Satan and other evil spirits or devils. Dante's *Divine Comedy* gives abundant examples of how this basic belief was elaborated. Exotic punishments were added. Eventually "limbo" was included in the realm of the excluded. It was a place of "natural" (vs. supernatural) happiness for unbaptized infants and for naturally good souls who died without committing mortal sin and before Christ decreed the necessity of baptism. Limbo was the device medieval theologians used to reconcile God's goodness with the apparent cruelty of condemning unbaptized infants and the virtuous of the pre-Christian era to hell.

A theological story or mythology accompanied this conceptual spirituality. Largely influenced by St. Augustine in the fifth century, the story ran along the following lines:

> In the beginning, God created the world good.
> But the first man and the first woman sinned.
> In so doing, they corrupted human nature and all of creation.
> God was angered as a result.
> He closed the gates of heaven for which human beings had been destined.
> Jesus' sacrificial death reopened heaven's gates.
> The church provides safe passage through those gates in the form of baptism and the other sacraments.
> Those outside the sacramental system are excluded from heaven and justly condemned to hell's eternal punishment.

A Medieval Totalitarianism

This medieval conceptual spirituality and its accompanying mythology was clearly totalitarian. Recalling Hinkelammert's description of totalitarianism, the middle ages' "state of grace system" might be described as:

> a movement which radically polarizes the world starting from the imagination of a perfect institutionality, and which passes from the social technique derived from this perfect institutionality to social terror. Totalitarianism reduces the subject to a single social relationship and isolates it in order to make the perfect institutionality appear as uniquely necessary. (*Democracia* 205)

The spirituality of the Roman Catholic Church during the Middle Ages and at the time of the conquest of the Americas fulfilled all elements of this definition. It expressly saw the Communion of Saints as a "perfect society," a perfect institution. In the final analysis, the church reduced all human beings to a single, all-important social relationship, that of believer to "Mother Church." Without affiliation to that body, human beings were doomed to meaningless and sinful lives intrinsically offensive to God. Unbelievers were destined to eternal punishment at the hands of a justly angry God. These totalitarian convictions led to social terror as resistance to conversion was deemed an offense that cried to God for vengeance. So shooting "heathen" women and children along with their husbands and fathers, their hanging, torture, starvation, deliberate infection with diseases all seemed justified on expressly theological grounds. The conquistadors were God's agents. They were merely doing the Lord's work by anticipating his punishment of unbelievers here on earth. In the sixteenth century (and afterward) this punishment was meted out not only to "Indians," but to others "outside the church" - to Jews, Muslims, African slaves, witches, and sundry "deviants."

Protestant Challenge

As seen in Chapter 4, the Catholic system was challenged by Martin Luther and the other Protestant Reformers beginning in 1517. Protestants judged the Catholic system as superstitious, excessively dependent on human effort, and unbiblical. To eliminate such features they insisted that God's grace alone was responsible for salvation (*sola gratia*); grace inspired a faith that was salvific even without pious works (*sola fide*); reformers insisted that the Bible was the sole standard of orthodox faith (*sola scriptura*). Nonetheless, Protestants retained the basic "state of grace" world vision in a drastically streamlined form. Their heaven eliminated the special status of the Blessed Virgin and of canonized saints. Luther and his successors did away with purgatory entirely and with the need for indulgences. They also drastically changed the realm of the church militant totally rejecting the notion of ecclesiastical hierarchy. The sacramental system was also gutted. For many sects, baptism and the Lord's Supper alone were retained, though Luther initially kept the sacrament of penance. Some denominations also retained confirmation. Similarly, sacramentals were set aside as Romanist superstition. Statues and paintings disappeared from reformed churches. In the realm of the lost, hell alone remained, limbo being eliminated as biblically unfounded.

But far from eradicating the Catholic "state of grace" model, Protestantism confirmed it. For the Reformers, there was still no salvation outside acceptance of the Gospel and baptism. The singularly reductionist social relationship was still understood in terms of church. And the "social terror" of the conquistadors was extended throughout North America by Puritans and others who pursued and slaughtered "pagan Indians" with self-righteous abandon. In this connection British Captain John Mason captures the operative totalitarian spirit that identified the slaughter of the "Indians" with the punishments of God.

> And indeed such a dreadful Terror did the Almighty let fall upon their Spirits, that they would fly from us and run into the very Flames, where many of them perished. [And] God was above them, who laughed his Enemies and the Enemies of his People to Scorn, making them as a fiery Oven: Thus were the Stout Hearted spoiled, having slept their last Sleep, and none of their Men could find their Hands: Thus did the Lord judge among the Heathen, filling the Place with dead Bodies! (Stannard 113-4)

CONCLUSION

The main direction of this chapter has been to argue that the West has successfully domesticated the resistance literature of the Judeo-Christian tradition. In effect, from the fifth century on, the entire biblical tradition has routinely been set on its head -- made to serve the interests of empire and become an enslaving rather than a liberating force (Hinkelammert *Sacrificios* 92). As a result, Christians within Western churches find themselves imprisoned in "caves," where the shadows representing the biblical tradition are just as deceptive as the other figures that pass on the wall depicting nonreligious dimensions of their culture.

> In this way, there emerges a world in which everything appears the opposite of what it is. The victim becomes the victimizer and the victimizer the victim. War is peace and peace is war. Love is hatred, and hatred is love. The Beast is God, and God is the Beast. Heaven is hell and hell is heaven (132).[7]

Reversals and inversions like the ones just reviewed have converted most versions of the Judeo-Christian tradition into what Hinkelammert calls an "ideological weapon of death." The contrary option for life leaves peace activists and educators with two alternatives. On the one hand, we can correctly identify the post-Constantinian religious tradition as essentially genocidal and repudiate it. In doing so, however, we must reckon the consequence of cutting off dialog with hundreds of millions who profess allegiance to the God of the Bible.

Alternatively (and this is our option), we can recognize the Judeo-Christian tradition as a source of powerful countercultural values, precisely subversive of the selfishness, individualism, and antihumanistic spirit that have become so central to the Western spirituality that lies at the heart of World War III. Rescuing the Bible's liberating thrust, obscured by 1,500 years of obfuscation and inversion, entails listening not only to Third World theologians, but to others who have preserved or recuperated the humanizing and subversive dimensions of Judeo-Christianity, including St. Francis of Assisi, the Anabaptists, the traditional peace churches, feminists, African Americans, the First Peoples of Abya Yala, womanists, and so forth. Only in this way is it possible to reverse the defeat which the biblical God of life has suffered in the theogony against the West's bestial legitimator of World War III:

> Idolatry is a sin against the first commandment. Of all the sins related to it, none is more scandalous than sin against the second commandment: "You shall not make wrongful use of the name of the LORD your God, for the LORD will not acquit anyone who misuses his name" (Exod. 20:7). It is blasphemy to use the name of God in defense of imperialism. In the United States, the theologians of the Institute for Religion and Democracy dare to compare multinational corporations with the Servant of Yahweh. This sin has fatal consequences when some bishops and priests become military officials, legitimating arms of war which are used to kill our people, justifying and facilitating total war, holy war. In some countries there are priests who not only serve as military chaplains, but who also give spiritual guidance to the directors of death squads. To invoke the name of the God of life to justify death and destruction is blasphemy. It is to scandalize the little ones (Mark. 9:42, 17:1-2). (Kairos Internacional 18)

NOTES

1. This was not to say, however, that Paul urged anarchism on his communities. Though the law responsible for upholding unjust orders was delegitimated, it still held binding power for the sake of order (Rom. 13: 1-7). Christians were to obey it,

when its norms did not contradict the dictates of faith understood as the anticipation of the new earth governed by love of neighbor (Rom. 13: 8-10). Evidently, Paul understood the institution of slavery as somehow compatible with the order willed by God; like other facets of the legal system, it was illegitimate, but still binding (Hinkelammert, *The Ideological* 147). According to Hinkelammert, Paul's position along these lines stemmed from his inability to conceive alternatives to the Roman legal system of his day. Absent criteria for reordering society in a practical way, Paul was forced to await "The Day of the Lord" for direct divine intervention to bring about the new creation (150). In the meantime, Paul's concern for order led him to pronounce the given political order as "illegitimate but binding." That is, it was condemned to disappear with the advent of the Day of the Lord. But for the sake of public order, it was in force during the interim.

Despite such protestations, Paul's preaching was seen as threatening to the Roman empire. That leaves us with a problem similar to that of the supposedly "other worldly" Jesus. It is hard to understand why the Romans would imprison, torture, and behead a nice tentmaker and rabbi for preaching sermons about personal salvation that had no relation whatever to public life. On the contrary, Paul's message was that a new world order was required. Because of this, Paul and his companions were seen as political threats. In Acts (17:6-7, 13), they are accused of inciting revolution, of preaching Jesus as king in place of Caesar. According to Tamez, Paul's crime was that he proclaimed Jesus as Lord in a time when the Roman emperor claimed centrality of power, glory and divinity (Tamez 95). Paul then took a stand against the idolatrous worship of Caesar, i.e., against putting state authority ahead of God's own (Rom. 1:23). This made Paul a subversive.

2. The Book of Deuteronomy, a peasant document originating from a farmers' rebellion in Judah in 640 B.C., indicates that rectification must take place much more frequently. Deuteronomy not only strongly endorses the Jubilee ideal; it goes so far as to proclaim mini Jubilees every seven years (sabbaticals), rather than waiting for the fiftieth year of remission. The purpose of sabbaticals centralized debt forgiveness:

> Every seventh year you shall grant a remission of debts. There will, however, be no one in need among you   Since there will never cease to be some in need on the earth, I therefore command you, "Open your hand to the poor and needy neighbor in your land. (Deut. 15: 1-11)

3. In this way, Anselm's thinking starts off the bourgeois revolution whose ethical axiom finds justice in the fulfillment of all laws, contracts, and debt obligations. Demanding payment of the unpayable ran directly contrary to the scholastic principle of the Middle Ages, which taught that no one is bound to do the impossible. From Anselm's position, it was a short step to blaming the poor for their inability to pay their debts. And from there it was an even shorter pace to perceiving poverty itself as a blameworthy state (Hinkelammert, *Sacrificios humanos* 86). Thus in modern thinking, the poor are rendered reprobate rather than God's elect (75). Their poverty is explained in terms of laziness and lust (87). Their "suffering" can therefore be ignored. In fact, as Malthus was to later explain, justice for the poor comes to mean honoring their right not to be given assistance. As Hinkelammert notes, Anselm's line of thinking eventually made modern Western society the most insensitive to poverty that has ever existed (88).

4. According to Hinkelammert, newer Latin American translations of the Lord's Prayer lead to a similar understanding of Jesus' paying the unpayable debt. The older Spanish and Portuguese translations in fact did read, "Forgive us our debts as we

forgive our debtors." But during the 1970s, the translation became, "Forgive us our offenses as we forgive those who offend against us." In this way, the Latin American versions of the prayer were made to resemble those used for a long time in the United States and Western Europe.

Significantly, the coincidence was manufactured precisely in the historical moment when those very developed regions were refusing demands for the remission of Third World debt (*La Deuda* 61). When asked about the change, translators admitted the influence of such considerations when they characterized the alteration as an attempt to avoid politicizing the prayer. But, of course, Hinkelammert notes, both translations are highly political. It is just that the interests of different classes are served by each version. More specifically, the new translation had the precise effect of reversing the meaning of the old one. For in the more traditional version, the duty of the lender was to forgive debts; the corresponding obligation of the debtor was to resist paying them. However, the new wording suggested that debtors should not offend creditors and should therefore pay their debts. And though the debtor must forgive the offense of the unpaid debt, the debt itself remains to be paid. There is no longer any question of forgiving debts as a fundamentally divine characteristic (62).

5. Hinkelammert bases his position that the quotation in italics was a later addition on four considerations:

(a) The text is apparently ignorant of the reigning custom of child sacrifice in Near Eastern patriarchal times. In such context, all good fathers would be willing to sacrifice their firstborn sons. There would have been nothing especially heroic about Abraham's intention. An audience without this knowledge would find a father willing to kill his son an admirable example of exceptional faith (*La Fe* 17).

(b) The text is incoherent with the overall thrust of the Abraham tradition, which is about a God who primarily dispenses life, not death.

(c) The additions are ambiguous. Even they do not explicitly say that Abraham's faith was found precisely in his willingness to kill his son. Instead, they pinpoint the patriarch's fidelity in his refusal to deny Isaac to Yahweh. Such negation could just as well indicate a refusal to deliver Isaac to death, in view of Abraham's dedication to the God of life. In the end, Hinkelammert notes, it is the reader's socialization that facilitates the common understanding of Abraham's faith (19).

(d) The story is easily seen as an example of a "divine temptation" tradition. It was not unusual for Israelite tradition to present God as commanding a "sinful" act and then as rewarding the one who disobeys the command (108-113).

6. Hinkelammert supports this perception when he points out that all conceptual spiritualities have their notions of heaven and hell. In *Democracy and Totalitarianism*, he examines traditional ideas of the Christian afterlife. These, he points out, took the earth as their starting point, and in a sense, as their end point too, since the various models effectively legitimate given social formations in relation to eternity (*Democracia* 244). Such legitimation was the function of all celestial imaginings down through the ages. In other words, heaven as well as earth has a history. Thus the concept of heaven was really the medieval era's imaginative depiction of the perfectly full human life and an indication of how to get from here to there (241). It reflected the conceptual spirituality of the late premodern period rather than the vision of the "new heaven and the new earth" found in the first century's Book of Revelation. As Hinkelammert puts it, "The medieval heaven is a feudal heaven. All humans have souls, but souls are feudaly arranged in hierarchical order. Heaven itself resembles a hierarchically-ordered feudal court with God as king over all, followed by the various clerical ranks, the aristocrats and ordinary folk who surround the court." (*Democrácia* 242)

Since earthly changes invariably required their counterparts in heaven, Hinkelammert argues, those who wished to change the earth had to alter the concept of heaven as well. Martin Luther found it necessary to alter drastically his followers' understandings of all dimensions of the afterlife. His denial of the Blessed Virgin's privileged place and elimination of canonized saints' status expressed not only a Christocentric and biblical theology but the democratic movements of his time as well. Thus "heaven ceased being a feudal court and was transformed into a heaven of souls all of which enjoyed equal happiness" (243). Even Marxist understandings of socialism and communism had to articulate anew as-yet-unrealized concepts of humankind's final destiny -- of fullness of life. The bourgeois had to do the same establishing their vision of the perfect society in terms of perfect market competition and its alleged universally beneficial consequences (241).

7. To Hinkelammert's list of inversions, we might add the following:

Whereas Paul sees the love of money as the root of evil; Western Christianity typically endorses capitalism, which understands the love of money (or at least desire for its unlimited accumulation) as the God-sanctioned root of society. Once again, as Mandeville put it in the eighteenth century, private vices produce public goods. Vicious conduct on the part of human beings, though perhaps punishable in the afterlife, ultimately makes this world a better place, since it causes economic growth (*Sacrificios humanos* 185-86).

Despite the miracles and pronouncements of Jesus and the teachings of Paul on resurrection, bodily life is unimportant in the eyes of God. The life of the soul and spirit is more important.

Payment of unpayable debts by blood is just. Forgiveness of debts leads to chaos and inferno.

The sacrifice of innocent humans for the sake of future blessings is demanded by God. Defending the right to life of actually existing humans is utopian and condemnable if it causes one to interfere with market laws.

God is the underwriter of (the U.S. form) of empire, since it really isn't empire but the defender of (market) freedom throughout the world.

God has made a "preferential option" for the rich, since their wealth is a sign of God's blessing. The poor suffer because of their laziness and unrestrained sexuality. Their poverty is a sign of the rejection by God.

Jesus is the example of the just person who pays unpayable debts with his own blood. Lucifer tempts debtors on the one hand to disown their unmeetable financial obligations. On the other, he tempts lenders to forgive unpayable debts.

Heaven is the place where disembodied souls go after death to enjoy the abstract pleasure of contemplating God. Hope in a Kingdom of God in history, creating a new earth inhabited by new men and new women with real bodies that eat and drink and enjoy bodily pleasure is diabolical.

The Eucharist is the celebration of a sacrificial death through which bread and wine transformed into Jesus' body and blood are eaten by believers, thus celebrating human sacrifice and the idea that life comes through death. Understanding the Eucharist as the celebration of the one who dedicated his body and blood (i.e., his very self) to providing food and drink so that all might have life abundantly is heretical (*Ideological* 193). Life does not come from life, but through death.

All of this has entailed the demonizing of the authentic Christian spirit of holy anarchism. Put even more starkly, Jesus himself has been demonized. This is most clearly illustrated in the inversion of the title, "Lucifer," which for the first three centuries of church history was exclusively given to Jesus, the Angel of Light who conferred on Christians the right to disobey empire's destructive laws. For that reason, Christians represented the demonic for Rome. Roman authorities connected the Christian Lucifer with diabolical resistance to the *Pax Romana* . That connection continued after Constantine, when, despite Christianity's acceptance, all resistance to empire was seen as Luciferean (129). Such identification has persisted through the centuries of Christianity's nearly invariable cooperation with Rome's successors. Thus today Free Enterprise Christianity links the devil, Lucifer, with humanists, war resisters, environmentalists, feminists, liberation theology, and with those guilty of the unpardonable sin of refusing obedience, debt payment, sacrifice, or simply the humble deference due the New World Order.

WORKS CITED

Calvin, Jean. *Calvin: Institutes of the Christian Religion.* Edited by John T.
    McNeil and translated by Ford Battles. Vol. 20 and 21. The Library of Christian
    Classics. Philadelphia, Pa.: The Westminster Press, 1960.
Dante Alighieri. *The Inferno: a verse rendering for the modern reader by John Ciardi.*
    New York: New American Library, 1954.
Deloria, Vine. *God Is Red.* New York: Grosset and Dunlap, 1973.
de Santa Ana. "Sacralizaciones y sacrificios en las prácticas humanas." *De la logica
    del sacrificio a la realizacion humana.* San José, Costa Rica: REDLA-CPID,
    1990, 7-20.
Duchrow et al. *Confidential Documents of the 17th Conference of the American
    Armies.* Mar del Plata, Argentina: 1987.
Hinkelammert, Franz J. *Democracia y totalitarismo.* San José, Costa Rica: Editorial
    DEI, 1987.
_____. *La deuda externa de América Latina: el automatismo de la deuda.* San José,
    Costa Rica: Editorial DEI, 1988.
_____. *La fe de Abraham y el Edipo occidental.* San José, Costa Rica: Editorial DEI,
    1991.
_____ . *The Ideological Weapons of Death.* New York: Orbis Books, 1986.
_____. "Nuestro proyecto de nueva sociedad en América Latina: el papel regulador del
    Estado y los problemas de la auto-regulación del mercado."*Pasos* 33,
    (Jan./Feb. 1991): 6--23.
_____. *Sacrificios humanos y sociedad occidental: lucifer y la bestia.*
    San José, Costa Rica: Editorial DEI, 1991.
Johnson, Paul. *A History of Christianity .* New York: Atheneum, 1977.
Kairos Internacional. *El camino de Damasco.* Managua, Nicaragua: Kairós
    Internacional, 1989.
Luther, Martin. "Preface to the Epistle of St. Paul to the Romans." *Martin Luther:
    Selections from His Writings.* John Dillenberger, ed. Garden City, N.Y.:
    Anchor Books, 1961.
Meyers, Ched. *Binding the Strong Man: A Political Reading of Mark's Story of Jesus.*
    New York: Orbis Books, 1988.
Pixley, Jorge. "Exige el dios verdadero sacrificios cruentos?" *Revista De
    Interpretacion Biblica Latinoamericana ,* no. 2: *Violencia, Poder y Opressión.*
    San José, Costa Rica: Editorial DEI, 1991, 109-131.
Stannard, David E. *American Holocaust: Columbus and the Conquest of the New
    World .* New York: Oxford University Press, 1992.
Starhawk. *Dreaming the Dark .* Boston: Beacon Press, 1988.
Tamez, Elsa. *Contra toda condena.* San José, Costa Rica: Editorial DEI, 1991.
Todorov, Tzvetan. *The Conquest of America.* New York: Harper and Row, 1984.

Weber, Max. *The Protestant Ethic and the Spirit of Capitalism.* New York: Charles
    Scribner's Sons, 1958.
Yoder, John Howard. *The Politics of Jesus.* Grand Rapids, Mich.: William B.
    Eerdmans Publishing Company, 1972.

6

Illusion: Utopia Is a Four Letter Word

To this point, we have argued that capitalism is a miserably failed system. While claiming hard-headed realism for itself, its belief that free markets can give us the best possible world is guided by a naively utopian functionalist spirituality and demands a heroic act of faith and of psychological denial. These acts are possible only by ignoring history itself, the impact of the system's 500 year Reich on the vast majority of the world's inhabitants, unbridled industrialism's brutal destruction of the natural environment, and the blatant contradictions between Free Market principles and our most cherished humanistic and religious convictions.

The present chapter will conclude our argument that the destructively utopian, totalitarian, genocidal, and ultimately *impossible* nature of the New World Order (NWO) stems from the model's lack of "moral imagination" -- of critical thought prioritizing human life ahead of institutional preservation that is merely self-referential. Lacking grounds for self-criticism, the NWO merely reiterates in secularized form the totalitarian structures of medieval conceptual spirituality, complete with ideas of heaven (the best conceivable world), earthly struggle (the best possible world), purgatory (the worst possible world), and hell (the worst conceivable world). By contrast, the alternative New Earth spirituality suggested below will locate grounds for self-critical thought about the possible, in human intersubjectivity excluding no one. In this sense, what we will term the "New Earth Order" embodies an act of "transcendent imagination" which we have been calling "moral" (Marguerite Rivage-Seul, *Harvard Ed* 162). That necessarily utopian act suggests discernment around commitments and policy directions, alliances and strategies.

NEW WORLD ORDER CONCEPTUAL SPIRITUALITY: THE IDEOLOGY OF GENOCIDE

Figure 6 attempts to illustrate our perception that the basic elements of medieval conceptual spirituality ("church" triumphant, militant, suffering) are retained in New World Order thinking.[1] So is a set of revised value sources, a kind of sacramental system and a well-defined realm of the lost. There also remains a largely secularized, but still theological story justifying social terror aimed at the elimination and eternal punishment of the unworthy.

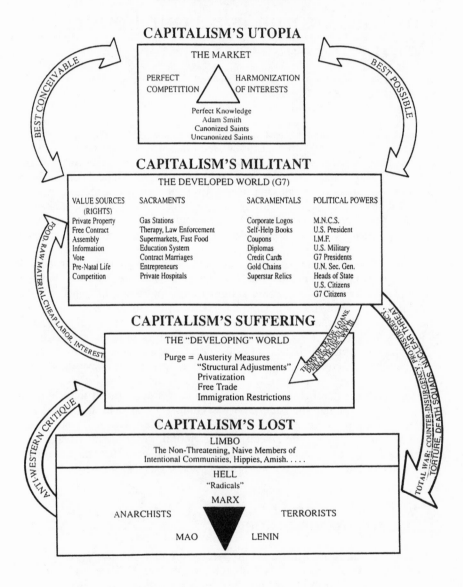

FIGURE 6
THE NEW WORLD ORDER

Capitalist Utopia

The topmost rectangle of the diagram represents the Free Market utopia, its vision of life's fullness.[2] In the Market System's "best conceivable" world, the market itself is the "Unmoved Mover" of the new order. It operates through the Holy Trinity of perfect knowledge, perfect competition, and harmonization of self-interest. The theory has it that if the market enables participants to know all relevant factors impacting economic choice, competition will drive them to produce the best possible products at the lowest possible costs; this will result in the greatest possible benefit for the greatest possible number.

As this system's fundamental prophet, Adam Smith occupies the place reserved for the Blessed Virgin in the medieval heaven. His fundamental concept of "invisible hand" ensures his priority of place; it represents the market system's concept of God. In fact, Smith saw the market in terms of Lord of life and death -- as the best means of controlling population, of deciding who shall live and who shall die (Hinkelammert, *"Nuestro Proyecto"* 11). Meanwhile, the stations formerly held by the seven choirs of angels have been taken by the great theorists of the monied class. As we have seen, these certainly include Ricardo, Malthus, Darwin, Spencer, and Keynes. Perhaps Weber and Popper, Hayeck and Friedman belong in their company as well, given Hinkelammert's indication that their theories have proven central to neocolonial control of the Third World (*Critica* 222). The storied role models filling the ranks of the "canonized saints" include the Vanderbilts, Rockefellers, Kennedys, Mellons, Danforths, Fords, Waltons, and a host of others who have made or maintained family fortunes by honoring the dictates of the Holy Trinity. The unsung, uncanonized heroes of free enterprise are countless.

The New Order Militant

According to the Free Market model, the secularized "church militant" belong, in effect, to the community of the saved. To the degree "best possible" at any given moment, they share the "sanctifying" life of the market. The militant live in countries that have achieved high standards of living because of their actual approximation of market ideals. In general, the G7 countries (the United States, Japan, Germany, Great Britain, Canada, France, and Italy) have currently attained this status. Their visible hierarchy runs from the international business community to the U.S. president, who is their chief executor. As such, the president enjoys "quasi-papal" powers of excommunication and interdict. He can remove heads of state from office or even contract their assassinations if they are not suitably obedient. Suffering under power reminiscent of papal interdict, whole nations today can be subjected to blockade, quarantine, or embargo if their leaders refuse debt payments, reject structural adjustments, attempt breaking the monopoly of developed nations on nuclear weapons, try to control their nation's resources for the benefit of their own people, or if they commit crimes of land reform or redistributions of wealth from the rich to the poor. The idea here is to cause so much suffering among subjects that the recalcitrant "prince" will submit to "church" discipline.

From the U.S. president, the chain of command runs more or less to the IMF, to the the U.S. military, to the presidents and prime ministers of the other six G7 countries, to the United Nations' Secretary General (who increasingly functions as the G7 coordinator of that international body), to the heads of other governments, to U.S. citizens, and finally to citizens of other G7 countries. This hierarchy has power because it controls the sources of the new salvation model's "sanctifying grace," natural resources, especially oil, the system's life's blood. Grace flows freely because the hierarchy ensures access to oil and the other less important raw materials that the system absorbs from another (underdeveloped) world.

The life's blood of the church militant is mediated through sacramental "channels of grace." Like their medieval counterparts, these sanctify key moments in life, but this time defined in terms of consumption. With only slight exaggeration, oil company service stations can be seen as types of baptismal fonts, dispensing the quasi-magical liquid that gets the system started and keeps it going. Supermarkets and fast food chains facilitate "eucharistic" meals offering artificially cheap foods imported from across the planet. Schools are the "catechism" classes that teach students commitment to First World consumption levels and to the status seeking that justifies vastly different lifestyles even within the First World itself (Illich, *Deschooling* 49-50). Graduation is the rite of confirmational passage that indicates pupils have learned their lessons well. Therapists provide private confessionals for middle-class and upper-class consumers unable to adjust to the requirements of consumerism for various reasons. Maladjustment in the lower classes receives a harsher "penance" administered by the courts, police, and jails. Rising expectations in terms of consumption draw men and women together to pool their resources according to marriage "contracts." Huge high-tech hospitals anoint the sick and prepare them for death. The increasingly gigantic malls representing the New Order's cathedrals, centrally locate its priesthood, the entrepreneurs who supply the developed world's need to connect to the market.

The system is buttressed by kinds of "sacramentals" that provide "passing helps" to commit acts of buying and selling. Corporate logos, superstar endorsements of products, and, above all, credit cards stimulate consumption. Celebrity relics, "holy pictures," and gold chains testify to one's "state of grace" (i.e., success or aspiration to success relative to market life.) The sacramentals are closely connected with the system's value sources, which, apart from those noted below, include advertising, the motion picture and television industries, schools and churches.

The main "value sources" of the New World Order model are largely secular and disembodied. In the modern and postmodern worlds, churches and personally identifiable church leaders (such as the Roman Catholic hierarchy in Chapter 5's Figure 5) provide only muted articulations of moral guidance. After the eighteenth century, their place was taken by various declarations of human rights as found in documents like the U.S. Constitution's Bill of Rights, and in the French Revolution's Declaration of the Rights of Man. These represent historical statements of utopian ideals deemed particularly important for the maintenance of the world order in question (*Democrácia* 138).

In the order governed by the Free Market, the right of private ownership of farms, factories, and other productive resources reigns supreme. It must be protected at all costs. In the same way, the right of producers to interact freely in the marketplace represents a right of high priority. To do so, however, people must be able to gather or assemble to bargain and trade. There must be free flow of information if the market's utopian ideal of "perfect knowledge" is to be approximated. The right to vote for government favorable to property holders is also important, as is the protection of prenatal life to ensure sufficient workforce competition to meet labor needs at low cost. In this system, however, following birth, the right to life is transformed into the right to compete (basically for scarce jobs, i.e., for life).

The New Order Suffering

The New World Order's total system has its purgatory too -- its "worst possible" world for those still hoping to enter the arena of superconsumption. The Third World falls into this category. But so do the newly "liberated" nations of Eastern Europe and even people in the G7 nations who have not yet attained their "piece of the pie." In the diagram those in purgatory are referred to as "developing" because of the model's traditional promise that those within its confines are "on the way" to the level of shopping "enjoyed" by the already "developed world." However, Nietzschean postmodernism largely agrees that pain will indefinitely remain the lot of the world's majority. The line between purgatory and hell is blurred accordingly.

Nevertheless, the "poor souls" in transition are punished for their failure to achieve. As nations they undergo hellish tortures termed "austerity measures," or "structural adjustments" requisite for "privatization" and "free trade" as described in Chapter 3. As individuals, the guilty must endure low wages and a lack of education, health care, social security, and retirement benefits. The idea remains that the process of purging will teach the "church suffering," the virtues long since learned by the "saved," allowing the successfully competitive to finally consume at levels which ensure the greatest good for the greatest number. Transition to that beatific level is hastened by "indulgences" in the form of bank loans and credit -- the most effective ways the church militant help the church suffering under the aegis of the market. In all of this, as we have seen repeatedly, starry-eyed free marketeers blissfully ignore the physical impossibility of the Third World ever approaching First World consumption levels. Or, once again, if that unpleasant fact of life *is* recognized, it is accepted ahead of time (by the well-off) on behalf of the suffering as the latter's "best possible" situation.

The Lost

Some, however, are excluded even from purgatory. Their crimes are unforgivable since the sins they have committed marginalize them entirely from the system of salvation. Such crimes deny the market's very bases -- private ownership, free markets, unlimited horizons of income, the ultimately binding nature of business contracts. Two classes of condemned belong here, one consigned to "limbo," the other to the torments of hell proper. Those in limbo represent relatively no threat to the market. In varying degrees this category of the lost "drop out" from the system they judge as harmful. Tribal peoples (especially where genocide has made their numbers insignificant), religious groups such as the Amish, neohippies, and members of intentional communities reject the "American Dream" and so will never enjoy the rapture connected with the "American Way of Life." They are the unfortunates allowed to live naively in "natural happiness" as opposed to enjoying the mechanized, cybernetic, high-tech pleasures of the New Order.

The more dangerous and absolutely anathematized by the Market System's hierarchy seek to destroy market order, typically aspiring to replace it with the "chaos of socialism" - understood as the "worst conceivable" world (Hinkelammert, *Critica* 204). In hell a trinity of devils reign: Marx, Lenin, and Mao Tse-Tung. Besides communists and socialists, hell includes Islamic fundamentalists, nationalists, anarchists, and other revolutionaries and contrarian radicals. All of these are classified as "terrorists." They and those they influence and control are deserving of death. Total war is waged against them including low- and high-intensity expressions. Both counterinsurgency and proinsurgency measures are employed, depending on the relations of the diabolical agents to political authority. Disappearances, torture, death squads, "punitive" and "preemptive" raids, and even use of nuclear weapons are legitimized in wars against the "evil empires" involved. The theological story or mythology accompanying this conceptual spirituality summarizes the reasons why:

> God created the world with the "Big Bang."
> He set up laws to direct it, e.g., gravity, inertia . . .
> Among God's natural laws those governing the Market have special importance:
> supply, demand, wages, competition. . .
> To disobey such laws trangresses human rights to property, profit and
> freedom of markets.
> Such abuse must be curbed, e.g., by blockade, embargo, boycott, "contra"
> wars.
> Deaths occurring in the process are regrettable but necessary.
> For there can be no genuine human life outside the market system.

A Post-Medieval Totalitarianism

Clearly, the spirituality of this secularized "communion" contains all the elements of totalitarianism as defined by Hinkelammert. The order represents a "perfect society" literally with no alternatives tolerated. In the final analysis, it reduces all human relationships to a single linkage defined by market participation. Aside from that relationship, human beings are doomed to meaningless lives to which death is preferrable. Such totalitarian convictions lead to social terror. The shooting of women and children along with their husbands and fathers, their hanging, torture, starvation, and subjection to diseases all are justified on hard-headed theoretical grounds. The marines, contra soldiers, and IMF collection agencies, the timber and mining companies destroying rain forests and native burial grounds are all transformed into agents of the God who established the market as "natural" and "realistic" as opposed to "utopian."

NEW EARTH SPIRITUALITY: THE REJECTION OF GENOCIDE

Our contention is that the employment of "moral imagination" as we have understood it reveals that market spirituality has both conceptual and practical alternatives. Those alternatives are revealed by changing the content of the utopia that we have seen as essential to any conceptual spirituality. The new content, we suggest, must be shaped by moral imagination that is essentially transcendent. Transcendental (moral) imagination is not totalitarian; it has a reference point outside particular systems of political economy. This contrasts with the exercise of New World Order imagination, which continually measures both the "best conceivable" and the "best possible" according to limits of perception dictated by an institution, the market itself (*Critica* 258). In Figure 6, this is indicated by the double arrows connecting "Capitalism's Utopia" with the diagram section designated "Capitalism's Militant."

By contrast, our New Earth Order (NEO) adopts human intersubjectivity as its transcendent reference point. According to Hinkelammert, this intersubjectivity, where men and women relate as persons rather than as objects acted upon, constitutes the essence of being human. In theological terms, it describes the experience of God. Striving for the practical realization of intersubjectivity reveals the limits of the possible. It enables the attainment of goals that would otherwise be thought impossible (Hinkelammert 1984, 275). The content of intersubjectivity is recognized and derived from meaningful work, from celebrations, and from experiencing love of neighbor.

It must be emphasized that the guiding spirituality depicted here is not arrived at by deciding that one set of arbitrarily chosen values is superior to another. Rather, its point of departure is life itself. Human beings must be alive to espouse any set of values whatever. The model therefore takes actually existing human life and its supporting natural environment as its baseline. It then asks, "What is necessary to preserve given life forms without dehumanizing exploitation?" In terms of economics, the NEO model responds that preservation of life requires "as much market as possible" and "as much planning as necessary" (cf. below). Humanization beyond that draws on the life-favoring traditions of tribal religions, feminine spirituality, world religions, and Western humanism. Together these yield a nonsacrificial conceptual spirituality for global intersubjective community as indicated in Figure 7.

FIGURE 7
THE NEW EARTH ORDER

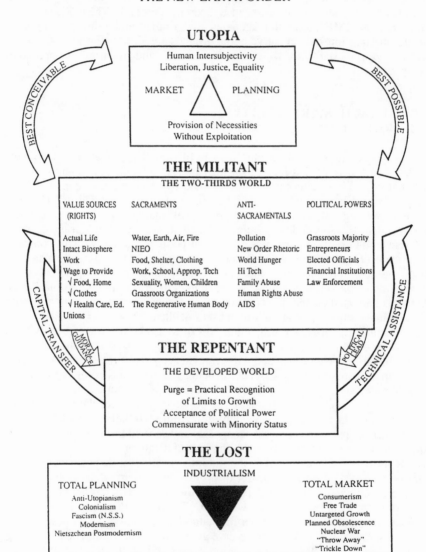

Obviously Figure 7 presents a conceptual model intended to counterpoint the totalitarian orders represented by the medieval church and New World Order configurations. It differs from those models, however, in that the entire depiction from "utopian critique" to "realm of the lost" represents a not-yet-realized possibility. Thus, all of the model's dimensions are "utopian" in the sense Hinkelammert says is necessary for any practice of the "art of the possible."

Nonetheless, as will become apparent below, all elements of the New Earth model are also grounded in concrete historical reality rather than in mere "pious wishes." This is true of the model's "heaven" or utopia. As already noted, its "best conceivable" world takes as its ultimate criteria of feasibility the maintenance of actually existing human life and of a life-favoring natural environment. Similarly, our model's inversion of New World Order realms of the militant (the "best possible" world) and suffering (the "worst possible") involve reversal of the humanly unacceptable character of life as experienced by Third World majorities. Also, the present model's region of the lost containing systems and concepts rather than people, rejects much of the New World Order's actual conceptual spirituality.

New Earth Utopia

Apart from what has already been described above, the New Earth model's utopia enshrines the goal of freedom understood as liberation and the values of justice and equality as necessary for attaining and preserving human intersubjectivity. The freedom sought here is the freedom of the world's poor from the dynamics of World War III as we have discussed it in our study. To reiterate, the goal of the desired freedom is the provision of life's necessities for everyone, without exploitation -- without premising anyone's standard of living on the inability of others to live. This critical utopia seeks liberation from the debt and sacrifice the New World Order imposes -- from the free enterprise system as we have seen it practiced in the Third World for the last 500 years. Vidales distinguishes this guiding vision pictured in Figures 7 from the goals of Figure 6:

> [T]he definition of development is conceived starting from the satisfaction of everyone's vital necessities in terms of a dignified life and the maximization of the people's potentialities guaranteeing that what governs the organization of work and production is communal logic, not that of business (which measures by gross product, quantity, income, accumulation). (*Utopía y* 112)

Similarly, our model's utopian realm enshrines justice and equality as guiding values. It desires a "level playing field," but this time where the disadvantages of the less well endowed (in terms of economic, technological, and political power) are remediated, by a corresponding restructuring of the economic and political "rules of the game." Such restructuring does not seek its justification in charity or in liberalism of the "bleeding heart" variety. Rather, it appeals to the history we have reviewed in Chapter 3. As we will see below, the concept of "reparation" is central here.

The base, then, of our model's "trinity" is clear. Its complementary elements distance themselves equally from the totalitarianism of market or of total planning as panaceas. On the one hand the model recognizes the productive, innovative, and incentive powers of free and fair competition. It therefore proposes "as much market as possible." This entails affirmation of the work ethic and of unequal income distribution and return on investment, without which economic output cannot be humanely optimal (*Democracia* 33, 41). (The model, however, expressly rejects the neoliberal position that income opportunities must be unlimited in order to stimulate optimal production.) On the other hand, Figure 7 advocates "as much planning as necessary" to ensure humane economic distribution and protection of the natural environment. These requirements place limits on investment return as well as on wages. For humanization is achieved in the continuum between maximization of output and income on the one hand and full employment (at a living wage) and environmental protection on the other (33-34).

The Militant

The realm of the "militant" belongs to those struggling against the reigning World Order model. Inhabitants of the "Two-thirds World" are located here. Like the earlier models depicted, they have their sources of value, their political hierarchy, "sacraments," and "sacramentals."

Sources of Value

Here, once again, value sources are depersonalized "human rights" rather than personally identifiable governing bodies with executive authority like the medieval church. (Even human rights groups like Amnesty International have no authority to implement their recommendations.) However, the human rights hierarchy in the present model reflects an economy organized according to what Hinkelammert and others term "the logic of the majority" (i.e., identifying the peasant and working class majority rather than the property-owning minority with the "general interest") (*Democracia* 151). Accordingly, the property rights of the latter group are not denied, but subordinated to the life requirements of the former. Here the right to life is not limited to *in utero* existence but extends comprehensively from conception to death. Actually existing human life is protected first and foremost; it can never be unwillingly sacrificed for the sake of future or potential life or for material prosperity. This principle of nonsacrificiality determines the rest of the value hierarchy. It protects the biosphere on which human life depends. It demands full employment at a living wage sufficient to procure nourishment, dignified clothing, and shelter. Health care and education and the right of workers to organize to protect their rights belong to the historically articulated ideals of the New Earth Order.

Political Powers

The political powers listed in the NEO also reflect Hinkelammert's majority logic. Here grassroots workers and peasants among the militant hold decisive power, without denying political rights proportional to numbers in the property owning classes. Both groups, in turn, elect representative officials drawn not from the ranks of professional politicians but from all societal groups. Elected officials oversee financial institutions and law enforcement agencies.

The Sacraments

Our model's channels of creation's basically free gift (life itself) are outward signs intended to communicate that inward reality. In this, they might be thought of as "sacraments" that Christian tradition understands as outward signs of an invisible grace. As we saw in Chapter 5, traditional Christian sacraments of baptism, penance, eucharist, confirmation, matrimony, holy orders, and annointing of the sick consecrated key moments in human life and employed foundational elements such as water, oil, fire, bread, and wine to lift faithful minds and hearts to the heavenly realm. Under pressures from WorldWar III and environmental destruction, we propose a reversal of that sacramental process. We suggest a vision that animated by a utopia of intersubjectivity (the experience of God in work, play, and love of neighbor), drives towards celebration of earthly elements themselves as historical embodiments of life. In effect, our heaven directs us back to earth to recognize and cherish the intersubjective there.[3] Here, then, seven sacraments of the New Earth Order:

The Sacrament of Earth. In the NEO, the earth itself is the fundamental sacrament. Without the earth, life is impossible. Its (baptismal) water, soil, air, and sunlight fire elicit veneration and the subordination of other goals to their preservation. These created elements embody the sacramentality of creation, which in so many religious traditions is *the* sign par excellence of God's life and immanence. For centuries, belief in the creation-mediated presence of God enjoyed prominence in Judeo-Christianity too, before Augustianian influence centralized Manichean beliefs about creation's corruption.

The Sacrament of Reparations. The New International Economic Order (NIEO), which, as we saw, was first proposed by Third World nations in April 1974, represents the New Earth model's sacrament of reconciliation. It calls for repentance and amendment not only in the developed countries but also among the elite and military of the underdeveloped countries. The extent of the reparation due the world's majority was indicated at a meeting of Third World Theologians who met in Sri Lanka in 1992. In response to Western bills for Third World debt, and in the spirit of biblical Jubilee, they proposed billing the Western Powers for "services (unwillingly) rendered" over the last half millennium. As reported by Joan Chittister:

> They intend to assess the value, interest added, of all the resources and labor
> and products taken from Third World countries in the colonial past in order
> to enrich the West. Think of it this way: They're going to send a bill for the

gold that was taken from the Americas with no recompense to them. They're going to send us a bill for the wages of black slaves that built the cotton industry in the United States. They're going to send us a bill for the oil and the bauxite and the titanium and the pineapples and the rice and the silk that has been drained out of hands of their children into the coffers of our own.They're going to send us bills for backpay for services rendered. They're going to send us a bill for rent and lease and property losses to Western governments and industries that simply appropriated their lands for our comfort and profit. They're going to send us a bill to cover the losses incurred through unfair trade policies that took their products at unfair prices and then charged them First World prices for First World imports. They're going to send us a bill for the relocation of people who have been starved out of their homes by Western policies and then denied immigration rights to the countries who enjoy the fruits of their exploitation. Because we've sent them our bill, they're going to send us theirs. Then we'll see who owes whom for what. Think about it awhile. Ask yourself what the Third World debt is really about. It's a great idea, isn't it? I mean, how else do you make a capitalist people understand the weight of their foot on the neck of another if you don't charge them for parking there? (17)

The Sacrament of Food. Penitential reparations would be used to provide shelter, clothing, and especially food -- the foundations of human life. Without these necessities of life, so closely connected with biblical traditions and with the elements of holy banquet, human beings cannot exist. In fact, lack of food in a world whose principal agricultural problem is food surplus represents the most devastating indictment of the reigning world order. In relation to that system, hunger transforms the famished into witnesses against the reigning system. As Dussel points out:

[T]he hunger of the oppressed, of the poor is a fruit of an unjust system. It shows that the oppressed person has no place in the system. The person in question is missing something; he or she is a non-being in the world. But fundamentally, structurally satisfying the hunger of the oppressed would entail the radical change of the system. As such, then, hunger is most subversive of the system. (48)

The Sacrament of Work. Vidales adds that the system cannot be subverted by handouts -- not by crumbs from the tables of the rich reluctantly allowed to fall in the direction of the poor. Instead (and here we arrive at the "sacrament" of spiritual adulthood) food, shelter, and clothing must be linked to schooling, to technology appropriate to local conditions, and especially to dignified work. This last element is absolutely crucial:

[T]he concept of "basic necessities" is indissolubly linked to the right to work, i.e. to stable employment and to an adequate salary allowing a just distribution of products to everyone. From this viewpoint, basic necessities are those which can and must be satisfied by means of just remuneration for employment available to everyone who has attained working age. In other words, the key to the satisfaction of basic necessities is full employment. (Vidales, *Teologia e imperio* 87-88)

The Sacrament of Children . As we have seen, children are the chief victims of World War III. From the perspective of moral imagination, they are outward signs of the grace to be obtained by overcoming their marginalization. More than any other expression, the advent of children constitutes the eruption of the new and of the real and possible future. Their openness personally embodies a type of utopian criticism that calls into question any order which threatens their existence. The mere presence of children represents a threat to given orders, as we see in the Oedipus myth. According to Alice Miller, children's inherent threat explains why cultures must subdue their offspring before the young have the chance to unleash their revolutionary potential (241). In other words, the newborn are exterior to the given, the organized, the traditional -- to the market. In that capacity, they occupy a vantage point from which to criticize what is; they are embodiments of a transcendent intersubjectivity (Dussel 96).

The Sacrament of Democracy. According to Dussel, children's potential for the new bears fruit in what he terms "the political moment" of human intersubjectivity. This brings us to the NEO's equivalent of ordination -- the exercise of leadership within the community. Here the fostering of genuine democracy is central. In fact, Moore-Lappé and Collins observe that more than anything else, democracy's absence in the Third World is responsible for widespread hunger there.

> Wherever people have been made hungry, power is in the hands of those unaccountable to their people. These antidemocratic governments answer only to elites, lavishing them with credit, subsidies, and other assistance. To protect the privileges of the wealthy minority, they increasingly funnel public resources toward the military. With increasing brutality, such governments fight any reform that would make control over food-producing resources more equitable. (6)

Accountability in the political realm has two dimensions. One is participation by the majority in their country's political life. This entails the fostering of grassroots organizations -- labor unions, women's organizations, youth groups, farming cooperatives and the like -- the very type of communities discouraged, undermined, and persecuted in the New World Order. Secondly, democratic accountability requires a strong central government with the interests of the majority at heart. Such governments are necessary to introduce the regulation of the market, which is essential to the recovery of the Two-thirds World.

The Sacrament of the Healing Human Body . The final "sacrament" of the humane earth order (evoked by consideration of medieval "extreme unction") is the regenerative human body itself. In terms of intersubjective fullness of life, the point here is to reidentify health-care with ancient practices of mutuality, self-treatment and harmony with nature rather than with a commodity to be purchased from those who control high-tech hospitals. As Ivan Illich argues, much of the technology involved in modern medicine is unproductive, counterproductive, and "iatrogenic" -- it often actually causes sickness.[4]

Accepting the regenerative powers of the body would detechnologize the practice of medicine, restoring to the healing process its necessarily intersubjective character and removing health care from monopoly by professionals and technicians. Illich is not alone in presenting this ideal. In 1975 the World Health Organization (WHO) advocated the deprofessionalization of primary health care as the single most important step in raising national health levels (224). Illich adds:

> If priority were given to equity in poor countries and service limited to the basics of effective medicine, entire populations would be encouraged to share in the demedicalization of modern health care and to develop the skills and confidence for self-care, thus protecting their countries from social iatrogenic disease. (237)

Antisacramentals

We do not need to devote much space to sacramentals in the Human Intersubjectivity Model. There are myriad "occasional helps" that can and do stimulate the church militant and suffering to perform "acts of virtue" aimed at reversing the sacrificial nature of the modern world order. These include the examples of "wholly" people, art, music, and the "great books" derived from revolutionary movements, East and West, North and South--not excluding those of the United States. The modern world's own humanist traditions, Marxism among them, suggest other sacramentals as do tribal faiths, feminist spiritualities and environmental movements. Sacramentals motivating action on behalf of liberation, justice and equality also derive from the world's great religions -- not least from the Judeo-Christian tradition, including reinterpreted medieval sacramentals. For instance, in these days of environmental degradation "holy water" might carry unexpected meaning.

But perhaps the most powerful material incentives to work on behalf of a New Earth Order are supplied by the underside of each "sacrament" described above. These might be understood as countersigns of life - as "antisacramentals." The degraded earth we have just mentioned--polluted oceans, water tables, and air, the New World Order and Free Trade Agreements themselves, statistics about the world's hungry, about unemployment, infant mortality, ratios of doctors to patients, and about population growth-- are relevant here. Even more so is the statistic-reflecting images, which, in the postmodern New World Order, flood the media. Representations of the starving are intended to pull people's heartstrings toward acts of charity. However, for those acquainted with New World Order spirituality and its alternative NEO paradigm, such images can stimulate action for justice.

The Realm of Suffering

The New Earth model reverses the G7 order's realms of the militant and suffering. The market system has the world's poor paying the price for a poverty inflicted on them by the 500 years of exploitation reviewed in Chapter 3. As Joan Chittister indicated, the developed world ironically bills the world it has actively underdeveloped -- apparently for the privilege of being raped by colonial and neocolonial regimes. Instead, the model at hand places the burden of paying for past sins squarely on the shoulders of those who have consumed a "free lunch" since the beginning of the sixteenth century. The burden is placed on our shoulders. And so we enter purgatory.

To the minds of many living in what amounts to the lap of luxury, the entry brings to mind the sign over Dante's hell: "Abandon hope all you who enter here." Indeed, the distinction between purgatory and hell is blurred for us. Developed world cultures have lost the Christian tradition's notion of *self*-sacrifice for the common good (vs. sacrifice of *the other* for the good of "the greatest number"). Hence if we change the world as it is, we are assured the "worst possible" world is at hand. The "civilization" which Europe has brought to the "backward" countries of the South will be overwhelmed and suffocated by barbarians.

In contrast, the NEO model insists that the developed world must cut back on consumption, redistribute resources, set full employment and environmental protection ahead of economic growth, move toward economic self-reliance, pay fair prices for foreign labor and resources, adopt new standards to measure economic prosperity; the list goes on and seems daunting indeed. The suggestion is, however, that like the medieval purgatory, our "worst possible" world is instead a place of salvation -- an antechamber to a better world -- the only *possible* world. The remaining alternative in the post-Cold War era is the hell of market totalitarianism with its attendant carnage and environmental devastation.

As Figure 7 indicates, the purgatorial process has three main dimensions leading to a fourth over-all purpose:

1. Elimination of false needs, wants, and ideas of happiness.

2. Acceptance of truth. This is revealed in the history and systemic analysis that proceeds from the Third World, and which we have tried to capture in our study. We in the North are an extreme minority. We consume far more than our share of the globe's resources. We have built our way of life on the backs of those we have colonized and neocolonized. Politically this realization must lead to a reordering of international political power -- according, by the way, to our own cherished democratic principles. This means giving proportional representation to the world's majority in decisions that affect them directly. Again, this now seems an impossible goal. It is impossible in the same sense that the fall of communism, the end of the Cold War, and the transition to majority rule in South Africa seemed a few years ago.

3. Reparation for the past. Requirements here are indicated by the two arrows in Figure 7 leading from purgatory to the realm of the militant. They include transfer of capital, technology, and training. Once again, the already quoted remarks of Joan Chittister are pertinent.

4. Humanization. Based on the right to full employment, humanization requires: (a) the satisfaction of human necessities (including spiritual and cultural needs); (b) active participation in political and social life, and (c) a degree of economic and social order sustainable within a healthy natural environment. The goal of meeting these requirements determines the degree to which elements of

given economic systems must become public property and the degree to which economies require planning (*Democracia* 58).

The Realm of the Lost

The realm of the lost in the New Earth model partially agrees with the spirit of the New World Order model. Figure 7 recognizes the inviability of the "perfect planning" utopian framework espoused by the Soviet Union and critiqued by Hinkelammert in his *Crítica a la razón utópica* (123-156). At the same time, figure 7 consigns to hell the New World Order's "perfect competition" horizon. This, no doubt, renders the New Earth framework unacceptable to those who see the present order as "without alternative" and as the best of all possible postmodern worlds. However, the reasons for rejecting this "inevitable" order have already been explained; they are the very matter of the chapters that have preceded this one. With those arguments in mind, the conceptual spirituality indicated in Figure 7 commits to eternal perdition the guiding utopian concept behind the New Order and its cult of free markets, free enterprise zones, free trade agreements, and free global economy. Along with that commitment, it rejects as eternally lost allied concepts of neocolonialism, modernism (with its implicit faith in automatic progress), fascism (especially as it appears in Third World "National Security States"), undifferentiated growth, postmodernism in its necrophilic form, consumerism, planned obsolescence, "trickle-down" economics, "throw away" society, nuclear war, and World War III.

Above all, the antiutopian utopia of the New World Order finds its place in hell. As Hinkelammert points out, the (impossible) utopia of New World Order postmodernism desires a world without utopias. It would eliminate utopian thinking from the human race by discrediting such thinking entirely. But the project, of course, is self-contradictory on at least two counts. To begin with, a world without utopias is itself utopian. Human beings are by all accounts, inherently imaginative; their thinking cannot be forever confined to the parameters of the given. Even more to the point (and secondly), the New World Order's "antiutopian utopia" refuses to recognize the utopian ideals central to the New World Order's "perfect competition" model. As already explained, eliminating utopian thinking would eradicate Free Market theory itself. All of this amounts to a denial of "moral imagination," which, we are arguing, is the necessary antidote to the horrors of World War III. Figure 7 says to hell with all unimaginative thinking of the (hypocritically) antiutopian kind. [5]

THE PRACTICE OF CRITICALLY UTOPIAN SPIRITUALITY

Grasping the continuities and discontinuities between the structures we have reviewed here is important for anyone wishing to assume an active, intelligent posture before our changing world. Even more important, clear awareness of where we are coming from will help direct our own efforts at peacemaking and political education. Those directions begin not merely with a conscious conceptual spirituality, but with a world vision grounded in history and the kind of structural analysis we find in the work of Third World scholars, which we have tried to reflect. This means possessing and communicating historical consciousness and global awareness characterized by the exercise of "moral imagination." Practically speaking, the exercise of moral imagination in this sense should affect peace educators and activists on at least four levels-- those of commitments and policy directions, alliances and strategies.

Commitments and Policy Directions

First off, each of us must decide where we stand in relation to the conceptual spiritualities and "shadows" we have examined to this point. Indecision here will keep our activism confused and directionless. We will lurch from issue to issue, from crisis to crisis, from situation to situation, randomly and arbitrarily focused without any coherent vision of the world.

Defining Identities

On the one hand, clarifying our own conceptual spiritualities entails defining our identities. Are we patriotic "Americans" who basically support "our" country's institutions and policies? Are we liberals, who think the world's needed changes can take place within existing political and socioeconomic frameworks? Do we imagine pseudoleaders are the problem; that they have caused us to stray from cherished historical traditions? Will locating the right set of elected officials somehow alleviate the problems we have summarized under the general heading "World War III"?

Or, alternatively, are we radicals in the sense of people who, on the basis of deep historical, structural, and spiritual analyses have decided that the leaders of the world's rich nations, like the system they serve, are pathogenic? Are we ready to conclude that the system of free market totalitarianism has always exploited the world's poor -- that it has created our planet's problems and is therefore incapable of solving them in an unregulated way? Can we decide that no matter who is in charge, no matter how great their goodwill or how deep their religious faith, the problems we have been describing will never be ameliorated in any significant way because the frame of reference our leaders use is hopelessly utopian, deeply flawed and even idolatrous?

It is indispensable to answer such hard questions of personal and group spirituality if we hope to end World War III. Deciding them will focus and change the activities of our grassroots organizations and will alter teaching content and methods. We must decide whose side we are on. Most of us resist defining our commitments, even provisionally. But, of course, that decision not to decide is in itself a political choice. It is a confirmation of the status quo -- of the world war against the poor.

The Necessary Political Direction

Say, then, that we decide that World War III is a reality, and that countries like our own are its perpetrators. Say we choose to think more historically and structurally. Say we also conclude that the Judeo-Christian tradition and that of the West in general has come to represent an oppressive spirituality of destruction. What if we recognize the historical facts and their demonstration of free market capitalism's complete failure, its systematic destruction of its own human and environmental bases, the disastrous consequences of its system of debt and of its version of economic "development"? What if, in short, we recognize our location in something like Plato's cave, and decide to escape, viewing the world through the prism of moral imagination and of intersubjective spirituality? What practical directions would that yield in terms of rebuilding our political projects and of informing our teaching? We believe moral imagination sends us along the following paths chosen under the conviction that the fates of the First and Third Worlds are inextricably linked.

• Our overall goal must be the ecological well-being of all. Dignified lives for actually existing human beings must be the measure of policy. No visions of future utopias (market or otherwise) can justify the sacrifice of a single living human being. As the U.S. founding fathers once claimed for another set of propositions, these are self-evident truths.

• It is similarly self-evident that policies that destroy the environment on which human life and economic systems depend must be rejected. Here we must come to the conclusion that the constantly resurfacing choice between jobs and environment -- between the spotted owl, snail darter, clean air, clean water on the one hand, and jobs, economic growth, overwhelming pollution, and toxic waste on the other -- should not be glossed over. The choice *is* between the environment and jobs if we leave it to a totalitarian Free Market to structure our lives. We cannot have it both ways. The reiterated dilemma -- economic well-being or the environment -- is an indication of the sickness of our system, including its hopeless utopian and necrophilic character. We suggest the system's priorities must be changed to embrace both the full employment necessary to economic prosperity and the environmental safeguards required to preserve the natural environment. By itself, the free market system cannot possibly deliver here.

• This means that unregulated free marketism must be set aside as a fetish. As we have seen repeatedly, neoliberalism represents an updated worldwide version of laissez-faire thinking with all the disastrous consequences Dickens and others made so evident in the nineteenth century. As we saw in our introduction and in Chapter 3, millions of economic decisions taken each minute and driven by ultimately short-term profit considerations with little and/or merely "voluntary" concern for their environmental impact, inevitably destroy the ecosphere. The "free" market is not a self-evident good either for human beings or for the planet in general. On the contrary, without regulation it represents a hopelessly utopian, unrealistic, necrophilic, and pie-in-the-sky arrangement.

• Only strict control guided by global vision can save the environment and the human lives that are sacrificed each day to the sacred cow of free marketism. As we saw in Chapter 2, controls must restrain naturally destructive market mechanisms; their purpose cannot be to make the market operate more efficiently merely in terms of capital accumulation. In other words, "government regulation" is not a self-evident evil. It is now more necessary than ever.

• Government regulation is especially imperative in the Third World where economies are weak and where there is very little tradition of "civil society" -- that is of government by the nonelite. Third World parliaments, congresses and national assemblies must therefore take decisions based on the welfare of the least well-off -- in favor of the majority of their citizens. For those without power from money and friends in high places, representative government is a main source of protection of their jobs, families, health, education, and futures. President Reagan was wrong when he said, "We don't have a problem with government; government *is* the problem." Government of the people, by the people and for the people may be *the* problem for the rich; its absence is the problem for the poor and for ordinary citizens everywhere, but especially in the Third World.

> At this time in history, particularly in the Third World, we need strong states because it is only strong states that can undertake massive social reform such as land reform, and it is only strong states that can negotiate with international capitalism. And I am not referring here to the kind of back scratching with the IMF that some leaders in the South engage in. The challenge for those of us in the South is to come up with governments that have a nationalistic and popular base strong enough to enable them to negotiate. (Rakamora 80)

• Accordingly, governing bodies in economically underdeveloped countries must be allowed to protect their comparatively weak local industries and producers from competition with international giants. That was actually the path followed by capitalism's "success stories" such as Singapore, South Korea and Taiwan (Muzaffar 82). "Protectionism," in other words, is not a four-letter word.

> [I]f multinational corporations have the right to trade without any tariffs imposed on their products or the right to invest in the Third World countries without any conditions imposed on their investments, we can predict that the Third World countries which are already very much marginalised in the world economy, will be even more marginalised. In their domestic sphere, where they have a substantial share of the domestic economy and product, Third World countries will also become marginalised by the transnational companies. (Khor 21)

• All of this means that policies of "structural adjustment" must be rejected. As we have seen, the phrase refers to the integration of Third World economies into a global arrangement where they compete with giant First World corporations. Structural adjustment entails "privatization" of national industries and services and the consequent reduction of government assistance to society's least well-off (again, the majority in the Third World). Structural adjustment also involves government intervention in the economy to make market mechanisms function more efficiently in terms of capital accumulation rather than income distribution. This only widens the gap between the super rich and the abysmally poor.

• Similarly, debtor cartels must be supported. Recognizing the largely fictitious nature of Third World external debt, it is important not to be fooled by plans to refinance, restructure, partially "forgive," or otherwise stop short of completely invalidating that debt. Lesser measures are largely public relations ploys on the part of the banking industry and its government representatives both in the First and Third Worlds. Supporting debtors' cartels and other measures on behalf of working people in the Third World benefits First World workers. It is part of resisting the New World Order process of "downward harmonization" that would serve the interests of international business by driving First World wages toward the level of their weaker foreign competitors. The process is already well under way -- to the great detriment of workers in the developed world.

> Workers in the North would be the beneficiaries of efforts to end austerity and reject low-wage export-oriented policies in the South. (Brecher and Costello 75)

• In other words, working people in the North should support worldwide "upward harmonization." This means adopting the best features of the quality of life (vs. the quantity of consumption) of the world's most adequately remunerated working people as the benchmark for working people everywhere.

> Harmonization upward is both a means and an ultimate goal. It is a means to improving the lives of those whose conditions are harmonized upwards and to reducing their downward pull on the conditions of others. Fully realized, it means a life of greater quality and equality for all. (74)

• Upward harmonization entails clarification of standards for quality of life. Obviously, First World, and especially U.S. levels of consumption are neither universalizable nor (given their impact on the environment) desirable. Opposite convictions, however, constitute the unspoken premises of mainstream rhetoric about economic growth and its necessity. Undifferentiated goals of simple "economic growth" are ultimately self-destructive. The exercise of moral imagination demands the rejection of such suicidal, wildly utopian spirituality. As Stierle has indicated, the standard G.N.P. measurement is essentially deceptive. New indices of national welfare must be adopted which centralize the very elements considered "externalities" in traditional market models--the environment, the unpaid work of homemakers, the informal economy, and so forth.

Alliances and Strategies

Coming to grips with a conceptual spirituality for peacemakers dictates new alliances and strategies for establishing and maintaining them. The needed changes will not come directly from the formal political process -- not from elected leaders whose mindsets invariably reflect a New World Order spirituality totally lacking moral imagination. Energies, we judge, are better placed in people's movements independent of government. The helpful grassroots alliances at home are familiar. They include the Rainbow Coalition and "Green" parties and organizations of various shades. But to serve a New Earth Order, alliances must stretch beyond our borders. Their starting conviction should be that we have to act globally -- internationally -- to solve our problems at home.

> We have learned to reverse the old slogan, "Think Globally, Act Locally." We learned you have to act globally to succeed locally -- you have to go to Brussels to save your farm in Texas. It was really important for farmers in different parts of the world to see their common circumstances and to develop win/win approaches, rather than being played off against each other. (Mark Ritchie, quoted in Brecher and Costello 75)

"Win/win" strategies based on leaving our "cave" epitomize the exercise of moral imagination. It may well entail locating our false competitors, acquainting ourselves with their living conditions and the goals, strategies, and programs of their working people and grassroots organizations. Working people in Berea, Kentucky, for instance, might directly inform themselves of the conditions of their counterparts employed by industries with installations both in Berea and in Mexico, Taiwan, or Malaysia. Thus Kentuckians might initiate correspondence with Mexican "people's organizations," perhaps arrange exchanges of delegations, and formalize relationships in terms of "sister" cities, communities, or workplaces -- all with the goal of educating themselves in the direction of harmonization upward.

But it is not enough to acquaint one's community with the conditions of people actually employed in sister situations -- especially when those with jobs may represent the privileged ones in contexts characterized by widespread unemployment. Grassroots relationships of dialog are also necessary with those displaced by multinational presence in Third World settings. These too are often organized in activist groups with their own analysis, goals, and strategies.

The vision here is of a one-world strategy for workers. But in the New World Order characterized by cooperative imperialism and harmonization downward, strategies must differ from similar movements in the past.

> Of course, a global strategy cannot be identical to the national labour strategies of the past. There are greater variations in culture, economic conditions, political jurisdiction, and power structures across different countries in the world than within any one country. New technologies, changing forms of economic organization, and expanded emphasis on such concerns as environmental protection and gender equality mean that all labour strategy, local and national as well as transnational, will be different

from the past. To pursue transnational cooperation, labour movements will often have to function far more independently of their national governments, work more closely with allies, and encourage rather than impede the networking activities of their own rank and file. Nonetheless, at the core of a one-world strategy for labour must lie the traditional labour orientation toward harmonizing conditions upward so that they do not instead harmonize downward. (Brecher and Costello 73)

Pressuring Multinationals

Similarly, the present World Order calls for new kinds of pressures on multinationals with installations in the Third World and on institutions such as universities, which invest heavily in such corporations. Efforts to condition investment of university endowments on observance of "The Sullivan Principles," in the case of South Africa, offer a model in a radically different global context.

In a general way, the People's Plan for the twenty-first century (PP21) provides guidance for such international cooperation among pressure groups. Launched in Minamata, Japan, in 1989, PP21 designated five themes of special concern for transborder focus. The last one has been the special concern of the present study.

> (1) Humankind and Nature - From destruction to harmony;
> (2) Liberation from Oppression - Creating new society and culture;
> (3) Overcoming Rule by the Strong- Changing the state and changing international relations;
> (4) Taking Back the Economy - From a relationship between things to a relationship between human beings; and
> (5) For a Common Future - Ethics and spirituality for people's solidarity. (Christian Conference 72)

Along these lines, the case of Mexico's "maquiladoras" yields a concrete example both of international cooperation between workers on both sides of the border, and of standards to which transnationals can be held, to impede the process of downward harmonization. "Maquiladoras" is the name given to the nearly 2,000 multinational factories located along the U.S.-Mexican border. Nearly half a million Mexican workers are employed there working for wages one-tenth those paid for similar work in the United States. Most of the workers involved are women. All live in what the *Wall Street Journal* termed "abysmal living conditions and environmental degradation" (quoted in Brecher and Costello 74).

Recognizing the links between such conditions and those of U.S. working people, groups from the United States have allied themselves with Mexican worker organizations to form the Maquiladora Coalition. They apply pressure at stockholder meetings to persuade multinationals to observe standards of conduct aimed at reversing the dynamic of harmonization downward.

The code spells out provisions for environmental protection, such as disclosure of all toxic chemical discharges, use of state-of-the-art environmental control technologies, and return of all hazardous materials to the country of origin. It requires that workers be notified of hazardous materials and that worker-management health and safety commissions be established. It bans employment discrimination based on sex, age, race, religious creed, or political beliefs. It requires equal pay for equal work, protects workers' right to organize, and demands disciplinary measures against sexual harassment. It discourages barrack style living arrangements, demands regular inspection of existing barracks by an internationally recognized human rights organization, and calls for contributions to trust funds for infrastructure improvements in maquiladora communities. The code incorporates many labour and environmental standards already required by Mexican law but poorly enforced in the maquiladoras. (75)

This project illustrates what is meant by "harmonization upward." The point is not to eliminate the maquiladora industries, but rather, to make the hard-won labor standards in the United States and other economically overdeveloped countries applicable throughout the world. The hope is that this will not only eliminate Third World "abysmal living conditions and environmental degradation," it will discourage capital flight to underdeveloped countries, thus saving jobs at home as well.

In summary, then, Brecher and Costello list the fronts on which the battle against harmonization downward at the hands of transnational corporations (TNCs) is fought. They include:

transnational solidarity and mutual aid among workers and their allies; making the protection of labour rights a condition of international trade, investment, and lending; international corporate campaigns to force TNCs to comply with codes of conduct; challenges to the ruinous "structural adjustment" policies of the World Bank, International Monetary Fund, and other international financial institutions; national economic strategies based on grassroots economic development, expanding employment, rising wages; and resistance to the use of international "free trade" agreements to impose worldwide harmonization downward. All involve transnational coalitions of people's organizations helping themselves by helping each other. (74)

CONCLUSION

These, then, are the new directions for peace activists and educators. The vectors emerge from a conceptual spirituality guided by moral imagination. Movement verges away from the shadows of isolationism, "Free Trade," and "Market Totalitarianism," along with their policies of structural adjustment, debt rescheduling, and high or low-intensity conflict -- military or financial. New paths lead toward North/South solidarity, toward recuperation of the Judeo-Christian tradition of community concern and selflessness, toward recovery as well of the West's humanistic tradition. But in all cases, situations must be judged and texts must be re-read from the viewpoint of the victims of World War III.

That viewpoint leaves us with conceptual conclusions that sound as common sense and obvious as the little boy crying out, "The emperor is naked!" Real capitalism is a clearly bankrupt system; it has created far more misery than its disastrously failed "real socialist" counterpart. Only starry-eyed utopians believe that the unaided market can solve the very problems it has created over the last 500 years. Feasible solutions must put people and the welfare of the planet ahead of all institutions, including the Free Market.   Various combinations of economic planning and market must be implemented throughout the world. A thousand flowers must be allowed to bloom. Market totalitarianism is as unacceptable as any other form. Speaking both morally and practically (in terms of human and environmental survival), the rich and powerful cannot continue to force their doomsday system on the world. Planning must protect the natural environment and ensure dignified jobs for everyone. Internationally, reparations are due from the economically developed world to the Two-thirds World, which the rich have plundered for their own benefit. Vast transfers of capital are required. All debts must be forgiven. Locally, work, not welfare or "foreign aid," must provide adequate income for everyone as the ticket to a healthy diet, respectable shelter, and decent clothing. Providing such work involves disobedience to "technological imperatives," and adoption of technologies appropriate to the goal of full employment. Only when that goal has been reached is it morally possible to employ "labor saving" technology or to plan for economic growth in favor of differentiating wealth. All of this is humanly possible now -- infinitely more so than the creation of a humane and healthy world or of a sustainable global economy through free markets and trade.

To these conclusions, market utopians will reply: "Impossible!" "Unrealistic!" "Utopian!" We can think of no better reply than Jonathan Schell's observation relative to nuclear war but equally pertinent to the topic at hand:

> Realism is the title given to beliefs whose most notable characteristic is their failure to recognize the chief reality of the age, the pit into which our species threatens to jump; "utopian" is the term of scorn for any plan that shows serious promise of enabling the species to keep from killing itself (if it is "utopian" to want to survive, then it must be "realistic" to be dead); and the political arrangements that keep us on the edge of annihilation are deemed "moderate," and are found to be "respectable," whereas new arrangements, which might enable us to draw a few steps back from the brink, are called "extreme" or "radical." With such fear-filled *thought-stopping* epithets as these, the upholders of the status quo defend the anachronistic structures of their thinking, and seek to block the *revolution in thought* and in action which is necessary if [hu]mankind is to go on living. (Schell 161, italics added)

It is time we exit the cave!

NOTES

1. Franz Hinkelammert suggests that all conceptual spiritualities have their notions of heaven and hell. In *Democracy and Totalitarianism*, he examines traditional ideas of the Christian afterlife. These, he points out, took the earth as their starting point, and in a sense, as their end point too, since the various models effectively legitimate given social formations in relation to eternity (*Democracia* 244). Such legitimation was the function of all celestial imaginings down through the ages. In other words, heaven as well as earth has a history. Thus the concept of heaven was really the medieval era's imaginative depiction of the perfectly full human life and an indication of how to get from here to there (241). It reflected the conceptual spirituality of the late premodern period rather than the vision of the "new heaven and the new earth" found in the first century's Book of Revelation. As Hinkelammert puts it, "The medieval heaven is a feudal heaven. All humans have souls, but souls are feudally arranged in hierarchical order. Heaven itself resembles a hierarchically-ordered feudal court with God as king over all, followed by the various clerical ranks, the aristocrats and ordinary folk who surround the court." (*Democrácia* 242)

Since earthly changes invariably required their counterparts in heaven, Hinkelammert argues, those who wished to change the earth had to alter the concept of heaven as well. Martin Luther found it necessary to alter drastically his followers' understandings of all dimensions of the afterlife. His denial of the Blessed Virgin's privileged place and elimination of canonized saints status expressed not only a Christocentric and biblical theology but the democratic movements of his time as well. Thus "heaven ceased being a feudal court and was transformed into a heaven of souls all of which enjoyed equal happiness" (243). Even Marxist understandings of socialism and communism had to articulate anew as-yet-unrealized concepts of humankind's final destiny -- of fullness of life. The bourgeois had to do the same establishing their vision of the perfect society in terms of perfect market competition and its alleged universally beneficial consequences (241).

2. Naively, market theorists refuse to recognize their own utopianism. However, as Hinkelammert indicates, all exercises of politics as "the art of the possible" inevitably employ utopian concepts (*Critica* 21). Politics in market societies is no different. It must use ideas of the best conceivable world and of the worst conceivable world, of the best possible world and the worst possible world. None of these concepts is empirical. All of them, however, represent necessary horizons towards which "the art of the possible" is directed. Utopian concepts become destructive, however, when their necessary function as guidelines is forgotten -- when the impossibilities of their undiluted historical implementation are ignored. Such blissfully utopian ignorance is embedded precisely in contemporary Free Market rhetoric.

Needless to say, defenders of the market system have traditionally recognized the dangers of utopian thought relative to socialism. In fact, they actively crusade against all utopias (i.e., against human hope, especially for the dispossessed). Karl Popper, for instance, points out that socialists who wish to create heaven on earth inevitably produce hell (167-68). Apart from validating our point about the continued relevance of medieval concepts of afterlife, Popper's observation is well taken. We agree that attempts to implement socialist ideals of "perfect planning" ended in disasters well known to all. However, Popper's point ignores the utopian nature of the "realistic" capitalism he contrasts with socialist utopias. Consequently, he fails to see that attempts to incarnate his theory's Free Market "heaven" create hell for the world's majority. Or if he does see hell fire in the Two-thirds World, he's willing (a priori) to accept inferno for those others as their "best possible" situation. Hinkelammert is among the few to perceive this undeniable truth and courageously declare it.

3. What follows is a very exploratory attempt to sketch a re-visioned sacramental system in the spirit of our entire inquiry. It has tried to "imagine the real" - i.e. to move from abstract, falsely spiritual worlds to the concrete, material reality which the Two-thirds World experiences as so oppressive. This is the world, we reiterate, with which critical thinking must become acquainted. In the context of sacramentality, we recall the directions of DEI scholar, José Hinajosa already quoted on p. 50:

> Considering the sacraments from a philosophical point of view leads us to discover the sacred in the material, not as an intent -- valid for Christians -- to encounter the presence of God in everything, but as the necessity to value things themselves and to discover their capacity to communicate something more and different from what appears on the surface. A sacrament thus understood is a sign of something else. As Leonardo Boff puts it: "The human world, even the material and technical is never only material and technical; it is symbolic and loaded with meaning." (11)

4. Intersubjective healing in the context of critical utopia involves recognizing that much sickness also finds human causes outside the medical model. Sickness, in other words, is often "antisacramental"; it is a countersign of life, potentially indicating the socioeconomic arrangements responsible for disease (Illich, *Medical Nemesis* 131). In some ways, then, true healing involves rejecting the socially anesthetizing effect of modern hospitals and medicine, which enable people to cope with oppressive social formations rather than change them.

> As long as disease is something that takes possession of people, something they "catch" they can be discharged from any political responsibility for having collaborated in increasing the sickening stress of high-intensity industry. An advanced industrial sociey is sick-making because it disables people to cope with their environment and, when they break down, it substitutes a "clinical" prosthesis for the broken *relationships*. People would rebel against such an environment if medicine did not explain their biological disorientation as a defect in their health, rather than as a defect in the way of life which is imposed on them or which they impose on themselves. The assurance of personal political innocence that a diagnosis offers the patient serves as a hygienic mask that justifies further subjection to production and consumption. (165)

5. The theological "story" supporting the New Earth Order departs from the Augustinian, Genesis-based narrative that undergirded the medieval "Communion of Saints" model. Even more so does it reject the basically Deist theology implied in New World Order thinking. Instead, the NEO model finds narrative support in the Exodus traditions, which, as we saw in Chapter 5, are authentically central to biblical faith, reflecting what we called the "moral imagination of God." The reflection is vital to theologies of liberation and runs as follows:

> Historically speaking, Israel's God first revealed divine power by liberating a group of slaves from Egypt.

Yahweh gave Israel a covenant to form a just community where widows, orphans, slaves and foreigners were specially protected.

Israel's leaders often broke the covenant oppressing the very people the Covenant centralized as God's own.

Unfaithful leaders were denounced by prophets who called them to task.

Repeatedly, Israel itself was victimized by surrounding empires (Assyria, Babylonia, Persia, Greece, Rome . . .)

In such circumstances, prophets announced a new future kingdom.

Jesus appeared in the tradition of the prophets, denouncing covenant infidelity and announcing a new future for the faithful.

He proclaimed a "Kingdom" -- the reign of God where a New Covenant would be in force.

He raised the hopes of the poor.

He evoked the ire of the Jewish and Roman authorities.

An alliance of temple and empire executed him.

His followers became convinced he was raised from the dead.

They formed a kingdom community of faith sharing all things in common and showing special concern for the poor rather than for institutions like the temple and its law.

Baptism was a sign of commitment to that New Covenant community where written expressions of God's law were understood as subordinate to human welfare.

Christians hoped for the *coming* of God's kingdom, for a new heaven and a new earth.

Christians today inherit this people-centered faith.

Questions of the afterlife are best left in God's hands.

WORKS CITED

Brecher, Jeremy, and Tim Costello. "People's Transnational Coalition."*Third World War*. Hong Kong: CCA - International Affairs, 1991, 73-78.

Chittister, Joan. "Third World poor to send bill for all we owe them." *The National Catholic Reporter* (14 May 1993): 17.

Christian Conference of Asia, International Affairs. *Third World War*. Hong Kong: CCA - International Affairs, 1991.

Dussel, Enrique. *Filosofia da Libertação*. São Paulo, Brazil: Edições Loyola, 1977. English translation: *Philosophy of Liberation*. New York: Orbis Books, 1985.

Hinajosa, José Francisco G. "Esta Viva La Naturaleza?"*Pasos* 38, (Nov./Dec.1991): 1-12.

Hinkelammert, Franz J. *Crítica a la razón utópica*. San José, Costa Rica: Editorial DEI, 1984.

_____. *Democracia y totalitarismo*. San José, Costa Rica: Editorial DEI, 1987.

_____. "Nuestro proyecto de nueva sociedad en América Latina: el papel regulador del estado y los problemas de la auto-regulación del mercado." *Pasos* 33, (Jan./Feb., 1991): 6-23.

Illich, Ivan. *Deschooling Society* . New York: Harper and Row, 1972.

_____. *Medical Nemesis* . New York: Bantam Books, 1976.

Khor, Martin. "The Recolonisation of the Third World." *Third World War*. Hong Kong: CCA - International Affairs, 1991, 21-24.

Miller, Alice. *For Your Own Good: Hidden Cruelty in Child-Rearing and the Roots of Violence*. New York: Farrar, Straus, Giroux, 1983.

Moore-Lappé, Frances, and Joseph Collins. *World Hunger: Twelve Myths* . New York: Grove Press, 1986.

Muzaffar, Chandra. "Spirituality, Culture and the Struggle for a Future." *Third World War*. Hong Kong: CCA - International Affairs, 1991, 80-85.

Rakamora, Joel. "Rebuilding Anti-Imperialist Solidarity." *Third World War*. Hong Kong: CCA - International Affairs, 1991, 78-80.

Rivage-Seul, Marguerite. "Moral Imagination and the Pedagogy of the Oppressed." *Harvard Education Review*, 57 (May 1987): 153-169.

Schell, Jonathan. *The Fate of the Earth* . New York: Knopf, 1982.

Stirle, Wolfram. "La verdad de la realidad: implicaciones metodológicas en el encuentro de teologia y economia." San José: DEI, Project: Invited Researchers Workshop, 24 Apr. 1992.

Vidales, Raúl. *Teologia e Imperio* . San José, Cost Rica: Editorial DEI, 1991.

_____. *Utopía y liberación: el amanecer del indio* . San José, Costa Rica: Editorial DEI, 1988.

Works Cited

Arenal, Sandra. "They Won't Pay for My Hands." *Trading Freedom: How Free Trade Affects Our Lives, Work and Environment.* John Cavanaugh, John Gershman, Karen Baker, and Gretchen Helmke, eds. San Francisco: The Institute for Food and Development Policy, 1992: 66-67.

Arendt, Hannah. *Totalitarianism.* New York: Harcourt, Brace and World, 1951.

Avrigan, Tony. "Should We Bank on the World Bank?" *The Tico Times* (21 Feb. 1992): 2.

Barney, Gerald O. (Study Director). *The Global 2000 Report to the President: Entering the Twenty-First Century,* vol. 1. Washington: U.S. GPO, 1980.

Berry, Thomas. *The Dream of the Earth.* San Francisco: Sierra Club, 1988.

Bowman, Robert. "The Strategic Defense Initiative." Lecture delivered at the University of Kentucky, Lexington (17 Apr. 1986).

Brecher, Jeremy, and Tim Costello. "People's Transnational Coalition." *Third World War.* Hong Kong: CCA - International Affairs (1991): 73-78.

Bryan, William Jennings. *The World's Most Famous Court Trial: Tennessee Evolution Case.* Cincinnati: National Book Company, 1925.

Buchanan, Keith, and Anne Buchanan. "Global Class War: A Review Article on *A Fate Worse than Debt." Race and Class* 30, no. 3 (Jan.-Mar. 1989): 91-97.

Calvin, Jean. *Calvin: Institutes of the Christian Religion,* edited by John T. McNeill and translated by Ford Battles, vol. 20 and 21: The Library of Christian Classics. Philadelphia: The Westminster Press, 1960.

Carroll, Peter N., and David W. Noble. *The Free and the Unfree: A New History of the United States.* New York: Penguin, 1988.

Chittister, Joan. "Third World poor to send bill for all we owe them." *The National Catholic Reporter* (14 May 1993): 17.

Chomsky, Noam. *Ideology and Power: The Managua Lectures.* Boston: South End Press, 1987.

_____. *Turning the Tide.* Boston: South End Press, 1985.

Christian Conference of Asia, International Affairs. *Third World War*. Hong Kong: CCA - International Affairs, 1991.
Committee of Santa Fe. *A New Inter-American Policy for the Eighties*. Washington, D.C.: Council for Inter-American Security, 1980.
Dante Alighieri. *The Inferno: A verse rendering for the modern reader* by John Ciardi. New York: New American Library, 1954.
Deloria, Vine. *God Is Red*. New York: Grosset and Dunlap, 1973.
Descartes, René. *Descartes Selections*. Ralph M. Eaten, ed. New York: Charles Scribner and Sons, 1927.
de Santa Ana. *La práctica económica como religion*. San José, Costa Rica: Editorial DEI, 1991.
_____. "Sacralizaciones y sacrificios en las prácticas humanas." *De la logica del sacrificio a la realizacion humana*. San José, Costa Rica: REDLA-CPID, (1990): 7-20.
Dierckxsens, Wim. "Hacia el desarollo sostenible? Después de la Perestroika y la guerra del Golfo Pérsico." *Pasos* (Numero Especial Jan. 1991): 5-17.
Drake, Stillman. *Discoveries and Opinions of Galileo*. Translated with an introduction and notes by Stillman Drake. New York: Doubleday Anchor Books, 1957.
Duchrow et al. *Confidential Documents of the 17th Conference of the American Armies*. Mar del Plata, Argentina, 1987.
Dussel, Enrique. *Filosofia da Libertação*. São Paulo, Brazil: Edições Loyola, 1977. English translation: *Philosophy of Liberation*. New York: Orbis Books, 1985.
_____. *Para Uma Ética Da Libertação Latino-Americana*. São Paulo, Brazil: Edições Loyola, 1980.
Galilei, Galileo. "The Letter to the Grand Duchess Christina." *Discoveries and Opinions of Galileo*, 175-216. Translated by Stillman Drake. Garden City, New York: Doubleday Anchor Books, 1957a, 175-216.
_____. "The Starry Messenger." *Discoveries and Opinions of Galileo*: 27-58. Translated by Stillman Drake. Garden City, New York: Doubleday Anchor Books, 1957b, 175-216.
Gallardo, Helio. *Crisis del socialismo historico: ideologías y desafíos*. San José, Costa Rica: Editorial DEI, 1991.
_____. *Elementos de politica en América Latina*. San José, Costa Rica: Editorial DEI, 1989.
_____. "Francis Fukuyama: el final de la historia y el tercer mundo" *Pasos* 28, (March/April 1990): 1-9.
_____. *Fundamentos de formacion política: análisis de coyuntura*. San José, Costa Rica: Editorial DEI, 1990.
Galeano, Eduardo. *Las Venas Abiertas de América Latina*. Mexico: Siglo Veintiuno editores, 1980.
Garostiaga, Xabier. "World Has Become a 'Champagne Glass.'"*The National Catholic Reporter* (27 Jan. 1995): 3.
George, Susan. *A Fate Worse than Debt: The World Financial Crisis and the Poor*. New York: Grove Wedenfeld, 1988.

_____. *How the Other Half Dies*. New Jersey: Rowman and Allanheld, 1977.

Girardi, Giulio. *La conquista de América: con qué derecho?* San José, Costa Rica: Editorial DEI, 1989.

Hedström, Ingemar. *Somos parte de un gran equilibrio*. San José, Costa Rica: Editorial DEI, 1988.

Heilbroner, Robert L. *The Worldly Philosophers*. New York: Simon and Schuster, 1969.

Hinajosa, José Francisco Gómez. "Esta Viva La Naturaleza?" *Pasos* 38 (Nov./Dec. 1991): 1-12.

Hinkelammert, Franz J. "Capitalismo sin alternativas?" *Pasos* 37, (Sept./Oct. 1991): 11-23.

_____. *Crítica a la razón utópica*. San José, Costa Rica: Editorial DEI, 1984.

_____. *Democracia y totalitarismo*. San José, Costa Rica: Editorial DEI, 1987.

_____. *Dialetica del desarrollo desigual*. San José, Costa Rica: Editorial Universitaria Centroamericana, 1983.

_____. "El Mercado como sistema autoregulado y la critica de Marx." (Manuscript made available to "invited researchers," March, 1992, DEI, San José, Costa Rica.)

_____. *La deuda externa de América Latina: el automatismo de la deuda*. San José, Costa Rica: Editorial DEI, 1988.

_____. *La fe de Abraham y el Edipo occidental*. San José, Costa Rica: Editorial DEI, 1991.

_____. *Las Armas Ideologicas da Morte*. San Paulo: Edicões Paulinas, 1983.

_____. "Nuestro proyecto de nueva sociedad en América Latina: el papel regulador del estado y los problemas de la auto-regulación del mercado." *Pasos* 33, (Jan./Feb. 1991): 6-23.

_____. *The Ideological Weapons of Death*. New York: Orbis Books, 1986.

_____. *Sacrificios humanos y sociedad occidental: lucifer y la bestia*. San José, Costa Rica: Editorial DEI, 1991.

Holland, Joe and Peter Henriot, S.J. *Social Analysis: Linking Faith and Justice*. New York: Orbis Books, 1983.

Illich, Ivan. *Deschooling Society*. New York: Harper and Row, 1972.

_____. *Medical Nemesis*. New York: Bantam Books, 1976.

Jaggar, Alison. *Feminist Politics and Human Nature*. Sussex: Rowman and Littlefield Publishers, Inc., 1988.

Johnson, Paul. *A History of Christianity*. New York: Atheneum, 1977.

Kairos Central America. *A Challenge to the Churches of the World*. Managua, Nicaragua: Antonio Valdivieso Center, 1988.

Khor, Martin. "The Recolonisation of the Third World." *Third World War*. Hong Kong: CCA - International Affairs, 1991, 21-24.

Kinzer, Stephen. *Bitter Fruit: the Untold Story of the American Coup in Guatemala*. Garden City, N.Y.: Doubleday, 1982.

Klare, Michael T., and Peter Kornbluh, eds. *Low Intensity Warfare*. New York: Pantheon Books, 1987.

Locke, John. *Two Treatises of Government*. New York: New American Library, 1960.

Luther, Martin. "An Appeal to the Ruling Class of German Nationality as to the Amelioration of the State of Christendom." *Reformation Writings of Martin Luther,* vol. 1, Bertram Lee Woolf, ed. New York: Philosophical Library, 1953.

_____. "Preface to the Epistle of St. Paul to the Romans." *Martin Luther: Selections from His Writings.* John Dillenberger, ed. Garden City, N.Y.: Anchor Books, 1961.

Malthus, T.R., and A.M. Malthus. *An Essay on the Principle of Population; or a View of Its Past and Present Effects on Human Happiness,* vol. 1. London: T. Bensley, 1807.

Marx, Karl, and Friedrich Engels. *Capital,* Trans. by Samuel Moore and Edward Aveling. New York: Modern Library, 1906.

_____. *The Manifesto of the Communist Party,* Trans. by Samuel Moore. Moscow: Foreign Languages Publishing House, n.d.

Meadows, Donella H., Dennis L. Meadows, Jorgen Randers, William W. Behrens III. *The Limits to Growth.* New York: New American Library, 1972.

Mesarovic, Mihajlo, and Eduard Pestal. *Mankind at the Turning Point: The Second Report to the Club of Rome.* New York: E.P. Dutton and Co., 1974.

Meyers, Ched. *Binding the Strong Man: A Political Reading of Mark's Story of Jesus.* New York: Orbis Books, 1988.

Miller, Alice. *For Your Own Good: Hidden Cruelty in Child-Rearing and the Roots of Violence.* New York: Farrar, Straus, Giroux, 1983.

Mires, Fernando. *El discurso de la naturaleza: ecologia y política en América Latina.* San José, Costa Rica: Editorial DEI, 1988.

_____. *En nombre de la cruz.* San José, Costa Rica: Editorial DEI, 1989.

Moore-Lappé, Frances, and Joseph Collins. *Food First.* New York: Ballantine Books, 1977.

_____. *World Hunger: Twelve Myths.* New York: Grove Press, 1986.

Mora, Arnoldo. "Los protagonistas de la conquista de América." *Pasos* 36, (July/Aug. 1991): 12-16.

Muzaffar, Chandra. "Spirituality, Culture and the Struggle for a Future." *Third World War.* Hong Kong: CCA - International Affairs, 1991, 80-85.

Nelson, Jack. *Hunger for Justice.* New York: Orbis Books, 1980.

Nelson-Pallmeyer, Jack. *Brave New World Order.* New York: Orbis Books, 1993.

_____. *War against the Poor: Low-Intensity Conflict and Christian Faith.* New York: Orbis Books, 1989.

Nkrumah, Kwame. *Neo-Colonialism: the Last Stage of Imperialism.* London: Panaf Books Limited, 1965.

Olson, Mancur and Hans H. Landsberg. *The No-Growth Society.* New York: W.W. Norton and Co., 1973.

Paley, William, D.D. *Natural Theology; or, Evidences of the Existence and Attributes of the Deity.* London: Baldyn and Co., 1819.

Pixley, Jorge. "Exige El Dios Verdadero Sacrificios Cruentos?" *Revista De Interpretacion Biblica Latinoamericana ,* no. 2: *Violencia, Poder y Opressión.* San José, Costa Rica: Editorial DEI 1991, 109-131.

———. *Historia sagrada, historia popular: historia de Israel desde los pobres (1220aC. a 135 d. C.).* San José, Costa Rica: Editorial DEI, 1991.

Plato. *Dialogues of Plato.* Trans. by B. Jowett. 2d ed. vol 3 *Republic.* Oxford: Clarendon Press, 1875.

Policy Planning Study (PPS) 23 , (Feb. 24 1948, FRUS 1948), I (part 2). Quoted in Noam Chomsky, *Turning the Tide.* Boston: South End Press, 1985, 48.

"Report of Committee on Factory Children's Labour." *Parliamentary Papers,* 1831-1832, vol. 15, 95-97, 192-194.

Ricardo, David. *The Works of David Ricardo.* Piero Sraffa, Ed. Cambridge: Cambridge University Press, 1951.

Richard, Pablo. *La lucha de los dioses: los idolos de la opressión y la búsqueda del Dios liberador.* San José: Editorial DEI, 1989.

Rivage-Seul, Marguerite. "Moral Imagination and the Pedagogy of the Oppressed." *Harvard Education Review,* 57 (May 1987): 153-169.

Schell, Jonathan. *The Fate of the Earth.* New York: Knopf, 1982.

Schumacher, E.F. *Small Is Beautiful: Economics As If People Mattered.* New York: Harper and Row, 1973.

Smith, Adam. *An Inquiry into the Nature and Causes of the Wealth of Nations.* Edinburgh, 1806.

Stannard, David E. *American Holocaust: Columbus and the Conquest of the New World.* New York: Oxford University Press, 1992.

Starhawk. *Dreaming the Dark : Magic, Sex & Politics.* Boston: Beacon Press, 1988.

Steffan, Heinz Dieterich. "América Latina entre el capitalismo utópico y la democracia mundial." *Pasos* 51, (Jan./Feb. 1994): 9-13.

Stirle, Wolfram. "La verdad de la realidad: implicaciones metodológicas en el encuentro de teologia y economia." San José: DEI, Project: Invited Researchers Workshop, 24 Apr. 1992.

Swift, Jonathan. "A Modest Proposal." *The Writings of Jonathan Swift.* Robert A. Greenberg, and William B. Piper, eds. New York: W.W. Norton and Company, 1973.

Tamez, Elsa. *Contra toda condena.* San José, Costa Rica: Editorial DEI, 1991.

Tinbergen, Jan, (Coordinator). *Rio: Reshaping the International Order, A Report to the Club of Rome.* New York: New American Library, 1977.

Todorov, Tzvetan. *The Conquest of America.* New York: Harper and Row, 1984.

Vanderslice, Lane. "Land and Hunger: El Salvador." New York: Bread for the World, Background Paper #54, June 1981.

Vidales, Raúl. *Teologia e imperio.* San José, Cost Rica: Editorial DEI, 1991.

_____. *Utopía y liberación: el amanecer del indio* . San José, Costa Rica: Editorial DEI, 1988.

Watson, Alexander F. "U.S.-Latin America Relations in the 1990s: Toward a Mature Partnership." Address before the Institute of the Americas, La Jolla, California, March 2, 1994. U.S. Department of State Dispatch, Vol. 5 #11 (March 14, 1994): 153-157.

Weber, Max. *The Protestant Ethic and the Spirit of Capitalism.* New York: Charles Scribner and Sons, 1958.

Yoder, John Howard. *The Politics of Jesus.* Grand Rapids, Mich.: William B. Eerdmans Publishing, 1972.

Zinn, Howard. *People's History of the United States.* New York: Harper and Row, 1980.

Index

About the Authors

D. MICHAEL RIVAGE-SEUL is Professor of General Studies and Religion at Berea College in Kentucky.

MARGUERITE K. RIVAGE-SEUL is Coordinator of Women's Studies and Lecturer in the General Education Program at Berea College.

ISBN 0-275-95201-0

9 780275 952013

90000>

HARDCOVER BAR CODE

EAN